Social Mobility and the Legal Profession

This book will be crucial reading for students across a variety of disciplines. A broadly socio-legal text, using a mixed-methods design combining grounded theory with an in-depth case study, this research explores a rarely-seen facet of the legal profession. Sociologists studying the practical effect of sociological concepts from theorists such as Bourdieu and Weber; those studying the legal profession from the sociological, legal or psychological angles; anyone examining elite professions; management students examining the operation of professional associations and the ways in which these mobilise to take action on controversial topics; those studying the role and creation of outreach schemes: all will find something of interest in this monograph. For those within the legal profession itself it also provides a look into an oft-hidden world: that of the English Bar. A notoriously secretive profession, traditional, elite and suspicious of research – the case study evaluating an outreach programme sheds light on how this fascinating world operates when trying to engage in progressive steps. Through the eyes of a professional association seeking to improve socio-economic diversity in the profession through instituting an access programme focussed on work experience, it examines not just how professional association action may succeed or fail, but why.

With foreword by Lord Neuberger, former President of the Supreme Court and Chair of the Working Party on Entry to the Bar.

Elaine Freer is a criminal barrister at 5 Paper Buildings (Chambers of Miranda Moore QC and Julian Christopher QC), where she prosecutes and defends in criminal and regulatory matters in the Youth, Magistrates' and Crown Courts. She is also a Fellow at Robinson College, Cambridge, where she holds a part-time post as a College Teaching Officer, supervising undergraduate students in the modules of Criminal Law and Criminology, Sentencing and the Penal System. Prior to pupillage she completed a PhD in Law at Keele University, which examined the operation of professional associations, focussing on an attempt to improve social mobility at the Bar.

Social Mobility and the Legal Profession

The case of professional associations and access to the English Bar

Elaine Freer

LONDON AND NEW YORK

First published 2018
by Routledge
2 Park Square, Milton Park, Abingdon, Oxon OX14 4RN

and by Routledge
711 Third Avenue, New York, NY 10017

Routledge is an imprint of the Taylor & Francis Group, an informa business

© 2018 Elaine Freer

The right of Elaine Freer to be identified as author of this work has been asserted by her in accordance with sections 77 and 78 of the Copyright, Designs and Patents Act 1988.

All rights reserved. No part of this book may be reprinted or reproduced or utilised in any form or by any electronic, mechanical, or other means, now known or hereafter invented, including photocopying and recording, or in any information storage or retrieval system, without permission in writing from the publishers.

Trademark notice: Product or corporate names may be trademarks or registered trademarks, and are used only for identification and explanation without intent to infringe.

British Library Cataloguing-in-Publication Data
A catalogue record for this book is available from the British Library

Library of Congress Cataloging-in-Publication Data
A catalog record for this book has been requested

ISBN: 978-1-138-05269-7 (hbk)
ISBN: 978-1-315-16764-0 (ebk)

Typeset in Galliard
by Swales & Willis Ltd, Exeter, Devon, UK

This book is dedicated to:

Rex and Beryl Freer;

5 Paper Buildings,
who embody everything wonderful about the Criminal
Bar, and make the other bits bearable,

and

the memory of
Dr Catherine Seville (1963–2016),
who believed in second chances.

Contents

Statutes and cases		viii
Foreword		ix
Preface		xii
Acknowledgements		xiv
Abbreviations		xvi
1	Social mobility and the professions in the 21st century	1
2	Social mobility and the legal profession: getting in and getting on	28
3	Conceptualising professional associations: powerful or power-hungry?	47
4	Values, attachment and professional associations	66
5	The importance of individuals within professional associations	98
6	Transformative action for social mobility: radical innovation or maintenance of status quo?	121
7	Wider constraints on interventions by professional associations: challenges within and challenges without?	152
8	Putting theory into practice: general themes for access schemes	182
9	Conclusions	209
	Postscript	214
	References	217
	Index	227

Statutes and cases

Statutes

Legal Services Act 2007

Cases

Lawson v Edmonds [2000] I.R.L.R. 391

Edmonds v Lawson [2000] I.R.L.R. 18

Foreword

The lack of social mobility has been seen as a problem in this country for some time, but it is only relatively recently that it has come to the fore as a truly important issue. And of course, it is an important issue for at least two basic reasons. First, justice: it is simply unfair that a person has significantly reduced prospects of success in their future life because they come from a family background which happens to be relatively disadvantaged in social or economic terms. Second, excellence: if it is impossible, or even very difficult, for a person from a disadvantaged background to enter the professions and other publicly valuable posts, it is statistically inevitable that society is being deprived of some of the best people for those important jobs. Those two reasons also underlie another powerful reason for improving social mobility. The injustice of poor social mobility inevitably generates feelings among much of the population of alienation and political disaffection, and the injustice and the reduction in excellence inevitably generate a lack of respect for, and a loss of confidence in, the professions and other national institutions. All this in turn threatens the stability of society.

A deficit in justice, a shortfall in excellence and a threat to stability, all of which are generated by lack of social mobility, are particularly relevant to the Bar. The barristers' profession is nothing if it is not dedicated to justice, excellence and the rule of law. Accordingly, it should be very concerned about the current lack of social mobility. The fact that it is from the Bar that many judges, indeed the great majority of senior judges, are selected reinforces the expectation that the Bar should be dedicated to improving diversity, and in particular to improving the most difficult element of diversity, social mobility.

I describe it as the most difficult element with some confidence. This is because, after I had been invited to chair a committee set up by the Bar Council in 2006 to investigate how the Bar could improve access generally, it quickly became apparent to me that social mobility was the biggest problem. At that time, it did not get as much publicity as gender and ethnic factors. But, so far as gender and ethnic diversity are concerned, it seems to me that, in terms of access (as opposed to career progression) great advances have been made compared, for instance, with the time when I started off my career as a barrister forty years ago. Sadly, no such claim can be made in relation to social diversity. While things may have, I believe and hope, got a little better, social diversity in terms of access still remains a very serious problem, and very serious problems need very careful analysis if they are to be tackled successfully.

For this reason alone, it would be right to thank Elaine Freer for writing an in-depth and up-to-date book of social mobility and access to the Bar. But there are many other reasons to be grateful for this book.

The basic idea of writing the study with particular reference to professional institutions is especially valuable. After all, if the Bar is to do something about improving the social background profile of its members, it is to the institutions of the Bar that we must primarily look if there is to be any hope of significant and sustained improvement. Of course, as the author says, there are also things which individual chambers, even individual barristers, can do, and it is good to read that there are steps which are being taken by individuals and by institutions.

Another significant aspect of the in-depth investigation undertaken by the author is her analysis of the various initiatives and steps which have been taken to improve social background diversity at the Bar, in particular the Pegasus Access and Support Scheme (PASS). In this book, she assesses their past and likely future success, in so far as that is possible, and she very sensibly does not make exaggerated claims in favour of or against any initiative or step. She is suitably dispassionate and appropriately cautious when the evidence is equivocal or unclear.

Another valuable feature of this book is that it draws on studies done and research carried out in relation to other areas of work outside the Bar, which is especially significant because relatively little analytical work has so far been done in relation to the barristers' profession in relation to this issue. In this connection, it is somewhat dispiriting to read that the author considers that the barristers' profession is rather behind the curve when it comes to improving social background diversity. In fairness to the Bar, this can arguably be explained by the particularly close connection which is generally (but arguably mistakenly) believed to exist between past academic achievement and future professional success in relation to the barristers' profession. Because the education system in England and Wales is so skewed in favour of those whose parents can afford the fees payable at first-class private schools, significant social imbalance would seem to follow almost ineluctably.

Having said that, it is only fair to add that there are many outstanding public-sector schools, but they do not represent anything like the same proportion of all public-sector schools as the outstanding private schools do of all private-sector schools. It is also only fair to acknowledge that many private-sector schools are doing far more than they did in the past to improve things in the form of scholarships and assisting public-sector schools. Nonetheless, these factors do not address the fundamental social diversity problem; nor do they begin to justify any sort of complacency.

I mention that partly in order to draw attention to the fact that there is a limited amount that the Bar and other professions and employers can do in order to improve social mobility. The problem originates early on and is attributable to aspects of the society in which we live. All that can be expected of the professions and employers is that they seek to address, allow for and ameliorate a problem which is inherent in our current social, economic and educational systems. But that does not mean that the professions and employers are justified in doing nothing. On the contrary. The very fact that there is an endemic problem imposes on all those who benefit from the system, and particularly those who play a public role, and above all those concerned with justice, a strong moral obligation to do all that they reasonably can to ameliorate the present unsatisfactory situation in this country so far as social mobility is concerned.

Apart from being a thoughtful and well-researched study, this book is very practical. It is clear from what the author says that there is a lot more to be investigated and a lot more to be done, and very usefully she includes a significant number of interesting suggestions in that connection. Having said that, it is right to record that the Inns of Court and the Bar Council, as well as chambers and individual barristers, did take serious and sustained steps with a view to improving diversity of access to the Bar following publication in November 2007 of the report of the committee to which I have referred. However, the melancholy truth is that these steps have met with pretty limited success. This book suggests a new way forward, and I welcome it and hope that it will be carefully considered and appropriately acted on by everyone concerned with social justice and maintaining the excellence and reputation of the Bar.

> David Neuberger,
> September 2017

Preface

> But there's another big social problem we need to fix. In politicians' speak: a 'lack of social mobility'. In normal language: people unable to rise from the bottom to the top, or even from the middle to the top, because of their background.
>
> David Cameron, then Prime Minister, address to the 2015 Conservative Party Conference

Social mobility at the Bar was never going to be an uncontroversial topic. On hearing my PhD project, many responses encompassed 'social mobility at the Bar? Presumably you've found that there isn't any?' As my thesis progressed it was clear that it was not quite that simple, or quite that bad. What was clear was that it could be, and needed to be, much better. Inner Temple took a laudable step towards improving access to the profession in launching PASS, and then funding research into its efficacy.

The challenges of promoting social mobility across the professions are significant. I cannot suggest that this book even attempts to solve those problems. They are rooted in many areas, including education, tradition, poverty and long-established social and business practices. What this book does seek to do, however, is to explore how professional associations may examine their own profession's approach to social mobility, and what power they may have to influence that approach. These are questions applicable to all professions, not just the legal profession. In most organisations there are patterns of cultural reproduction which cause or encourage social stratification. Wherever these patterns occur it is possible to stop them, but that requires action to be taken by individuals at all levels to critically analyse how their recruitment processes contribute to perpetuating such stratification. Through the case study of PASS I aim to highlight how access programmes targeting increasing socio-economic diversity within a profession may be structured and delivered to maximise their effectiveness in tackling the processes and assumptions that lead indirectly to the reproduction of socio-economic stratification. In this respect also the book is of much wider interest than to the legal profession – it offers suggestions that any organisation wanting to encourage greater diversity of entrants, or institute an access programme, may find helpful.

One way in which reproduction of social stratification occurs is when attributes considered by the profession to be a pre-requisite are more easily attainable by candidates from certain socio-economic demographics. In this study, work experience was notionally available to anyone who applied for it. But this apparent simplicity overlaid complexities. Those with family or friends in the legal profession could often access work experience without their achievements or abilities being subject to scrutiny. This enabled them to gain knowledge of the profession and consequently make more convincing applications for pupillage. Those students without family links in the profession had to apply through external processes for work experience. These processes were fiercely competitive, and favoured traditional demonstrations of merit and knowledge of the profession more easily gained and displayed by 'traditional' students – those from more privileged socio-economic backgrounds. This meant that 'non-traditional' students, with no family background in the profession, became trapped in a vicious cycle which reduced their chance of entering the profession. Their potential was often not recognised by those selecting work experience students through the external applications. For example, if they had attended a low-performing school by whose standards their achievements were excellent, but were not regarded as competitive against other applicants, they were often dismissed, and did not secure work experience. Similar observations can be made in other jurisdictions; for example, clerkships to senior judges in the USA.

Without the more detailed and nuanced knowledge that comes from observing a barrister in their day-to-day professional life in work experience, they struggled to demonstrate an informed interest in the profession. Without that first mini-pupillage, they could not secure further work experience to increase their knowledge. When faced with application forms and pupillage interviews requiring them to justify their career choice, they consequently lacked the detailed knowledge to answer those questions as convincingly and confidently as those who had accessed work experience.

A carefully-constructed and well-administered access programme can contribute significantly to the possibilities that a profession offers for aspirant entrants. PASS targeted the struggles many non-traditional aspirant entrants had in accessing work experience. It was a small-scale programme, but nonetheless the implications of the findings in relation to it are wide-ranging across professions, higher education and geographical reaches. At the time of writing, the world is considering, with Brexit triggered, and Donald Trump as the President of the USA, the effect in real and political terms of allowing large numbers of young people to be 'left behind' in disadvantaged areas. Without prospects to better themselves and seeking to fulfil untapped potential, this research is a timely examination of some of the ways in which disaffection of intelligent young people might be reduced in future. Even where participation in such a programme does not lead to entry to the profession offering the programme, it can disseminate general information to guide career choices, thereby assisting students in their decision-making processes and heightening aspirations. The role of programmes in engaging non-traditional aspirant entrants with professions at large cannot be underestimated.

Acknowledgements

Academically, this book owes its existence to an ambitious collaboration between Keele University and Inner Temple creating a PhD project under an ACORN studentship to examine the role of a professional association seeking to instigate change, and evaluate PASS. This was supervised by Professor Andrew Francis (now at Leeds University) and Professor Marie-Andreé Jacob at Keele, and Anthony Dursi and Benchers at Inner Temple. Without data and assistance from Inner Temple and the willingness and honesty of all participants I would have had little to analyse, and it is to them that I owe the most thanks. I am indebted to my examiners, Professor John Flood (now at Griffith University, Brisbane) and Professor Anthony Bradney, for their enthusiasm for my research, and their encouragement to seek a publisher. Andrew Johnson and Mark Bostock undertook proofreading; Sarah Lynch helped me navigate the world of publishing, and Routledge's Alison Kirk and Ruth Noble fielded myriad questions with patience.

Personally, this book owes its existence to many people. In research engaging so deeply with the importance of individuals' stories and work experience it would be wrong of me not to thank those people who shaped my path to the Bar. Most influential were mini-pupillages with Avik (now His Honour Judge) Mukherjee (formerly 1 High Pavement); Ken Millett (now Red Lion Chambers) and Angus Bunyan (2 Hare Court); and Stephen Hopper (5 Paper Buildings); whilst marshalling with Judge John Milmo QC offered a very different perspective. They all taught me far more than I suspect they realise. Financially, I could pursue this career due to scholarships from Lincoln's Inn, and the Kalisher Trust in conjunction with Cloth Fair Chambers.

In 2016 I completed pupillage and accepted tenancy at 5 Paper Buildings (Chambers of Miranda Moore QC and Julian Christopher QC). The dedication of this book to everyone there is deserved testament to how important they have been to the writing of this book, to my practice and to my happiness. I am especially grateful to Denis Barry, for his support as my first pupilmaster and since, and to Dominic Lewis, for not asking to sit somewhere else (and sometimes putting the kettle on). Without Andrew Johnson and Carolina Bracken this book would have been finished much sooner, and through the contributions of others it narrowly avoided: being called 'Part-heard in Milton Keynes' (JGN); having a soundtrack of music from *Jaws* (TAQC); including a picture of an Ewok (DAR), and being performed through interpretative dance (DJL). Without passing comments of interest and encouragement from many others when they saw me in chambers (or, once, Wood Green Crown Court – CR), it would never have been completed at all.

The combined demands of the Bar and the manuscript led to neglected friends, who were understanding about constant unavailability; a persistent lack of punctuality, and my increasing air of (seemingly inexplicable) freneticism. I hope that this book is some way to a satisfactory explanation (and apology). My colleagues at Robinson College, Cambridge, continued to be a vital source of intellectual energy and good company, as were all my students: special mention being deserved by Amelie, Chyna, Lizzy, Luisa, Mollie and Olivia, who never complained about Saturday Criminal Law supervisions as I balanced teaching with practice.

Finally, I owe everything to my parents for giving me opportunities that they did not have, and encouraging me to take them. My parents inspired my love of criminal law, and although my determination to join this bizarre, difficult and wonderful profession perhaps took them by surprise, their encouragement was unwavering. I was deeply aware during this research of my 'dual identity' – whilst my parents are from working-class families in Nottingham and left state grammar schools at 16 with some O Levels, I went to an independent secondary school. As the first in my family to go to university, I found it utterly bewildering, dropped out very quickly and had an unplanned year out working in which I applied again. I am grateful to Selwyn College, Cambridge for the incredible support I received there as an undergraduate, especially from Professor John Spencer and Dr Janet O'Sullivan. I consequently identified with elements of both the non-traditional aspirant entrants' experiences and of the traditional route into the profession.

I hope that initiatives to tackle a lack of social mobility will ensure that professional roles are open to all bright young people wherever they are from, and whatever their path. Talent that is harder to display is no less worthy of recognition.

Elaine Freer
5 Paper Buildings, Temple
Robinson College,
Cambridge
September 2017

Abbreviations

BPTC	Bar Professional Training Course
BVC	Bar Vocational Course (forerunner to the BPTC)
BSB	Bar Standards Board
COIC	Council of the Inns of Court
GDL	Graduate Diploma in Law
LPC	Legal Practice Course
LSA	Legal Services Act 2007
LSB	Legal Services Board
PASS	Pegasus Access and Support Scheme

1 Social mobility and the professions in the 21st century

The legal profession is an ancient cornerstone of the British establishment. For many centuries, wigged and gowned figures have been depicted with fascination by writers and television producers, often as white, male, and privileged. Statistics show that this is, to an extent, true. The most traditional areas of practice, such as chancery, remain the preserve of white, male Oxbridge graduates (72% male; 61% Oxbridge-educated and 97% white; Bar Council, 2014: 105). In most other practice areas, however, the picture is different (39% male, 21% Oxbridge-educated and 89% white at the Family Bar; Bar Council, 2014: 27, 105).[1] Nonetheless, research by Zimdars (2010) demonstrated that pupil barristers (those in the final, vocational, stage of training) do not reflect the university graduate population demographically, and that whilst participation rates of women and ethnic minorities compare favourably with other professions, there is not representative participation across socio-economic backgrounds compared to the university population. Recent statistics suggest that only 6% of barristers had parents in routine or semi-routine occupations.[2]

There are various causes of this under-representation of those from working-class backgrounds (referred to throughout this book as 'non-traditional aspirant entrants').[3] This research uses a case study of the Honourable Society of the Inner Temple (a professional association of the Bar)[4] to examine two wide,

---

1 Although the Working Lives Report was billed as a biennial survey of the Bar, it was not carried out in 2015, hence the reliance on data from the 2013 report, and other ad hoc data gathered by the Bar Council. Since the 2013 Working Lives Report there have been no statistics published showing the breakdown of attributes by practice area. At the time of writing, data is being collected for the 2017 Working Lives survey.
2 Laurison and Friedman, 2015.
3 Choosing nomenclature is in itself a delicate matter; this term is preferred as it features as the accepted definition in most specialist academic papers (see, for example, the Social Mobility and Child Poverty Commission's report 'Non-Educational Barriers to the Elite Professions' (Ashley et al., 2015)).
4 'Inner Temple' is the shortened name used throughout this research for the Honourable Society of the Inner Temple, one of the four Inns of Court; the professional associations of the Bar. Membership of one of the four Inns is a requirement for qualification and practise as a barrister in England and Wales.

inter-linked issues. First, how and why a professional association may seek to bring about change within its related profession, and second, the challenges experienced by non-traditional aspirant entrants seeking entry to traditional professions. In examining the second issue, the case study focusses particularly on PASS, a scheme developed by Inner Temple providing work experience at the Bar (usually called 'mini-pupillage') to non-traditional aspirant entrants. In evaluating how the scheme was developed and why, an important insight into the operation of traditional professional associations, and their relationships with their profession, is gained.

This book forms an analysis of a layer of activity, action and experience not usually investigated by researchers. This layer, however, is an important dimension of the profession's composition, and how the theoretical concept of professionalism manifests and influences the legal profession.

As legal professionalism develops (Francis, 2011) it does so in increasingly diverse ways. By studying its interplay with matters of access and increasing social mobility at the Bar, an additional perspective to the analysis of legal professionalism and access takes shape. This book also addresses a source of increasing societal tension: elite professions and their contribution, or perceived failure thereof, to social mobility, and continuing occupational closure.

Over the last forty years the legal profession in general, and the Bar particularly, has seen myriad changes. These have been structural, financial and practical. Whilst most solicitors are employed in firms, most barristers are self-employed. In 2015 there were 15,899 practising barristers,[5] of whom 12,757 were solely in self-employed practice, and a further 245 practised in dual capacity, taking work through both employed and self-employed structures.[6] Although alternative business structures of solicitors and barristers in joint practices were heavily encouraged, in practice they have been less commonly utilised (McMorrow, 2016). The reduced availability and dwindling sums of legal aid funding make practice areas such as Criminal, Family and Immigration increasingly fraught. When combined with an historical tendency towards social closure, ever-increasing fees for the Bar Professional Training Course (BPTC – a compulsory academic year taken after a qualifying Law degree), and stiff competition for pupillage (the final, compulsory, stage of vocational training), homogeneity of socio-economic background is favouring those from wealthier families. Furthermore, the focus on work experience and social conformity poses an additional challenge to entry for those unfamiliar with the profession, favouring aspirant entrants with social connections with legal professionals.

There is already a strong body of research examining access to the solicitors' branch of the profession in England and Wales by researchers such as Hilary Sommerlad and Iain MacDonald. Access to other practitioner roles, and

---

5 These are the most recent figures published.
6 www.barstandardsboard.org.uk/media-centre/research-and-statistics/statistics/practising-barrister-statistics [accessed 4th April 2017].

challenges for part-time Law students (Francis, 2011), have also been the focus of research. Meanwhile, research into the Bar, and especially access issues, remains scarce. Rogers (2010) researched the process of pupillage, and its role as socialisation. Flood (1981) performed an ethnography of barristers' clerks. Yet the Bar remains deeply suspicious of research, fiercely guarding access (Rogers, 2010: 40). Funding by a trusted professional association of the Bar, and the researcher's biography as a non-practising barrister, were therefore important in gaining access. This research also examines earlier milestones on the access pathway: access programmes aimed at sixth-formers and university undergraduates, reflecting evidence that disadvantage flowing from socio-economic background manifests early in life (Feinstein, 2003: 85), and consequently interventions to address it need to be carefully timed.

To engage with under-researched matters usually obscured from both the public and academic researchers, this research used a mixed-methods approach (Kuhn, 1977), which was qualitative-dominant (Morse, 2003). Central were two case studies consisting of original qualitative and quantitative data. The first, smaller, case study focussed on a programme called Pathways to Law (run by the Sutton Trust, and hereafter 'Pathways'), and gathered quantitative and focus group data from participating secondary school students. The main case study, of PASS (run by the Honourable Society of the Inner Temple), gathered a much wider range of data. As well as quantitative questionnaire data, focus groups were conducted with students, and interviews held with instigators and organisers of the programme, and a much larger sample of students filled in 'before' and 'after' questionnaires to allow exploration of potential effects of participating in the programme (see below).

The analysis of these case studies is informed by a theoretical framework which develops from a central-value-based model of professions, overlaid with a neo-Weberian social closure approach. This is interwoven with insights from Bourdieu's work on social capital and cultural reproduction, along with contributions from the understanding of organisational change and institutional entrepreneurship (e.g. Suddaby, 2010; Greenwood and Suddaby, 2006).

Through a close analysis of the process undertaken by a professional association seeking to instigate an access programme aimed at supporting demographic diversification, I argue that individual- and organisation-level factors are both of key importance. Their meeting in the right place and at the right time heavily influences whether a force for organisational change will be created, and if so, its efficacy in securing that change. By looking at an effort to influence a societally-sensitive matter by a deeply traditional profession we can identify factors affecting both the efficacy of action by professional associations generally, and those matters likely to affect the success of interventions aimed at improving social mobility. These illuminate core tensions both within professional associations, and surrounding access to the professions more generally.

I argue that the stories of those involved in a professional association access scheme, as student participants, creators, instigators, organisers and administrators, reveal the importance of inspirational and practical leadership, as well as the human capital that can be harnessed through emotional ties. The importance of these affective connections has been under-estimated in previous research. However, these personal stories also cast light on the embeddedness of some exclusionary practices, and the challenges to securing meaningful contributions to social mobility. A key challenge remains identifying and establishing programmes that can genuinely test the status quo, instead of reinforcing the 'otherness' of non-traditional aspirant entrants to the profession.

1.1 Wider policy and societal concern with social mobility

This research comes at a time when much of society is concerned with equality of opportunity, and the perceived elite nature of certain professions causes discontent.[7] The Government has made it an increasing priority,[8] with an extensive range of documents on its website concerned with social mobility matters,[9] including a speech by the then Prime Minister on improving life chances for people from all backgrounds,[10] and more recently a speech by Justine Greening opening the Left Behind Britain conference on the causes and consequences of declining social mobility.[11] In 2016, the Social Mobility Commission published its report 'State of the Nation 2016: Social Mobility in Great Britain'. This focussed on factors affecting social mobility at every life stage from birth through to obtaining jobs and housing. Noting that only one in eight children from low-income families will go on to become a high-income earner as an adult (Blanden and Machin, 2007), the report observed that there were much more complex factors than the traditionally-cited 'North–South' divide within England which influenced the possibilities for social mobility (2016: 128). Notably, many towns and rural areas, not only in the North, are being 'left behind' by the more affluent South East, financially and educationally (2016: 137).

Amongst commentators, discussion abounds as to whether social mobility is occurring,[12] and if it is, whether it can ameliorate inequalities in society.[13] Existing policy documents on social mobility (explored below) demonstrate particular pressure on professions to ensure that they are recruiting solely on merit and potential. However, such merit and potential may be demonstrated in various ways, especially by those who have not followed the educational system linearly, or have had their education otherwise disrupted. For many young people a lack of educational opportunities means that they are unable to demonstrate their potential in recognisable ways when applying for work experience or employment. Consequently,

---

7 Milburn, 2014: 10.
8 www.gov.uk/government/policies/social-mobility [accessed 7th August 2017].
9 www.gov.uk/government/organisation/social-mobility-commission [accessed 7th April 2017].
10 www.gov.uk/government/speeches/pm-speech-on-opportunity [accessed 7th August 2017].
11 www.gov.uk/government/news/left-behind-britain-narrowing-the-social-mobility-divide [accessed 13th April 2017].
12 Milburn, 2015.
13 Clark, 2015.

there is increasing pressure on professions to value transferable skills, and those demonstrated outside of the education system, equally with traditional educational achievements.

1.1.1 The policy background

Considering this widespread concern regarding social mobility, important context to the current research is provided by various policy documents from the last five years. In recent times 'social mobility' has become a much-used 'buzz-word' in political policy papers, but its central pre-occupation bears closer scrutiny. Defining social mobility is not straightforward. It can be defined as 'akin to equality of opportunity' (Crawford et al., 2011: 6) and the relationship between an individual's position on the income ladder in early life as compared to their income as an adult (Papademetriou et al., 2009: 1). When measured inter-generationally, it is expressed as 'the relationship between the socio-economic status of parents and the status their children will attain as adults' (Causa and Johansson, 2009: 5), whilst intra-generational social mobility is concerned with changes to position in the social hierarchy of an individual (Nunn, 2011: 5).

Social mobility can also be absolute – the social hierarchy of the entire society shifts, or relative – individuals move within the established social hierarchy (Nunn, 2011: 5–6). It is widely acknowledged that, as such an amorphous concept, it is easier to identify the drivers of social mobility than to pinpoint its exact conceptual definition (Crawford et al., 2011: 6), and these include education, skills and employment (Crawford et al., 2011; Papademetriou et al., 2009; Nunn, 2011).

Neither is measuring social mobility, nor the effect of programmes aimed at increasing it, easy. It is not until retirement that social mobility can be assessed if done by reference to earnings and occupation (Kennedy, 2010). Therefore, we know much more about social mobility of the generation in their sixties than the generation in their thirties, who may yet get promoted or progress to more prestigious jobs before retirement. This makes assessing 'current' social mobility somewhat challenging. The success of programmes aimed at increasing social mobility through intervention early in life, such as Sure Start, will not be known until the cohort who had access to such programmes is much older (Kennedy, 2010: 78–79). Assessing the effectiveness of current initiatives is difficult for the same reason as measuring current social mobility; social mobility is an event which continues over a person's working life, and therefore cannot be reliably measured until their working life has ended. Indeed, this is one limitation of the current case study; it is a snapshot of the interventions currently employed by Inner Temple. The long-term effects of PASS will only be known if follow-up, or ideally longitudinal, research is carried out in the future.

As Nunn et al. (2007: 69–70) conclude, factors dictating to what extent people are able to achieve intra- or inter-generational social mobility are also complex and vary between individuals. This was reflected by the views and experiences of the students who spoke with the researcher during this project. What actually motivated and constrained them, and their perceptions of those factors, was complex, varied and nuanced, meaning a 'joined-up' approach between Government departments, agencies and non-governmental organisations is necessary to improve social mobility by addressing those factors which inhibit it. Although social mobility is a measure of societal fairness, it needs to be considered in conjunction with other measures to gain an accurate picture.

Social mobility is perceived as desirable because it is inextricably linked to societal fairness, and so too to social cohesion. It is described as the manifestation of equality of opportunity, albeit that the gulf between formal and substantive equality may be vast (Nunn, 2011: 6). At its heart, social mobility is the progression of a person to the possession or achievement of attributes associated with a social class that is higher than that of their parents. In less eloquent terms, it may be synonymous with climbing the social ladder. Whilst some academics have suggested that this is a trait inherent in all, that everyone will attempt to emulate the behaviours of those above them in the social order (Bourdieu, 1984), for others it is a process that should be striven for across society. Determined attempts to 'cause' social mobility through external forces, however, are not straightforward due to huge variations in opportunities afforded to individuals to demonstrate their ability and access drivers of social mobility (Crawford et al., 2011: 6). This inequality of access to opportunities reinforces social stratification (Parsons, 1940), whereby society adopts a normative pattern, with individuals theoretically divided by the differentiation of roles, leading to a differentiation of goals for different social groups (1940: 845). Each group has different moral patterns, and compliance with these is inculcated at an early age (1940: 846), similarly to the inculcation of tastes documented by Bourdieu (1984). Differential evaluation of the values of each stratum leads to a hierarchy being created according to the desirability of the values of each stratum considered under six attributions; these include achievements, possessions, authority and power (Parsons, 1940: 848–9).

The current focus on (inter-generational) social mobility, upwards movement by an individual from their parents' social stratum, is largely due to political desires for its increase.[14] The UK lags far behind other similarly developed nations in ensuring that those of equal talent but from under-privileged backgrounds have the same chance of accessing the most respected professions as those with more privileged upbringings. What is illustrated clearly by current social policy documents is that the current research is contributing to narrowing a wide gap in the literature. Whilst there is a lot of general research into social mobility, and this can be combined with varied academic research focussing on non-traditional entrants to the profession as solicitors, and extensive research on the American Bar, there has been comparatively little written about the situation at the English Bar, and none of that has been recent. Meanwhile, there is increasing pressure on legal professional organisations to collect data giving more detail than ever before about

---

14 See text of the Prime Minister's 'One Nation' speech delivered on 22nd June 2015 – note 10.

applicants and entrants to the profession so that the attributes of entrants can be monitored. However, much of this data, although collected, does not undergo meaningful analysis to identify patterns and potential action in pursuit of change.[15]

Concern about a lack of social mobility at the Bar relates to three broader concerns. First, that if the Bar is not representative, individuals who are intimately concerned with the pursuit of justice may not be able to relate to, or understand, the needs of their lay clients. Second, for as long as this imbalance persists, progress towards a more representative judiciary will be difficult, as the pool from which many judges are drawn will be unrepresentative (e.g. Bindman and Monaghan, 2014: 6). Third, that talented young people who are capable of a career at the Bar are deterred from even attempting to join the profession because they think they will not succeed if they are from a lower socio-economic group (Sommerlad, 2007). Many young people from such backgrounds may be the first in their family to go to university, or the first to have hopes of entering a profession such as medicine or law. Young people in this group may find the prospect of the Bar a foreboding one. Reasons given for this by students who participated in this research included: stereotypes of the profession, feeling that they did not 'fit in' due to unfamiliarity with the profession's social norms, and a lack of access to information about the working practices of barristers and life at the Bar.

1.1.2 Importance of early intervention

Recent interest in this area has largely been triggered by the then Deputy Prime Minister, Nick Clegg, asking former MP Alan Milburn to undertake a comprehensive review of social mobility after the latter stood down at the 2010 General Election.[16] Whilst an MP, Mr Milburn had undertaken work examining social mobility, published in his 2009 report 'Unleashing Aspirations', and was later appointed as the Independent Chair on Social Mobility and Child Poverty (House of Commons' Education Committee, 2012), a role he filled until his resignation in December 2017. Mr Milburn accepted this role with his remit as 'considering how best progress towards the long-term goal of the United Kingdom becoming more socially mobile can be fairly assessed'.[17] Since 2010, there have, therefore, been documents produced both by groups representing specific professional groups (see documents below from the Bar Standards Board (BSB) and the Legal Services Board (LSB), for example), and also more general documents produced by groups aiming to increase social mobility across the population (for example, the Bridge Group and the Sutton Trust, significant independent charities promoting social mobility through inclusion in higher education).

---

15 For example, the BSB Handbook explicitly requires chambers to appoint a 'diversity data officer', who is responsible for collecting and collating data about members of chambers (2017: 73–75).
16 www.gov.uk/government/news/letter-to-alan-milburn-on-his-appointment-to-review-social-mobility [accessed 7th August 2017].
17 www.gov.uk/government/uploads/system/uploads/attachment_data/file/62364/milburn-clegg-letter.pdf [accessed 7th August 2017].

For a more comprehensive overview, it is helpful to begin by examining two significant documents from 'pre-Milburn' social mobility literature. Langlands (2005) 'examined the available evidence and reflected some of the genuine concerns expressed by professional bodies, universities and other higher education institutions and employers' (before the increase in university fees and the altered arrangements regarding repaying student loans). His Government-published report separated its recommendations for increasing social mobility into four categories, delineated by four stages usually required to enter a profession: initial decision-making prior to entry to higher education; application to higher education; period of study; and entry to and retention in employment (2005: 8–9). This research focusses on the fourth stage identified, entry to the profession, although it also engages with issues surrounding careers decision-making at secondary and higher education levels and experiences within the higher and vocational educational stages.

Existing research highlights that 'early intervention' in the education system is vital. Research conducted from birth shows how quickly those of high ability from lower social backgrounds fall below the performance of their higher-social-background-but-lower-ability peers from the age of 6 years (Feinstein, 2003: 85). This demonstrates how social stratification (Parsons, 1940) begins to manifest early in life. Such stratification is inherently linked to social mobility, as social mobility is the process by which individuals can move out of the stratum of their parents (inter-generational) or themselves progress from one stratum to another (intra-generational). This research focusses on inter-generational mobility, as the young people participating had their eligibility for PASS assessed according to criteria including parental education, and identifiers of parental income such as free school meal eligibility.

Early intervention is important to pre-empt and reduce such stratification. Targeting of resources at children from more disadvantaged backgrounds then needs to continue throughout their education to provide the resources and encouragement to enter higher education, and gain qualifications which will improve their chances of a stable, higher-entry-level job. Such ongoing support gives young people tools to assist movement up through levels of social stratification. Appropriate advice and information early in secondary education is needed to combat negative stereotypes of certain professions which may be especially prevalent amongst those from lower socio-economic backgrounds, that a certain profession 'isn't for people like them' (Langlands, 2005: 8). Such support then needs to continue into higher education: Jerrim, Vignoles and Finnie (2012: 22) demonstrate that, in comparison to the USA and Australia, England has the lowest percentage of people from the 'low socio-economic' group going to university, linked to poor school performance of many children from that group.

Such encouragement needs to continue through formal education and extend to the provision of careers information. Responses to the Milburn Review from the Bridge Group and the Sutton Trust highlighted the need for information and encouragement to be given to those with ability from lower socio-economic backgrounds at university level by those already in professional positions (Bridge Group, 2011: 2). This linking of professionals and non-traditional aspirant entrants is seen in the case study intervention, and mentioned by many participants as a valuable way of offering support and insight to aspirant entrants who may struggle to access accurate information about the profession otherwise. The need to counterbalance potentially erroneous advice from informal sources such as family and friends has been identified as a key role of careers advice in a literature review carried out by the Centre for British Teachers (now the Education Development Trust) (Hughes and Gration, 2009: 20).

Many practitioner participants in this research discussed the challenge of ensuring opportunities were available to young people with relatively poor grades from formal education but who showed potential through other attributes and transferable skills. They also highlighted that many students did not realise during their formal education how competitive a career in law was, and the grades required, until they had already sat examinations. Due to the strength of the research showing that employment, and chances thereof, is intrinsically linked to the ability of people to improve their social mobility, there has been significant engagement with professional bodies and education providers to explore how best they can assist in increasing social mobility. This engagement has been particularly strong in those professions where there has traditionally been a significant under-representation of those from lower socio-economic backgrounds, of which law is one. Data used by the National Equality Panel (2010: 329) showed that the percentage difference between the average family income of a typical professional and the average family income across the population was highest for lawyers (a 75% difference) compared to eleven other specific professions, and a collective twelfth category of 'other professions'. 'Unleashing Aspirations', colloquially known as the Milburn Report (Milburn, 2009), highlighted the lack of progress made in access to the professions, with a focus on four specific sectors: law, media, medicine and government/politics.

Langlands' report acknowledges that different professions face different particular challenges, but in addition to general themes relevant to many professions (2005: 14) two particular challenges faced the legal profession. First, that prospects, pay and working conditions were important factors in the choices made by graduates working in the profession. This reduced the likelihood of graduates working in predominantly legally-aided practice areas. Second, there remained issues surrounding social background and access, despite attempts to address diversity (2005: 53). It will be examined below how the legal profession's position has changed since 2005. Regrettably, Langlands considers only the solicitors' side of the profession, ignoring the Bar. There are significant differences in how the Bar and solicitors' firms operate (see 2.2), so this omission is unfortunate.

Similar concerns were raised in the Department for Work and Pensions report produced by Nunn et al. (2007). This report 'examined the factors that are facilitating and inhibiting social mobility in the United Kingdom in the early years of the twenty-first century', and looked particularly at the role that employment could play in social mobility. The authors assert that:

> Trends in social mobility are remarkably resistant to policy interventions. Those in higher social classes appear to have been able to take greater advantage of the opportunities created by policy interventions and more able to use a variety of additional social advantages to maintain their relative position. This may undermine the potential equalising benefits of universal public provision.
>
> (Nunn et al., 2007: 4)

The report does highlight, however, that employment opportunities are a crucial part of social mobility: 'people who have experience of unemployment are more likely to find themselves trapped in low quality "entry" level employment, with limited opportunities to progress' (Nunn et al., 2007: 4).

Therefore, it is clearly recognised that those measures aimed at increasing social mobility may themselves widen the gap between middle and working classes. This means that policy interventions must be carefully formulated and monitored to reduce this differential effect as far as possible. Furthermore, if social mobility is so resistant to policy interventions, it is necessary to ensure that any policy interventions utilised are radical enough to address the problem where it is most felt, and where intervention could lead to the most significant returns.

Increasing interest in social mobility, combined with increasing awareness of the difficulties faced by those from low socio-economic backgrounds in getting access to the 'top jobs', led to the commissioning of a report dedicated solely to social mobility in England and Wales: 'Unleashing Aspirations'. The report was wide-ranging, and included a large-scale consultation process with various bodies, both charitable and professional, with relevant expertise and experience in working to increase the accessibility of the best education and jobs to those from low socio-economic backgrounds.

Research shows that, compared to six other developed countries (the USA, France, Denmark, Sweden, Germany and Canada), Britain is displaying the least inter-generational social mobility when measured by the strength of the links between the earnings of fathers and sons (Kennedy, 2010: 78–9), and that rates of occupational mobility are lower than the international average for men and are at the bottom of the range internationally for women (National Equality Panel, 2010: 324–5). However, Kennedy also states that evidence suggesting that social mobility has declined in this country is 'far from clear cut', due to challenges of measurement (see 1.1.1).

1.1.3 Role of the professions in social mobility

Although professions had been key to increasing social mobility in the post-war era (Milburn, 2009: 16–17), they have subsequently contributed to its stagnation, with extrapolation suggesting that in the future, professionals will come from families that are in the top 30% of the population in terms of income (2009: 20). The report further highlighted existing research on the importance of factors affecting children's early years in their later life paths (2009: 26–41) and called for these to be ameliorated through policy-based interventions.

As well as interventions, advice has been issued to professional bodies on how to improve social mobility: an example being the Social Mobility Toolkit (2012). This was funded by the LSB and the General Medical Council, with support from the Chartered Insurance Institute and the British Dental Association; all professions which have traditionally struggled to recruit and retain those from lower socio-economic backgrounds. The toolkit is aimed at advising 'traditional' professional bodies and companies on understanding and monitoring social mobility, and best practice for improving access (2012: 4). It is hoped that by providing information on how best to recruit the strongest candidates for a position regardless of their background, professions will feel better able to adapt their recruitment practices to reflect best practice, and to monitor social mobility within their organisation to allow future evaluation of the effectiveness of current programmes.

Heeding criticisms levelled at the legal profession, a consultation paper by the LSB 'discusse[d] our policy proposals in relation to increasing diversity and social mobility at all levels of the legal services workforce. It focusses on the role of providers (firms and chambers) and approved regulators in this process' (2011: 1). The LSB is the independent body responsible for overseeing the regulation of the legal profession, and works with the 'approved regulators' (including the Bar Council and the Law Society, exercising disciplinary functions through the BSB and Solicitors' Regulation Authority (SRA) respectively) who undertake routine regulation of lawyers.[18] The LSB and approved regulators share eight regulatory objectives, and it is argued that increased regulation to promote these has contributed to a reduction in the power of professional associations such as the Inns of Court (see Chapter 7).

As an approved regulator under the Equality Act 2010, the LSB is now required to collect and monitor diversity data on those entering the profession. It therefore wanted to establish an evidence base on the profession's current demographic, and to gather information on attributes of applicants in the future, by developing new diversity monitoring forms (LSB, 2011: 2). The consultation was chiefly aimed at establishing the views of solicitors' firms and barristers' chambers on what questions should be asked of current and prospective lawyers, and how the information obtained should be released publicly to comply with the duty under the 2010 Act. Data on socio-economic status was only collected from new applicants by way of a question on their parents' education; a relatively basic measure.

The LSB therefore attached to the consultation paper a template questionnaire, and invited responses on its appropriateness. Of the responses accessed, the setting of targets caused most concern (something the LSB had said that it was 'minded to reject at this stage' in any event (2011: 3)), along with the requirement of very small organisations to publish their data, risking the identification of members with a particular disability, for example (response from the Inner Temple (2011)). There were positive comments about the intention to collect

---

18 www.legalservicesboard.org.uk [accessed 7th August 2017].

data on socio-economic backgrounds (response from Matrix Law).[19] In designing the template questionnaire, the LSB stated:

> We have sought advice from the Equality and Human Rights Commission (EHRC) on the best approach to measuring each characteristic. We have sought to follow an approach that complies with best practice and is aligned as far as possible with external datasets such as the national Census.
>
> (2011: 34)

This alignment will help transparency in assessing social mobility as it will be possible to draw meaningful comparisons between different organisations' datasets.

Although statistics show that those qualifying and entering practice as solicitors and barristers are more diverse now than previously (with significantly increased proportions of female and black and minority ethnic entrants (Bar Council, 2014: 9)), concerns regarding lower rates of retention and progression of people from those demographics remain, with high attrition at each stage from the BPTC, pupillage, and tenancy (Bar Council, 2011: 9–12). The Bar Council figures from 2012 clearly illustrate this problem; whilst just over 49% of those Called to the Bar were women, only just over 37% of barristers practising in England and Wales were women (2014: 16). Therefore, it is understandable that most replies to the LSB's consultation paper endorsed initiatives supporting social mobility, and contributed suggestions on how to do so more effectively. Not only does any initiative need to address the relatively low number of non-traditional aspirant entrants entering the profession, it needs to consider causes of the disproportionately high attrition rate. This requires understanding how non-traditional aspirant entrants experience the profession and factors influencing their decisions on career choice and progression. The role in this research of discussion in focus groups with non-traditional aspirant entrants was to explore their perceptions of the profession, and the challenges they face in entering it, in an interactional setting with peers and the researcher.

At a similar time, responses were also being composed to the Legal Education and Training Review (LETR) discussion paper 'Equality, Diversity and Social Mobility Issues Affecting Education and Training in the Legal Services Sector'. The LETR is a joint project of the SRA, the BSB and the Chartered Institute of Legal Executives (CILEx) Professional Standards, which provides a fundamental, evidence-based review of education and training requirements across regulated and non-regulated legal services in England and Wales. The BSB's Education and Training Committee's response to the LETR discussion paper makes particular reference to an anomaly found at the Bar; the fact that 'there is currently *no* "Equality Code" in place which requires all members of chambers' recruitment committees to undertake equality and diversity training.' (BSB, 2012: 1).

---

19 www.legalservicesboard.org.uk/what_we_do/consultations/closed/pdf/matrix_law.pdf [accessed 8th August 2017].

The final report of the LETR (2013) was extensive and made wide-ranging recommendations across every level of the legal training process. However, it made little in the way of recommendations directly addressing concerns arising in this research.

A progress report (Milburn, 2012) followed up the recommendations made in the 2009 Milburn Report, measuring progress against four criteria (2012: 11). First, raising aspirations; second, work experience and internships; third, recruitment and selection, and fourth, flexible routes into the professions. It concludes that, in testing economic times, increasing access has been side-lined; although some organisations have made significant progress, overall progress was characterised as insufficient (2012: 29). A lack of information at school age, narrow recruitment bases and the importance of work experience are indicated as particular challenges (2012: 29). Milburn praises 'real efforts' in his examination of the legal profession, but laments the amount remaining to be done (2012: 40), and specifies four areas requiring attention. These are the purpose of programmes; the sustainability and evaluation of programmes; embedding fair practices, and widening the recruitment pool (2012: 40–41). This research identifies and directly engages with all four of these issues.

The most recent research on this matter was published by the Social Mobility and Child Poverty Commission in June 2015 (Ashley et al., 2015), which found, in line with this research, that:

> despite [elite law and accountancy firms'] efforts to improve social inclusion over the past ten to fifteen years, these elite firms continue to be heavily dominated at entry level by people from more privileged socio-economic backgrounds. This can be attributed primarily to a tendency to recruit the majority of new entrants from a narrow group of elite universities, where students are more likely to have attended selective or fee-paying schools, and/or come from relatively affluent backgrounds. In addition, elite firms define 'talent' according to a number of factors such as drive, resilience, strong communication skills and above all confidence and 'polish', which participants in the research acknowledged can be mapped on to middle-class status and socialisation.
>
> (2015: 6)

The study used proxy indicators of economic and social status: eligibility for free school meals (indicating parental eligibility for benefits, or annual income of less than £16,190); whether the individual's parents attended university, or whether they were the first generation in their immediate family to do so; and third, whether they were educated at a state school, selective state school (grammar school), or private school (2015: 8). It identifies that one of the biggest barriers to social mobility in the workplace is a lack of social mobility in the applicant pool, which can itself be tracked back to a lack of social mobility at elite universities, from where most law and accountancy firms will recruit (2015: 9–11).

Most notably, the study reflects a key argument in this research – that programmes aimed at increasing participation require organisations to examine how they construct 'talent' in recruitment, as opposed to seeking to alter applicants' attributes:

> the focus of such initiatives has historically been on raising aspirations and changing the attitudes, behaviours and skills of potential professionals from non-traditional backgrounds. Though welcome, this emphasis neglects the 'demand side' causes of limited diversity, including the role played by current definitions of 'talent'. Unless elite firms further interrogate their own notions of talent, it is likely that those who participate in access schemes will continue to face barriers to entry and progression. Even greater progress would be made if firms reflected further on those characteristics which represent 'talent', and minimised those aspects of their current recruitment and selection strategies which tend to reproduce their existing work forces. Second, mainstream recruitment and selection processes advantage many of the most privileged members of our society, whilst social inclusion initiatives have focussed on some of the least privileged students. We suggest that marginal but still useful improvements to inclusion could be made if many more elite firms could also encourage suitably qualified students from 'ordinary' backgrounds to apply in significantly higher numbers and, critically, provide them with the support they need to succeed. At present, this group represents a 'missing cohort' of potential new professionals, who are arguably over-looked by existing initiatives to open access to the professions.
>
> (2015: 13)

1.1.4 What is the solution?

A recurrent theme in these policy documents is criticism of elite professions, such as the Bar, for failing to take sufficient action to recruit young people from diverse socio-economic backgrounds. Whilst there is often recognition that young people are emerging from education without the qualifications needed for such professions, this is identified as attributable in many cases to their socio-economic circumstances, not a lack of intellect. However, as professions continue to recruit largely by reference to selection criteria preferring traditional academic achievement, it is difficult for intelligent young people without these traditional markers of merit to gain access to the most prestigious professions.

Suggestions for increasing numbers of young people from lower socio-economic backgrounds in professions have usually centred around two main matters, though Ashley et al.'s report does present some more nuanced suggestions, as set out above. First, the provision of greater support throughout schooling, especially relating to decision-making about higher education, and second, improved links between elite professions and young people. Such improvement is often conceived of as being through mentoring schemes and provision of information.

At the core of any social mobility discussion is meritocracy; indeed, I suggest that the two concepts are inextricably linked. The corollary of everyone achieving according to their talents, unmediated by advantage or inhibited by lack thereof, is that no-one is restricted in their achievement by their background. Therefore, the two notions appear to be co-dependent.

These increasing concerns about social mobility and meritocracy have been particularly expressed in relation to the legal profession, and especially the Bar. Perceptions of the Bar as an 'old boys' network' and thus accessible only to those from higher socio-economic groups and with inside connections have brought the profession under scrutiny. Such scrutiny has fallen not on individual chambers, but on the whole profession, and the Inns of Court as professional associations which control initial admission to the profession by way of 'Call'. This process of admissions is described in the next chapter.

Before turning to the details of the research itself, however, a brief overview of the methodology used provides the context for the quotations and questionnaire responses on which this research relied. This is also a convenient point to explore briefly one of the reasons why so little research into the English Bar exists: access for researchers can be as complex to navigate as it can for non-traditional aspirant entrants.

1.2 Professional association as interventionist actor: Inner Temple's Pegasus Access and Support Scheme as case study

As a professional association, not directly employing barristers, Inner Temple may not seem the most likely body to implement an access programme. However, as the bodies responsible for the initial admission of aspirant entrants, the role of the Inns of Court (see Chapter 2) cannot be ignored in any discussion around the demographic composition of the profession.

As an historic and elite profession, the Bar has traditionally operated occupational closure (Larson, 1977). Whilst claimed to be necessary to protect standards, the increasingly rigorous academic entry requirements can be gained only through expensive courses. Information about the profession, and work experience within it, are difficult to access for those without informal links within it. Furthermore, a traditional educational path is usually expected (Francis and MacDonald, 2009). It may not be expected that an embedded professional association within a traditional profession would seek to change a longstanding status quo. Their field position within the profession is central, and therefore such an association could be expected to wield significant power such that it could make an alteration if it desired (Greenwood, Suddaby and Hinings, 2002). However, it would also be expected that such an organisation would have a strong attachment to the central value system due to its embeddedness, and therefore might not wish to alter a longstanding status quo. In the case study, this longstanding status quo was an acceptance of practices which indirectly facilitated social closure.

However, the professional association used as a case study in this research, Inner Temple, established and promoted PASS as an innovative programme aimed at overturning a notion previously regarded as crucial to the professional project, despite being an embedded professional association within a traditional profession. Inner Temple describes the programme on its website as:

> The Honourable Society of the Inner Temple, in association with participating Chambers, launched PASS in March 2012 to ensure that all students with the capability and determination to pursue a career at the Bar have the opportunity to undertake work experience (known as 'mini-pupillages') in barristers' Chambers, regardless of their background or personal networks. [. . .] PASS is aimed at specific groups that might face obstacles in progressing to the professions.[20]

PASS was established by Inner Temple in 2012. At the time of the data collection there had been one pilot cohort and two full cohorts. Applications are accepted annually. Successful candidates undertake their mini-pupillages over the remainder of the academic year at a time convenient to them and the chambers with which they are placed. Although the pilot cohort was relatively small, full cohorts since have been increasing in size (see Table 2 below), and it is hoped that this number will increase as more chambers sign up to be 'partner chambers' that accept students through the scheme.

There are currently sixty-one partner chambers, of which fifty-three are exclusively based in London, one is a London set with annexes outside of London, and seven are elsewhere in the country.[21] (The scheme is currently focussing on London-based chambers due to organisational constraints on extending it. It is hoped that it may be possible to extend it to more sets outside of London in the future.)[22] These chambers are of varying sizes and their expertise covers all practice areas, from general common law sets (e.g. 3 Paper Buildings) to specialist sets in media and information law (e.g. One Brick Court).

PASS is the first programme developed and run exclusively by an Inn of Court on this scale. It is run in partnership with chambers, who agree to give one or more mini-pupillage slots per year to PASS candidates. It also unites with COMBAR, the Commercial Bar Association, to provide additional funding and mentoring for five students.[23] Candidates are selected by Inner Temple

---

20 www.pegasus.me/?page_id=71 [accessed 17th July 2017].
21 Atlantic Chambers – Liverpool, Enterprise Chambers' Leeds' annexe, 37 Park Square – Leeds, Chartlands Chambers – Northampton, Guildhall Chambers – Bristol, Linenhall Chambers – Chester, No5 – Birmingham, St John's Chambers – Bristol; www.innertemple.org.uk/becoming-a-barrister/how-to-get-involved/pass/our-partners [accessed 19th November 2017].
22 www.pegasus.me/?page_id=71 [accessed 12th August 2017].
23 www.pegasus.me/?page_id=162 [accessed 17th July 2017].

by application forms, with some given a short telephone interview if deemed necessary for the Education and Training team to fully assess their application. The application form is designed to capture motivation and skills necessary for the Bar learnt in other contexts, as well as any educational and personal disadvantage that may have prevented the candidate from fully demonstrating their potential. Compared to many mini-pupillage application forms, the PASS form consists of a relatively small number of questions regarding academic achievements, requiring only a personal statement setting out the candidate's reasons for considering being a barrister, plus one academic and one character reference.

Salaried staff members at Inner Temple's Education and Training Department with specialist knowledge of access and education sift the applications. Traditional conceptions of merit are not rigidly applied, as staff are experienced in quantifying achievement in its context. Students select specialisms in which they are interested from a list of practice areas, and if possible are matched with chambers in that area.

Mini-pupillages offered through PASS are intended to be the same as any other mini-pupillage offered by that chambers to direct applicants in terms of work seen, activities undertaken and duration. However, the chambers is required to provide expenses to students who secure their mini-pupillage through PASS. The importance of this in enabling students to undertake the placements was articulated repeatedly by student participants.

1.3 Methodological notes

This research drew on data obtained through three techniques. Questionnaire data already obtained by Inner Temple during its own efforts to evaluate PASS prior to this research was used to direct a grounded theory approach, and further data to support and nuance the development of the theoretical framework was then obtained through questionnaires, focus groups and elite interviews.

1.3.1 Funding and access

The Bar is notoriously hard to access for academic research (see, for example, Flood's account of his ethnography of barristers' clerks (1981), and Rogers' writing on her research into pupillage (2010)). In this respect, the identity of the funding source (Keele University in conjunction with the Honourable Society of the Inner Temple) was very important. Not because it (knowingly) influenced the output of the researcher, but because the hurdle of access was largely overcome by Inner Temple's involvement, as a respected professional association trusted by practitioners. This gave credibility with participants, and probably influenced some interviewees' agreement to participate. Inner Temple collected and provided the questionnaire data; acted as intermediary between the researcher and the Pathways and PASS participants, and provided a location for the focus groups. I had no prior affiliation to the Inner Temple before beginning this research, ameliorating some of the possible 'bias' effects identified in existing research.[24]

Similarly, my own experiences influenced my approach to this research. I had undertaken mini-pupillages, completed the BPTC and been Called to the Bar by another Inn of Court. Financially that had been made possible by a major scholarship from my Inn prior to the BPTC, and the Cloth Fair Scholarship from the Kalisher Trust as I completed the BPTC. At the end of the first year of this research, I secured pupillage.

It is recognised, perhaps most saliently by ethnographers, that in data interpretation the meaning which the researcher takes from words and actions will be affected, albeit subconsciously, by their own knowledge and practices. As highlighted by Martens (2012) there are risks of researcher knowledge being projected onto the actions of participants. My antidote to this was to ask more questions to elicit more precisely the feelings of participants. With hindsight, this was perhaps also a subconscious nod to a feminist method of research, whereby the researcher attempts to elicit the understood meaning from participants themselves, as opposed to imposing their own meaning onto events (Kindon, 2003). Interpretation is crucial for this research (due to the use of grounded theory), so many quotations are included in the text so that readers can make their own interpretations.

As well as the downsides to 'insider researchers', there are undeniably advantages (Costley et al., 2010). Having knowledge of what can be a very idiosyncratic profession, and one which is complex and multi-layered, allowed me to gain the trust of participants. Although I never divulged my own experiences unless explicitly asked about them (in which case I disclosed the minimum possible), it enabled more detailed exploration of difficult issues with some participants, and potentially created confidence in the research, as it was being conducted by someone with an understanding of the professional context.

1.3.2 Design

A fixed mixed-methods design allowed a pragmatic combination of the strengths of both qualitative and quantitative research methods (Creswell and Plano Clark, 2011: 54). Questionnaires provided both types of data, and focus group and interview data added a depth, richness and array of lived experience. Due to the purpose of this research in investigating the ability of embedded professional

---

24 For example, in a meta-analysis of anti-depressant studies, those funded by a pharmaceutical company were likely to favour the drug of that company to an extent not found by non-industry-sponsored research (Bruce Baker et al., 2003) by up to a multiple of four (Becker-Bruser, 2010). 'Funding bias' or 'sponsorship bias' is a sub-category of 'experimenter bias', the researcher's desire to demonstrate results supporting a viewpoint desired by the funding body (Bero, 2013). I did not feel aware of any pressure to produce particular findings, or even necessarily to report positively on the programme.

associations to act on a divisive issue such as social mobility at the Bar, it was not possible to have a representative sample. Self-selection bias was inherent, as the sample relied on willing and available participants, and their possessing relevant knowledge of the research subject matter. Therefore, a purposive sample (for example, Sommerlad (2007), Francis (2004) and Braithwaite (2010)), was used.

It was important that varied viewpoints were gathered, so groups likely to have different perceptions of the programme's meaning and operation were identified. These were Benchers (elected senior members) and salaried staff of Inner Temple; representatives of participating chambers; representatives of other professional associations and chambers which were not participating, and students. With each of these groups slightly different information was being sought. In exploring the role that professional associations can take in addressing contentious issues within the profession, interviews were conducted with chambers' and professional associations' representatives. In interviewing Benchers, the hope was to gain an understanding of the motivation behind the intervention; why the Benchers had initiated action to improve social mobility through Inner Temple and had agreed to dedicate resources to such a programme. When interviewing salaried staff who administered the programme the focus was on how it ran in practice, and how this compared to the theory of it. Discussion of possible improvements was also common. With chambers' representatives, discussion centred around the relationship between the Inn and the chambers in running the programme, what a mini-pupillage at that chambers consisted of and how the chambers viewed mini-pupillages as an aid to entry to the profession. To consider the impact of interventions on their target groups students of both PASS and Pathways[25] participated in focus groups. This provided the crucial experiential element missing from much of the research in this area. In reality, data from interviews and focus groups with all categories of participants was relevant in every area of the research. Although focussing closely on PASS data, as a programme entirely constructed by Inner Temple, data from the Pathways focus group adds depth by including the experiences of younger aspirant entrants.

1.3.3 Ethics

Although biographical markers are used to give context when interview responses are quoted, none are so specific as to allow the combination of the quotation's content and the biographical markers to identify the speaker. This means they are necessarily scant, as the group of barristers involved explicitly with social mobility at the Bar is fairly small.

More generally, it was important that this research was conducted in a way that did not reinforce any negative connotations that non-traditional aspirant entrants

---

25 Pathways to Law is a programme aimed at sixth form students and run by the Sutton Trust (www.suttontrust.com/programmes/pathways-to-law [accessed 7th August 2017]). As part of the programme students spend one day at Inner Temple participating in activities such as debating, court visits and Q&A sessions with barristers.

might have of the profession. In exploring a programme aimed at tackling a socially-sensitive issue, the stakes were higher than simply complying with regulatory requirements. In pursuing the academic aim of assessing how and why a professional association was attempting to improve social mobility, it was important to be aware of related tensions, and the sensitive nature of some relevant matters. Taking care not to reinforce power imbalances or existing stereotypes was therefore a consideration, in the hope that participating in this research was part of a broader positive interaction with the profession for the students involved.

1.3.4 Prior preliminary data collection

Inner Temple had previously collected some data through questionnaires administered to students who had attended access events at the Inn. There were nine sets of data, representing nine different Pathways cohorts. There was a tenth event in November 2013 but questionnaire data for that was unavailable during the time that data was being collected and analysed. Therefore, it is not included in the data referred to, although the numbers were later obtained and are included in Table 1 for completeness. Table 1 below summarises the Pathways cohorts and their response rates.[26]

1.3.5 Data collection methods

1.3.5.1 Questionnaires

The response rates for individual days of the Pathways scheme, and the overall response by year cohort for PASS students, can be seen in Tables 1 and 2. Recent methodological research has suggested that response rates may not be as crucial to data reliability as previously thought (Holbrook et al., 2007).

For logistical reasons, it proved impossible to use focus groups as a method of data collection for the second full PASS cohort. Therefore, two questionnaires written by the researcher were distributed, one before the students undertook their placement, and another afterwards. This was in addition to the post-placement questionnaire written and distributed by Inner Temple, the answers to which were also provided to the researcher.

The 'before' and 'after' questionnaires written by the researcher were designed to allow some measure of attitudinal change through repeating some questions in both questionnaires. Due to the non-scientific research design, it is not possible to claim causation of any attitudinal changes through participation in PASS, but it allowed an exploration of potential changes in perception contributed to by the programme.

---

26 The exact questions varied between cohorts, and this is highlighted where relevant. Demographic data were not collected from the January and June 2011 cohorts or the February 2013 cohort. Where demographic data is referred to, the total number of responses is given for clarity. The content of the questionnaires used to collect data from the Pathways students was not determined by the researcher, though addressed the same broad issues.

Table 1 Participation and response rates of Pathways students to feedback questionnaires

Event	Location of students	School year group of students	Number of participating students	Number of responses to survey	Response rate
April 2010 (Pilot)	All institutions	Year 13	41	41	100%
January 2011	London	Year 12	114	110	96%
April 2011	Out of London	Year 13	78	73	94%
June 2011	London	Year 13	105	68	65%
December 2011	London	Year 12	140	139	99%
April 2012	Out of London	Year 13	62	62	100%
November 2012	London	Year 12	139	128	92%
February 2013	London	Year 13	28	25	89%
April 2013	Out of London	Year 13	77	56	73%
November 2013	London	Year 12	91 signed up (exact attendance unknown)	87	96% (based on 91 attendees)

Table 2 Participation and response numbers of PASS students to feedback questionnaires

Cohort	No. of students participating	Responses to Inner Temple's post-placement questionnaire	Responses to researcher's pre-PASS questionnaire	Responses to researcher's post-PASS questionnaire
Pilot	18 (13 actually undertook placements)	7	N/A	N/A
First	30	25	–	–
Second	48	17	31	16

The table above sets out responses to the questionnaires sent to PASS students; as can be seen, the number of responses varied greatly.

1.3.5.2 Focus groups

Focus groups provided qualitative data from the students themselves about the experiential elements of the Pathways and PASS programmes to add depth and credibility to the research through engaging with those at whom the programme was aimed. Focus groups were preferred over interviews for the student participants to encourage dialogue and discussion, and to access data from a greater number of students in a shorter period.

Three focus groups were conducted with the researcher. They were recorded and later transcribed. The first was with nine Pathways students, the second with four PASS students and the third with two PASS students. The groups were unrepresentative, and the members were unknown to one another (Merton, Fiske and Kendall, 1956). The first two focus groups were carried out at Inner Temple, and a third by conference call, with the researcher and both participants in their home locations. Each was scheduled to last for up to ninety minutes, and preliminary schedules of questions were used, though with flexibility depending on answers given (a semi-structured design; Noaks and Wincup, 2004: 79)

1.3.5.3 Interviews

Whilst focus groups were judged the most appropriate data collection method for the students, interviews were preferred for Benchers, Inner Temple staff and chambers' representatives. Speaking with these participants individually allowed for an exploration of nuanced views, and the possibility of discussing views which might not have been communicated in a group setting. Anonymity and confidentiality were assured in the letter of invitation, the information sheet and on the consent form, and interviewing of employees was done with the knowledge and permission of Inner Temple.

Table 3 Biographical abbreviations of interview and focus group participants

M/F	Male/female.
Inner/non-Inner	Denotes whether the interviewee was a member of Inner Temple (as a Bencher or barrister) or employed by Inner Temple in any capacity.
Other prof. assocs.	Denotes that the interviewee has membership of other professional associations, such as the Bar Council, BSB or similar bodies. It was decided not to be more specific than this to protect the anonymity of the interviewees.
Chambers' rep.	Interviewee was speaking in their capacity as the person in their chambers who deals with mini-pupillage applications, and by extension PASS participants, in those chambers.
Salaried	These interviewees were employed as salaried members of staff by the relevant organisation. They were not legally trained.
FG	Focus group.
1/2	Denotes which number focus group the speaker participated in (applies only to PASS participants).

Twelve separate individuals were interviewed one-to-one with interviews ranging in length from forty-five to ninety minutes, at a location of the interviewee's choice. Eleven interviewees were interviewed in person at their place of work, all of which were in London, with one exception. Most of these interviews were organised directly with the individual, although many were practising barristers and therefore clerks often assisted with scheduling as they had access to the interviewees' professional diaries. The twelfth interview was conducted by telephone after a face-to-face interview had to be cancelled at late notice due to professional commitments.

One chambers that did not participate in PASS but had instead created its own bespoke programme agreed to have a senior member interviewed as part of this research. This offered a point of comparison – what was another organisation doing to challenge social closure at the Bar, and in what ways did it differ from PASS? Where focus group or interview data is used, it is accompanied by relevant biographical detail coded as set out in Table 3.

1.4 Grounded theory

As illustrated in part by the non-representative sampling, this is explorative research, without hypothesis testing, to investigate an area of interest (Bachman and Schutt, 2011: 43). From this investigative approach, a grounded theory approach was utilised (Glaser and Strauss, 1967) whereby theories were formed and concepts developed flexibly as the research unfolded (Layder, 1993). Glaser and Strauss have defined grounded theory as 'the discovery of theory from data systematically obtained from social research' (1967: 2); clearly an apt description of this research. Although extensive literature reviews in relevant areas have been conducted, and views advanced on potential outcomes in this book, there is nonetheless no settled hypothesis that this research aims to prove or disprove as in the typical experimental model of research. In grounded theory knowledge of existing research is used to inform our analysis, as opposed to prescriptively directing it. Indeed, existing literature can itself be seen as 'data' within grounded theory, and used actively to integrate the knowledge produced by the research (Glaser, 1992). This also allows for the role and use of the researcher's own knowledge of the field, as discussed above.

A conceptual framework is established which introduces the reader to the existing literature that is later used to inform the analysis of the data collected in this research. In this way, the existing literature is very much an active element in this research; it is used to shape understanding of the data collected, as an aid to its interpretation, and to suggest how this research may build further upon existing literature through its exploration of a developed concept (social mobility) within an area that has been subjected to little academic analysis (the Bar).

Although originally conceived by Glaser and Strauss, grounded theory has since seen a split between its two 'founding fathers', with Strauss and Corbin (1990) advancing a different conception based on the 'basic of qualitative research' which was seen by Glaser (1992) as being overly prescriptive; he referred to it as 'full conceptual description'. Meanwhile, Charmaz (2000: 521) built upon Glaser's symbolic interactionism-inspired approach: '[b]y adopting a constructivist grounded theory approach, the researcher can move grounded theory methods further into the realm of interpretive social science consistent with a Blumarian (1969) emphasis on meaning, without assuming the existence of a uni-dimensional external reality.'

It is Charmaz's conception which is preferred in this research, as through it grounded theory offers the opportunity to emphasise the meaning attributed to professional associations, social mobility, and programmes aiming to promote it, by those who are involved in these within the Bar, and the students experiencing the programmes. As the experiential element of students on these programmes is so important to this research, as explained above, grounded theory allows accessing of the meaning attributed by participants, as opposed to one imposed by the researcher. Furthermore, as Charmaz (1995, 2002) notes, some elements held in common by all grounded theories lend themselves to exploratory research such as this, most notably the simultaneous collection and analysis of data, the creation of analytic codes and categories developed from data and not by pre-existing conceptualisations (theoretical sensitivity), and discovery of basic social processes in the data.

Whilst not suited to an experimental method, this research is akin to that identified by Crooks (2001) as especially suited to grounded theory: '[Grounded theory] is ideal for exploring integral social relationships and the behaviour of groups where there has been little exploration of the contextual factors that affect individual's lives.' In light of the arguments advanced that both the English Bar and the situations of aspirant barristers from disadvantaged backgrounds have been rather neglected by research, the need for a theory that allows the lack of specific research in this narrow area to be taken into account demonstrates a particular attraction of grounded theory.

From data generation in grounded theory, three types of coding usually take place: open, axial, and selective (Strauss and Corbin, 1990; 1998). *Open* refers to the process of generating initial concepts from the data. *Axial* refers to the development and linking of concepts into conceptual families through a coding paradigm, and *selective* coding is the formalising of these relationships into theoretical frameworks. This coding is 'kept active' by a constant interrogation of the data for meaning by the researcher as they code (Glaser, 1978). The aim is that enough data will be collected whereby 'saturation of concepts' is reached; that is not the point where no more data can be collected, but the point at which collecting more data will not cause any more categories to be created or generate greater conceptual knowledge of the categories existing (Glaser and Strauss, 1967: 61). These coding exercises took place with the assistance of NVivo software, and the development of an initial document which examined the themes found in the interviews, so that these could be linked to one another and to overarching theoretical concepts.

From this point, it was possible to develop a 'core category' around which the generation of theory occurs (Glaser, 1978: 73), and to which all categories were linked. As it should account for most variations in data, it tends to be a more highly abstracted category than others within the formed theory, but should still be firmly grounded in data. A weakness of the theory, however, is that the method of developing this core category is regrettably vague.

A further criticism levelled at grounded theory is that it is not 'rigorous' due to its basis in inductive conclusions, amongst other reasons (see Gasson, 2004: 85–92), although this is clearly a value-laden and comparative term in itself; a process that is rigorous in one sense may not be in another, yet it may still objectively be rigorous. Charmaz also defends grounded theory: 'Weaknesses in using the method have become equated with weaknesses inherent in the method' (1990: 1164); thus, properly conducted grounded theory is defended by its supporters as being equally rigorous as other methods. Indeed, it also has its own criteria for assessing the reliability of grounded theory-based research (Glaser, 1978):

(a) Fit and relevance – how well do the categories relate to the data and derive from constant comparison and conceptualisation of the data?
(b) Workability – to what degree are the categories integrated into the core category that emerges?
(c) Modifiability – are all the concepts that are important to the theory incorporated into it by the constant comparison process? A modifiable theory can be altered when new relevant data is compared to existing data.

A further 'test' for the rigour of grounded theory has been suggested by Melia (1996): that of whether the grounded theory produced from the data creates a 'plausible story'. In research which places so much weight on the interpretation of data by participants, as opposed to its construction and meaning imposed upon it by the researcher, this is an important test of rigour for this method, and one that demonstrates its value in research such as this, which is aiming to expose a rarely-studied area of the legal profession to academic research.

In this research, the grounded theory model led to a framework emerging from the data that emphasised the role of individuals within organisations when seeking to alter manifestations of central values. It became clear that PASS would not have begun without the particular efforts of a small group of individuals. They came together to effectively utilise the increased power resulting from their combination of elite status within the professional association, and the professional knowledge of access and education. The theoretical framework resultantly focusses on the role of individuals within the wider context of a professional association, and how they may influence the actions of the professional association. A co-existent framework that emerged was that of constraints; both those operating on the professional association and those operating on non-traditional aspirant entrants. Both sets of constraints exerted significant influence on the efficacy of a programme, and contributed to a portrayal of the Inner Temple as operating from a basis of generally diminished power of professions and their professional associations. The next chapter will set out the existing literature which forms the conceptual framework used for analysis. In keeping with a grounded theory approach, this existing literature is also treated as data in itself, strengthening the conclusions drawn through the symbiosis of current research and new data and arguments.

1.5 Overview of the book

This chapter has examined the background of general research and societal interest in social mobility which led to this research. However, the depth of this research focusses on a specific subsection of a specialised profession, requiring an initial introduction to the structure of the profession and its workings. Many of these structural aspects are key to an understanding of the context of the professional association and how its operation may be constrained. Therefore, this book proceeds initially with Chapter 2 briefly describing the landscapes of the Bar and Inner Temple. It then addresses the interplay between the profession and social mobility, before setting out the key arguments made in the rest of the book. Chapter 3 sets out the evolution of our understanding of professional associations, and their movement from the more powerful position they have historically occupied to a new, more precarious location. Chapter 4 considers the key matters for a professional association; those values that are, or have previously been regarded as, central to a professional association. It also explores why, in the case of the Bar, social closure has featured as a component of the central value system; how this value system is perceived externally, and what may motivate a professional association to seek to alter the composition of the central value system.

Chapter 5 then moves towards a consideration of the methods by which a professional association may be an interventionist actor, focussing on how such an organisation may be able to use its power and influence within its profession to effect change on the central value system. Specifically, the role of internal dynamics, loyalty and the motivations experienced for developing or engaging with such a project are explored, and management change literature is used to assess whether this change is likely to be successful in the longer term. Relevant to this are matters such as institutional entrepreneurship and the crucial distinction between management and leadership.

Chapter 6 also moves more deeply into the case study, examining PASS itself, beginning by introducing work experience in the form of mini-pupillages, its importance at the Bar, and how it is usually obtained by aspirant entrants. It then considers why Inner Temple has chosen to channel its action into a programme focussing on work experience, and whether a programme which focusses on causing non-traditional aspirant entrants to conform to the established norms is a truly radical innovation. It concludes that it is not as radical as some might try to portray it, and that a more innovative programme would be one which challenged the existence of these norms and encouraged the recognition of ability demonstrated differently.

Both Chapters 5 and 6 have raised the issue of the potential importance of individual agency within professional associations, and Chapter 7 analyses this importance in the light of post-professionalism, as identified by Kritzer (1999), and constraining factors on professional associations' ability and choice to act in altering the profession itself. These constraints are analysed in terms of their sources, and the degree of control over these sources held by a professional association. Particularly at the Bar, these constraints are mainly external, such as legislation, and those operating on the target audience of interventions. These constraints suggest that professional associations are no longer masters of their own destiny as they had previously been perceived, and the reasons for this are analysed towards the end of this chapter. It is argued that the role of individual agency has been overlooked in the academic literature on professional associations specifically, and that it would not be possible for a professional association within a conservative and traditional profession to be interventionist in a divisive area such as access without significant human capital and individual agency within the association. Furthermore, the links made between employed individuals at the different sites of professional power at the Bar also appear to have been overlooked. Although outside of the scope of this research, this is highlighted as an area for potential further research.

Chapter 8 brings together existing research and findings from the current project to suggest attributes for a successful access scheme, examining what factors are likely to have the greatest impact on the efficacy of an intervention. Concluding, Chapter 9 draws together the threads examined into thoughts on the operation of professional associations in traditional professions, their sources of power, constraints on that power, and how it can be used to pursue an alteration in the central value system subscribed to by a profession.

2 Social mobility and the legal profession
Getting in and getting on

Having set this research within wider societal interest, this chapter begins by explaining the somewhat complex structure of the profession, how the components inter-relate and the path that must be woven between them to enter practice. It then explores a brief history of the demographics of the Bar, before developing the theoretical framework used and the key arguments consequently arising from this research.

2.1 Structure of the Bar

2.1.1 Chambers: power in autonomy

Chambers are unique structures in which a group of self-employed barristers rent office space and hire clerks (and sometimes administrative staff) by each barrister paying a regular sum in chambers' fees and rent. Chambers are not usually corporate entities (although some chambers are run as small business, e.g. Matrix)[1] but a group of individuals benefitting from economies of scale by jointly hiring property and staff. Chambers were an important element of this research, as they chose whether to participate in PASS; a decision itself of interest. They were also key to the operation of PASS, as the programme required incorporation of PASS mini-pupils into chambers' regular mini-pupillage programme. As is described in Chapter 6, this led to variations in student experience affecting the efficacy of PASS.

Chambers' governance is usually through committees comprised of tenants. Most tenants will sit on a committee for a set term, before they are succeeded by another tenant. Consequently, committees may lack consistency and continuity, despite the magnitude of decisions often taken by them. Furthermore, membership of committees is voluntary (although in smaller chambers pressure may be exerted on tenants so that each committee is 'complete'), but as the barristers involved are self-employed, it is often difficult to devote extensive

1 www.matrixlaw.co.uk/about-us [accessed 17th July 2017].

time to committee roles. Interviewees recognised that this made the running of chambers-based access programmes very difficult, and this recognition contributed to a wider implicit understanding that chambers were not the best organisations to establish programmes:

> Part of the problem [lack of programmes] at the Bar is that we are all self-employed very busy practitioners and we all take on voluntarily different roles within chambers.
> (Interviewee 10, Inner, F, Bencher, other prof. assocs.)

As well as each chambers operating autonomously, there is no unifying body to which all must belong. Internal practice therefore varies between chambers, challenging consistent and cohesive action across the profession as no over-arching body has coercive power (besides regulatory objectives fulfilled by the BSB – see 2.1.4). All barristers must belong to an Inn to practise, so members of each of the four Inns of Court are found within any chambers. The prevalence of self-employment at the Bar (80.2% if counting those solely self-employed, 81.7% if those practising in dual capacity are included, in 2015; BSB, 2017) means a more fragmented profession. Sets of chambers – even in Central London – are smaller than leading City solicitors' firms.

This requires Inns to foster strong links with individual members if those members are to feel included by the professional association, something interviewees felt Inner Temple did particularly effectively. This was an important base for establishing PASS, as Inner Temple members encouraged their chambers to participate. Many barristers are also members of specialist Bar associations which are often practice-area-based (e.g. the Family Law Bar Association, or FLBA),[2] or are linked by some other practice attribute (e.g. Young Legal Aid Lawyers)[3] or personal characteristic (e.g. the Association of Women Barristers).[4] It is often through these sub-committees that barristers both network and innovate within the profession.

The relationship, and particularly the level of control possible, between chambers and Inns of Court is highlighted in this research. Whilst chambers are autonomous, the links that the Inns of Court can forge with individual practitioners may significantly influence their chambers in co-operating with an Inn of Court. In PASS the power of co-dependency was illustrated, with each body taking on the necessary elements of PASS with which it was equipped to deal. Inner Temple had the administrative resources, whilst chambers had the practitioners. Without both of those elements, the scheme would not have been tenable. Overall, this system seemed to cause relatively little friction or disagreement.

---

2 http://flba.co.uk [accessed 17th July 2017].
3 www.younglegalaidlawyers.org [accessed 17th July 2017].
4 www.womenbarristers.com [accessed 17th July 2017].

2.1.2 Inns of Court: community in fragmentation

The Inns of Court, once a barrister has qualified, are of relatively less practical importance than whilst a student, although they do monitor and provide opportunities for compulsory Continuing Professional Development (CPD). However, participants in this research emphasised that many barristers retain a loyalty to their Inn developed as students, and this early development was supported by the attachment already claimed by some PASS participants to the Inn. As a student member undertaking the BPTC, there is a requirement that twelve Qualifying Sessions are attended, consisting of dinners; intensive, heavily-subsidised, residential advocacy training, or talks by prominent lawyers or legal academics. Furthermore, many students are financial beneficiaries of their Inns, as scholarships are awarded by all four Inns. More and larger scholarships are awarded for the BPTC, but some smaller sums are awarded to pupils. The Inns also undertake other activities such as attending university careers' fairs and hosting Dinners to the Universities (when students attend formal dinners at the Inns). The Inns also participate in access work to varying extents: Middle Temple has developed the Access to the Bar Awards[5] and Inner Temple participates in Pathways and has developed PASS.

The Inns are largely practitioner-run through a committee structure, with a small base of salaried staff. Thus, some barristers continue to be heavily involved in Inn-based activities throughout their careers, as described by this interviewee. Loyalty of this kind became a prevalent theme in this research (see Chapter 4):

> I started off because I was involved with the Qualifying Sessions Committee which I chaired and I then went on to Chair the Education and Training Committee [. . .] for four or four and half years, something like that, so it was through that I became involved in the oversight really of the Inn's activities because the Outreach Committee is one of our sub groups. I had previously been involved with the Bar Council social mobility programmes. I was firstly on the 'C' Working Party and secondly I was the Chairman of the Working Party that set up the Social Mobility Foundation scheme.
>
> (Interviewee 9, M, Inner, Bencher, other prof. assocs.)

2.1.3 Representative body: Bar Council – position without power

Alongside the Inns are the Bar Council and the BSB. It is not possible to put the Inns and the Bar Council and BSB into a hierarchy, as they do not exist for the same purposes and their composition is very different. It is, perhaps, more accurate to set out the position as the Inns operating in parallel to the Bar Council and BSB.

---

5 www.middletemple.org.uk/members/special-interest-groups/access-to-the-bar [accessed 7th August 2017].

Social mobility and the legal profession   31

The Bar Council is the representative body of barristers, both employed and self-employed. It used to serve both representative and disciplinary functions. However, s.1 of the ('Legal Services Act 2007 LSA') created the LSB and required the separation of representative and disciplinary functions, the latter now fulfilled by the BSB.[6]

The Bar Council is comprised of officers (the Chairman, Vice-Chairman and Treasurer), who are elected by members each May, and serve for a term of a calendar year from the following 1st January.[7] Membership consists of around 115 barristers who are elected or represent the Inns, circuits and other interest groups. The work of the Bar Council is carried out through sixteen committees, each with a specific specialism or focus. Their work is supported by the secretariat, which provides policy and administrative support. The committees are made up of both members of the Bar Council and co-opted individuals. It was possible during this research to speak to practitioners and salaried staff who currently sit, or have sat, on Bar Council committees, particularly the Social Mobility and Education committees, allowing an insight into the internal – and often hidden – operations of a professional association within a profession little explored by research. This research reveals the interaction between the Bar Council and Inns of Court. It also suggests that the Bar Council is perceived in generally negative terms by many practitioners, compromising its ability to take innovative action, although the perception of its efficacy varied significantly even amongst former elected members.

2.1.4 Regulatory and disciplinary body: Bar Standards Board

The BSB fulfils the regulatory and disciplinary functions which were previously also found within the Bar Council. The BSB is made up of fifteen people, a combination of lay people (the majority, since 2012) and barristers. The Board is assisted in its work by three non-voting Special Advisers. The current Chair in 2017 is Sir Andrew Burns KCMG, a former diplomat,[8] and the Director is Dr Vanessa Davies, a non-practising barrister.[9] Similarly to the Bar Council, the BSB takes most of its action through committees, of which it has five, all reporting to the Board.[10] The BSB is described for completeness, as it did not play a notable role in this research.

The Inns of Court are the focus of this research, particularly their actions as a professional association in moulding the profession itself. As described above,

---

6 Although some unrest remains about the genuine nature of its independence; www.legalfutures.co.uk/latest-news/lsb-bar-council-interfered-independence-bsb-cab-rank-rule-changes [accessed 7th August 2017].
7 www.barcouncil.org.uk/about-us/who-we-are/officers [accessed 7th August 2017].
8 www.barstandardsboard.org.uk/about-bar-standards-board/how-we-do-it/our-governance/our-staff/chair-of-the-bar-standards-board [accessed 20th March 2017].
9 www.barstandardsboard.org.uk/about-bar-standards-board/how-we-do-it/our-staff/director-general-bar-standards-board [accessed 20th March 2017].
10 www.barstandardsboard.org.uk/about-bar-standards-board/how-we-do-it/our-governance [accessed 20th March 2017].

the Inns of Court occupy an unusual position within the legal profession. To better understand their role, a brief recounting of their role in the Bar's historical approach to social mobility is of interest. Without understanding where a professional association has come from, it is difficult to see where it might be heading. First, however, some practical explanations of the most common route of entry to the profession are set out.

2.2 Route to practise

To practise at the Bar, a person must be 'Called' by their Inn of Court. There are four Inns of Court: Inner Temple, Middle Temple, Gray's Inn and Lincoln's Inn. An aspiring barrister can choose which of the four they wish to join, and there is widely regarded as being little material difference, although the amount and distribution of scholarships may influence choice. Membership of an Inn is a pre-requisite of practice, meaning every barrister joins as a student, undertakes Qualifying Sessions, is Called and then remains a member of their Inn whilst they are practising.

Call is a ceremonial occasion which requires a person to successfully complete a qualifying Law degree or the Graduate Diploma in Law (GDL), the BPTC, twelve Qualifying Sessions at their Inn, and to have a character reference as a fit and proper person. Once Called, a person can begin pupillage; the final vocational stage of training and a pre-requisite for practice. Competition for pupillage is intense: each year those completing the BPTC number around double the number of pupillages available. Furthermore, candidates can apply for pupillage up to five years after completing the BPTC (Rule rQ029; BSB, 2017: 150) meaning that the cumulative number of those applying for pupillages in any year is much higher than the number of those completing the BPTC that year. Many who complete the BPTC do not secure pupillage.[11] There are many elements that chambers will look for when selecting pupils. At the paper sift stage attention will be paid to academic ability, written communication, work experience and other indicators of commitment to the Bar. From the paper sift a much smaller number will be selected for interview. At first interview, candidates will be assessed on their oral communication skills and interpersonal skills by a small panel of chambers' members, and may be given specific oral or written advocacy exercises to complete. At many chambers, interviews go to two rounds, with the second interview often being more demanding and with a larger panel of tenants.

The process is undeniably rigorous for any candidate, but statistics (including the disproportionate number of privately- and Oxbridge-educated barristers)

---

11 For example, for the cohort who started the BPTC in 2013, by 31st March 2017 fewer than 50 percent had begun pupillage (BSB, 2017a: 81). These statistics are unfortunately not presented in the most accessible manner, making it impossible to give an exact percentage.

suggest that those from particular demographics are more likely to succeed. This sits ill at ease with a commitment to equality of opportunity regardless of background, and the possibility of high achievement based solely on intellectual ability. Research, however, suggests that other factors such as educational and socio-economic circumstances significantly affect a young person's chance of successfully entering the profession (Sullivan, 2010).

Ultimately, if an aspirant entrant cannot succeed in this process, they will not be able to practise, despite having formally obtained entry to the profession through the completion of the BPTC and being Called by an Inn. As the statistics show that there is a diverse body of students undertaking the BPTC (Bar Council, 2011: 9–12), it appears that the attrition of students from lower socio-economic backgrounds between the BPTC and practice occurs at the stage of securing pupillage.

A key element to securing pupillage has been identified as work experience (Francis and Sommerlad, 2009). Often called 'mini-pupillages' at the Bar, work experience allows an aspirant entrant to experience the reality of day-to-day life at the Bar, speak to those already in practice, observe areas of law that may not be covered by their degree course, and assimilate those almost imperceptible behaviours that will allow them to fit in within the profession.[12] Furthermore, it facilitates making contacts within the profession – practitioners who can assist by giving advice, encouragement or even valuable 'inside information'. For many traditional aspirant entrants, they already have such contacts through family, friends or their educational establishments, providing advice and guidance during the process of applications for pupillage, and possibly leading to the provision of a mini-pupillage, arranged informally through the contact. This allows traditional aspirant entrants access to a crucial opportunity to fit themselves for the Bar, and gain valuable knowledge and understanding, without having to go through the highly competitive process of applying for mini-pupillage. Some interviewees admitted that many chambers receive so many applications even for mini-pupillage that many may go unread and unprocessed, often due to the other demands on the time of the barrister trying to both administer the scheme and run a busy practice of their own.

Thus, there is often an inequality of opportunity between traditional and non-traditional aspirant entrants of access to mini-pupillages. Such opportunities allow those who secure them to fulfil objective selection criteria requiring the completion of mini-pupillages, and to be better informed both about the profession itself and the life of a practitioner. However, they also allow aspirant entrants to be more convincing in their future applications, through exposure to the expected social norms

---

12 Throughout this book, when 'work experience' is referred to, it usually means 'mini-pupillage', as opposed to general legal work experience, unless there are clear contextual markers suggesting otherwise. Data collected suggested that students and practitioners both felt that legal work experience that did not take the form of a mini-pupillage, such as time in a solicitors' firm, was not ascribed the same value as mini-pupillages. It is suggested that this is because such work experience does not expose aspirant entrants to the specific social norms of the Bar (see Chapter 4).

seen at the Bar. Data gathered illustrated that the opportunities for this experienced by traditional aspirant entrants in family, educational or social settings were not experienced by non-traditional aspirant entrants. Similarly, the experience of non-traditional aspirant entrants in this research was that they struggled to secure work experience, and especially mini-pupillage, as they did not have familial and informal contacts whom they could approach to secure such experience. In direct application processes, they were also overlooked, which was itself something they attributed to not yet having been able to secure mini-pupillages, causing a vicious circle and feelings of discouragement. For these reasons, Inner Temple focussed an access programme on the provision of mini-pupillages to non-traditional aspirant entrants. For the importance of mini-pupillages as a process of socialisation to be understood, an overview of how the Bar has approached social mobility in the past provides helpful context.

2.3 Social mobility at the Bar over the 20th century

> There was no shortage of snobbery and anti-Semitism, and juniors still suffered arrogant or condescending treatment at the hands of some of their seniors, but the days when Bethell had provoked Neate to assault him in court and the Bar had sent Adolphus and Andrews to Coventry for fighting with umbrellas were long over.
>
> (Ashton, 1924: 25)

Whilst there have been no in-court assaults between counsel or fighting with umbrellas in many years (to the author's knowledge),[13] the snobbery mentioned has remained a perceived barrier to the Bar. Over the years, the process for admission has, thankfully, evolved from times when new members were chosen solely at the discretion of whichever barristers happened to be present at the relevant time; at Lincoln's Inn each candidate had to be approved by the Bar Table (those barristers dining in on the night that they were proposed for admission – Polden, 2010: 1080). Whilst this veto could be over-ridden by Benchers (Lincoln's Inn Black Books, iv, 113, 119–20, 128 – cited in Polden, 2010: 1080), it likely privileged those who could capitalise on links within the profession, propagating social closure.

Prest's work on the composition of the Bar in the 16th and 17th centuries suggested that social closure may not, in fact, have been as rife as might have been expected. In a sample of 115 men (5% of those Called between 1590 and 1639), he discovered that they were a more diverse group than may be expected (1986: 87). It is hard to fully appreciate what social diversity existed at the Bar at that time, as Prest's research suggests that recording practices were less than

---

13 When I read this quotation to a colleague their immediate reaction was to act out a duel with an (imaginary) umbrella with the Silk leading them in an upcoming trial, with whom they were experiencing some frustration. Perhaps the true difference of nearly 100 years is therefore one of self-restraint, as opposed to a lack of desire.

scrupulous, as the Inns wished to maintain their status as 'honourable societies' and therefore, in some cases, appear to have left unrecorded, or deliberately mis-recorded, the social origins of some entrants (1986: 87–91). Prest argues, however, that his further research suggests that many were not, in fact, from elite or landed-gentry backgrounds; the backgrounds of many were obscure, and some claims to high social status were dubious, at best (1986: 91). This is supported by the variety seen in the men's educational backgrounds (1986: 109), with a number not educated to university level (and, indeed, some express advice at the time against a university education, suggesting instead experience after education before practice, or a liberal arts-style degree as opposed to the direct study of Law (1986: 111)).

As the only 'gatekeepers' of the profession, the Inns had acquired the right both to lay down general requirements governing entrance and to exclude either from admission or Call those whom they felt undesirable (for example, no Inn would admit a man rejected by another Inn (Brady Leigh, 1827: 33)). Once again, this further contributed to the Bar developing the 'caste-like' appearance of which Larson (1977: xv) is so critical, with those already within the profession choosing those to join who resembled themselves. Each Inn of Court was governed by its Benchers, a 'self-perpetuating body of unrestricted size who added to their number as and when they chose' (Polden, 2010: 1078). The admission requirements applied vacillated between ethnic, moral, social and religious, and even these were applied inconsistently (Prest, 1986: 107), creating a currency of privilege as opposed to merit.

Furthermore, the Benchers' or other relevant members' decision was final, with no right to appeal. This was despite the fact that there were no procedural safeguards to ensure fairness – as illustrated by the method employed by Lincoln's (described above) – and selection could, at best, be arbitrary (or dependent on the amount of alcohol consumed by the Bar Table that evening). In 1825, Lincoln's Inn decided that its Visitor (arbitrator of disputes between individual and organisation) did not have jurisdiction to interfere with those regulations on the admission of students (Cocks, 1983: 22), removing an avenue by which an aggrieved refused aspirant entrant may have taken action. In this respect, a step forward was taken in 1837, when appeals were first allowed against refusal of admission, whereas previously it had only existed against refusal of Call after having been admitted. At this time, Lincoln's also abandoned the Bar Table veto (Polden, 2010: 1081). It remained the case that any woman who applied for admission was automatically refused on the grounds of her gender alone, without any consideration of her merit (Mossman, 2006). This stranglehold over admission, however, was to come back to haunt the Inns when, in the 1830s, the profession perceived them as being responsible for a downturn in the Bar resulting from the sorts of 'low-character' men whom they had been admitting (Cocks, 1983: 24), demonstrating the key role played by the Inns as professional associations in governing entry.

The most progressive Inn at this time seems to have been Middle, which had abandoned the long-held tradition of ordering the dining tables by seniority, now preferring a more democratic approach (Polden, 2010: 1087). It consequently attracted a large proportion of less demographically traditional entrants. Non-traditional entrants at that time mainly consisted of those from London University and mature entrants, but Middle Temple also saw an influx of students from the empires, and its diversity was possibly attributable in part to it providing the most generous scholarships (Polden, 2010: 1087).

However, an emphasis on the background of entrants continued to predominate, and an insistence that the Inns of Courts fulfilled their titles of being honourable societies meant that there was almost certainly a refusal to truly record the background of entrants if they were 'plebeian' (Lemmings, 1990: 11–13). Such was the strength of feeling surrounding this that James I made an edict which, although it had neither legal nor practical force, decreed that only sons of gentlemen be admitted to the Inns. Despite it lacking effect, the Inns did not make any formal provision for the sons of poor men to work to the Bar, in the way that Cambridge and Oxford allowed such men to come up as 'servitors or sizars', who paid for their board and tuition by doing menial labour for their college (Lemmings, 1990: 22). This meant that, in practice, entry was impossible for those who did not have access to independent means. Undoubtedly, part of the reason for this lack of provision was as a result of those already admitted by the Inns holding rather unprogressive views on the matter: '(the early Victorian Bar) had traditional values which made any sort of change the subject of extremely contentious debate within the profession itself' (Cocks, 1983: 55). This attention to membership flows, in a large part, from a desire to defend the status of 'profession' in a society that conflated 'elite' with 'exclusive'.

As Cocks writes (1983: 5), 'the modern Bar, with its distinctive blend of old and new ideas, was largely the creation of Victorian advocates'. This historical background provides context to the current access challenges facing the profession. It also allows an appreciation of the significant roles that have been played by the Inns in the development of the Bar and its identity as a profession.

The Bar has always faced certain problems to which the Inns have had to respond, namely funding and over-crowding, partly attributable to its status as an elite but predominantly self-employed profession. Its response to these problems set a backdrop for current concerns and approaches towards greater access. The Bar's loose-knit structure and self-employed nature made any institutional response to over-crowding difficult. The Inns did, periodically, attempt to put in place new obstacles, occasionally as a concerted effort by all four Inns, but on other occasions just a single Inn took steps towards restricting entry (Polden, 2010: 1019).

This illustrates that the problem of how many people should be allowed admission to the Bar, and whether it is appropriate to attempt to restrict entry, is not a new problem for this profession. The barriers that the Inns erected varied; there were 'disqualifying occupations', for example, and if you were engaged in such an occupation you could not be admitted to the Bar at any of the Inns. Inner Temple, acting alone in 1829, restricted its entry by imposing an entrance examination, examining candidates in 'classics and general studies of a liberal education' (Polden, 2010: 1019). However, the other Inns did not follow suit, and Inner Temple, rather than losing potential students due to this additional hurdle, discarded the examination in the 1840s.

Nonetheless, there were complaints throughout the 1830s and 1840s about the perceived lack of work available as a result of the Bar increasing in size (Cocks, 1983: 57). The early to mid-1800s were a turbulent time for the Bar and a time during which the Inns, Cocks suggests, actually played only a small role in the profession as a whole, and did not always do this in a way that made them popular within the profession. In Victorian times, it was possible, having been Called, for a barrister to 'forget his Inn for the rest of his life' (Cocks, 1983: 2), with most of the matters concerning a barrister being concentrated instead in the Circuit Mess on each respective circuit throughout the country. Cocks does concede that the Inns could be of real importance during this period, but it seems that they were more commonly regarded as self-involved, lost in their own world and contributing relatively little to the life of the profession (1983: 6). This is in sharp contrast to the views of participants in this research on the modern-day relevance of the Inns.

In the past it was easy to join an Inn if you had money, as it meant that no enquiry would be made into your character (Cocks, 1983: 1–2). This is closely related to class issues: although there are invisible boundaries in place caused by perceptions of tradition and exclusivity, there is also the very tangible barrier of being able to afford the training that is necessary to become a barrister. Even in the 1800s a university-educated Bar student might expect to spend £400 per annum and another £600 on board and lodgings (Duman, 1982: 47–8). Even post-Call, one was not guaranteed an immediate income, and Edward Cox thought that even considering the expenses of only five attendances at Sessions and a restricted attendance on circuit, a barrister would need at least £272 per annum from savings or another income off which to live until he was financially self-sufficient through his own practice. It would be necessary to find this sum for some years, as it usually took more than five years to show a profit at the Bar (Cox, 1852: 39–40), and this figure is supported by Duman (1982: 57), who suggests £250–£300 using handbooks on the profession from the time. Consequently, those training for the Bar and in their junior years of practice needed familial financial support, a second job or significant savings of their own upon which they could rely.

It was likely that only those from relatively privileged backgrounds would have either financial support from their families or savings of their own, and the Inns were restrictive about what sort of second job was considered suitable for a young barrister, demonstrating the power of the Inns at that time. Indeed, the Inns can still refuse Call to someone who cannot obtain a 'proposal for Call' (similar to a character reference),[14] although the denial of such a reference now would only

---

14 The Inns arrange pre-Call interviews with a Bencher or Master for aspirant entrants without existing connections; www.innertemple.org.uk/education/students/call-to-the-bar?showall=&start=1 [accessed 7th August 2017].

exist on much more serious grounds. However, the key issue here remains that of maintaining the elite character of the profession: in the past it was held to be incompatible for young barristers to supplement their fees with other employment, and the need to be in chambers or in court when that elusive brief arrived precluded another job which required regular work (Polden, 2010: 1034). Many young barristers took on university fellowships teaching Law (Duman, 1982: 59).

In the modern day, the role of the Inns continues to evolve, although their main role is often perceived as the provision of Qualifying Sessions, scholarships and CPD training. Increasingly, they are also undertaking more activities focussed on students studying at sixth form or university level, to promote the profession. However, this seemingly narrow remit may in fact disguise the power that is held by the Inns as professional associations of the Bar.

2.4 Getting in and getting on: mini-pupillages and access

Mini-pupillages have been identified as a key stage in the process of securing access to the Bar. A mini-pupillage is work experience; a period of between one day and a week shadowing one or a number of barristers from a set of chambers as they go about their professional lives. It may fulfil many roles: it allows students to see the daily life of a barrister, gain helpful knowledge by meeting and speaking with those practising, experience areas of law outside degree syllabi, and fulfil a formal requirement for many pupillage applications.

For all these reasons, it has been identified as offering a unique opportunity for identity formation (Francis and Sommerlad, 2009: 65), as it exposes students to the social norms and behaviours expected at the Bar. These consist of the unspoken and assumed rules ('doxa') according to which social interaction and behaviour is conducted within the social field ('habitus') of the profession, and is known to those within it (Bourdieu, 1984). Habitus is the physical embodiment of cultural capital (see below). For those from non-traditional backgrounds, who are often without informal contacts within the profession, it is argued that securing such exposure is harder than for their counterparts from traditional backgrounds, reducing opportunities to assimilate norms and practices of the Bar. This formed part of the reasoning behind the Social Mobility Commission's call for a statutory ban on unpaid internships (2016: 144).

2.4.1 Identity and 'fitting in'

Sociologists have explored the formation of social orders within society, where members of higher social strata will seek to exclude entrants from lower strata to maximise the benefit to those inside the closed group, a phenomenon called 'closure' (Weber, 1947: 188). This process was also identified by Weber as occurring in the occupational context (1947: 193). Professions often become real communities, and this means that members have permanent affiliation, identity, personal commitment and general loyalties (Larson, 1977: x). Therefore, despite supposedly being open to all of academic ability, professions such as medicine and law (Freidson, 1970) do, in fact, operate closure so that the established community can consider closely those whom it allows to be admitted. It is likely to admit only those who display 'traditional intellectuality' (Larson, 1977: xv), and those aligned outwardly with existing members (Abel, 1988: 48–9).

There has been debate concerning whether the professions as a whole are immune from, or neutral to, class structure (Larson, 1977: xiv). Whilst they may initially appear so, in that most professions notionally operate as meritocracies, and admission is ruled only by the achievement of certain requirements (usually academic), it may be that those qualifications will be more easily accessible to those from certain socio-economic demographics, operating as a barrier to entry for those from lower socio-economic groups. Therefore, as Larson later states (1977: xvi), both objectively and subjectively, professions are outside and above the working class, as occupations and as social strata. This supports an earlier contention by Goode (1957) that professions are in fact separate social groups, incorporating the internal commonality and shared experience of any community.

This allusion to professions as both occupations and social strata echoes the assertion by Freidson (1994) that the two concepts may join as one in some circumstances, including in the law. De Tocqueville stated that the absolute need of assistance in legal matters in England due to their complexity, and the public's high opinion of the ability of the legal profession, tend to separate it from the public and erect it as a distinct class (de Tocqueville, 1899, trans. Reeve, 1946: Chapter 16). Even the walled Inns of Court, centrally located in London yet also hidden, and the security measures which now pervade courts, set lawyers and their locations of practice out of the physical path of many lay people.

This research does not subscribe to the notion that a profession is a class, rather seeing it as a conflation, but the two concepts are clearly strongly linked. The fact remains that individual professional status is still an undeniably middle-class attribute and a typical aspiration of the socially-mobile children of industrial or clerical workers (Larson, 1977: xvi).

2.4.1.1 Social norms: Bourdieu's social capital and aesthetics

One possible contributory explanation for the under-representation of non-traditional aspirant entrants at the Bar can be found in Bourdieu's (1984) work on social stratification. Bourdieu proposes that society is split into 'class fractions' (1984: xxix), and three elements determine into which class fraction a person falls. These elements are social capital, cultural capital and economic capital. Their formation is triangular, with Bourdieu placing cultural capital apart from social and economic, both of which he portrays as acquired over time and dependent upon the cultural capital which a person already possesses.

He emphasises the dominance of cultural capital from the very beginning of his analysis, by stating that 'differences in cultural capital mark the differences between the classes' (1984: 69). This highlights that social capital cannot be learned, and neither can it be accumulated at a later age through education (1984: 15). Therefore, if it is postulated that a non-traditional aspirant entrant's access to the profession will be inhibited by their lack of social capital, intervention by a professional association is unlikely to assist. Manifestations of social capital are developed at a young age, and as such an intervention by a professional association at secondary school or university level is unlikely to engage with the target group early enough to make any alteration to this. Even if it could engage early enough to shape the markers of heightened social capital, serious ethical questions would arise (and it is argued that it is unlikely to be ethical). Later chapters consider the possibility of the greater transformative nature of recognising intellectual and practical potential relevant to the Bar over the outward manifestation of socio-economic class. Discussion of the ethicality of an earlier intervention is returned to in Chapter 8.

Bourdieu claims that how a person chooses to present their social space to the world (i.e. a person's aesthetic dispositions) demonstrates that person's social status and thereby distances them from lower social groups (1984: 468–9). A person's social class is displayed in their demeanours and self-presentation (1984: 32). Social closure may easily be propagated as there are external signifiers by which a person's class may be identifiable – such as their clothes (Thornton, 1996: 226) and their speech (Bourdieu, 1984: 58).

The development of aesthetic dispositions is largely determined by a person's social origin, rather than being accumulated over time, as demonstrated by Bourdieu's assertion that cultural capital is the most important, with economic and social capital occupying more subsidiary positions. The acquisition of cultural capital, key to the formation of aesthetic disposition, depends heavily on 'total, early, imperceptible learning, performed within the family from the earliest days of life' (1984: 59). The role of class is so important in the acquisition of these characteristics because 'The "young" can accept definitions that their elders offer them' (1984: 480), and these definitions form the basis of more nuanced preferences:

> [Taste] functions as a sort of social orientation, a 'sense of one's place,' guiding the occupants of a given ... social space towards the social positions adjusted to their properties, and towards the practices or goods which befit the occupants of that position.
> (1984: 468–9)

Bourdieu believed class distinction and preferences are:

> most marked in the ordinary choices of everyday existence, such as furniture, clothing, or cooking, which are particularly revealing of deep-rooted and long-standing dispositions because, lying outside the scope of the educational system, they have to be confronted, as it were, by naked taste.
> (1984: 77)

Social capital is identified by Bourdieu as a way in which the status of elite elements of society are preserved; those who do not display cultural signifiers of belonging to the upper class will be prevented from entering the 'circle' of a group or profession. Bourdieu (1984: 474–5) identifies that most people will seek to identify themselves with those higher on the social ladder, and to demonstrate their difference from those perceived as lower on the ladder. Therefore, many people adopt cultural signifiers of the next 'rung of the ladder', hoping that they will be perceived to belong to that group.

Existing research into non-traditional students at the Bar has illustrated the strong link between educational and social capital (Zimdars, 2010: 130), supporting Bourdieu's theory that with cultural capital as the bedrock upon which those are situated, the challenges for non-traditional aspirant entrants are not easily tackled by a professional association. For example, emphasis is often put on subtle factors, such the way in which women used their physical attributes and sexuality in a professional context (Sommerlad, 2007: 200; Thornton, 1996: 226), and the way in which they adapt their behaviour to distinguish between professional and non-professional contexts (Francis, 2015: 192).

As noted above, however, the ethicality of intervening on matters perceived by many to be elements of self-expression (albeit that the way that expression is used has class distinctions) is a complex question. Tocqueville observed that, due to the nature of the law, lawyers are usually inherently conservative, and the predominance of historical customs adds to this conservatism a taste and a reverence for what is old (de Tocqueville, 1899, trans. Reeve, 1946: Chapter 16). Such an observation is particularly pertinent with more recent criticisms of the Bar for being 'an alien environment for those who are not used to Chapel, Grace and dining' (Dame Jocelyn Barrow, writing in her report as Chair of the Committee of Inquiry into Equal Opportunities at the Inns of Court School of Law (1994), quoted by Abel, 2003: 183), which are customs from times gone by, and ones likely to be unfamiliar to those who did not attend collegiate universities. Thus, this 'taste and a reverence for what is old' often manifests itself in the preservation of traditions which are themselves exclusive. If non-traditional entrants are not willing to conform to or accept these traditions (and this may be an even more significant issue for those who are from other cultural or religious backgrounds) then they are at risk of feeling uncomfortable within the profession, and may ultimately leave – this is an example of a 'habitus' of the legal profession as described by Bourdieu. There is a tension to be resolved between increasing access and preserving those classical origins which are felt to be so important to a traditional profession and its sense of community.

Professional development requires a student to adopt a certain identity and inner dialogue of being value-free and neutral, and consequently the habituation for an aspirant lawyer is to become a 'disembodied, bleached out professional' (Wilkins, 1999), despite everyone being gendered, raced and classed (Collier, 2002). There is support for such a Bourdieusian perspective from empirical studies which show that workplaces usually operate, albeit often unintentionally, systems of power relations which are imbued with race, class, gender and other social category distinctions (e.g. Haywood and Mac an Ghaill, 1997).

In any organisation, cultures are created that may become subsumed within the professional ideology. Bourdieu describes how the knowledge of these cultures (doxa), and the accepted responses to them within a social group (habitus), can demarcate those who are within the group from those who are 'outsiders'. Under a Bourdieusian perspective these social constructions, even if they shift in content over time, often are such that non-traditional entrants feel uncomfortable within the profession. This can have the outcome that they eventually feel that they have to either leave or assimilate the characteristics required by the culture to make their continuation within the profession less uncomfortable (Lee, 2000; Wilkins, 1999). A non-traditional entrant may feel forced to extinguish markers associated with their lower socio-economic status, and instead adopt those associated with higher socio-economic status which they associate with lawyers (Sommerlad, 2007: 201). Whilst there are students from non-traditional backgrounds who may wish to challenge the presumptions and homogeneity of the legal profession, their attempts to do so are hampered by the fact that they struggle to gain the initial access to the profession required to readily make such a challenge, which can only really be effective if coming from within the profession (Battilana, 2006: 660).

In a profession which attaches such significance to history and tradition, there will be many students for whom the 'ease of a comfortable situation' (Bourdieu, 1984: 255–6) is much more easily obtainable within the legal profession due to their standard educational route and links to the professions through friends or family. Those who have no such links may struggle to obtain the knowledge and guidance that they need from within the profession whilst seeking to enter it to make a 'comfortable situation' for themselves. Their struggles in obtaining the all-important work experience are documented extensively by Francis and Sommerlad (2009), and more briefly by Sommerlad (2008).

One reason why entry to the profession is more difficult for non-traditional aspirant entrants is that firms more easily recognise an aspirant entrant who demonstrates the normative professional identity and has followed a recognisable pathway of traditional education (Francis and MacDonald, 2009), extra-curricular activities and work experience (Francis, 2011: 37–8). Without these, students struggle to present themselves as serious candidates. Traditional candidates are already familiar with the ways and norms of the field which they are seeking to join, enabling them to imitate the behaviours expected and fit into the profession comfortably (Bourdieu, 1984: 255–6).

Francis and Sommerlad (2009: 65) identify work experience as a 'hidden moment' in cultural reproduction that was crucial for students to assimilate behavioural knowledge that they would need to present themselves as convincing candidates for the legal profession. As well as the demand for limited places, there are additional barriers to completing work experience which disproportionately affect non-traditional students. Research shows that work experience is an essential pre-requisite to finding a job in the legal aid sector (Young Legal Aid Lawyers, 2013: 22), and that consequently unpaid work experience represents a significant barrier to social mobility at the Bar (Young Legal Aid Lawyers, 2013: 19; Francis and MacDonald, 2009: 239).

Aspirant entrants therefore may be disadvantaged by their non-traditional status as they seek to enter the profession. Not only are they likely to have very little knowledge of the profession, they struggle to access an opportunity to obtain such knowledge: work experience. The importance of historic and ritualistic practices, along with the value placed on work experience, contribute to the occurrence of social closure at the Bar, by subtly and subconsciously propagating the notion that anyone who is not accustomed to such traditional behaviours and with existing links to the profession will feel like an 'outsider'.

The provision of mini-pupillages has therefore been crucial as a method of 'gate-keeping'; both the way in which it is secured, and the experience of the mini-pupillage itself, are likely to disadvantage students from non-traditional backgrounds. Thus, work experience has been a key dimension of social closure at the Bar. Therefore, for a professional association hoping to improve access, increasing the opportunities for non-traditional aspirant entrants to undertake mini-pupillages makes this 'moment of identity formation' more widely available, allowing them to make informed choices about careers in the legal profession and present themselves as serious candidates.

There is also, however, an element of mutuality; as non-traditional aspirant entrants are exposed to the profession, so the profession has an opportunity to both assess aspirant entrants and market itself to them. For traditional applicants, social capital (Bourdieu, 1984: 69) and their recognisable educational paths mean that they are more likely to secure mini-pupillage through chambers' direct application processes, and therefore have easier access to this mutual exposure.

Ostensibly, the use of work experience as an entry criterion is a way of securing the best candidates; from the profession's point of view it is clearly in its best interests to recruit the best candidates. Evidence suggests that direct legal work experience is one indicator that the profession perceives as being possessed by the best candidates. However, it is argued that, due to the barriers identified in this research, the importance of work experience to those making recruitment decisions may be unjustified. This argument is advanced on the basis that whilst a profession would be expected to set its entry criteria such that the best candidates succeed, the importance attached to mini-pupillage is only delivering the best candidates from a certain subset; those from traditional backgrounds. Therefore, those from non-traditional backgrounds who may in all material ways be equally good are disadvantaged. The result is that the profession does not access the best candidates overall whilst it privileges direct legal work experience in the form of mini-pupillages, as it has done thus far.

2.5 Key arguments

Having established that social closure remains a defining feature of the professional project within a post-professional[15] landscape, this research explored the factors restricting social mobility in the context of entry to the Bar. Through

---

15 The term 'post-professionalism' was coined by Kritzer (1999). It refers to the sociological state of professions experiencing a decline in power and influence (p. 715) leading not to the extinction of the professions, but rather to a re-shaping of them forced by external conditions. Kritzer defines such re-shaping as including the increased use of technology within the profession, increased specialisation leading to segmentation, and a loss of exclusivity of knowledge and practice rights (p. 720).

the case studies, I then sought to identify to what extent it is possible for an 'embedded' professional actor to disrupt patterns of social closure manifested within the profession. Where there was an effort to disrupt these patterns, that required evaluation of the institutional factors and individual actors who were driving interventions aimed at supporting increased social mobility (or purporting to do so). In the case study of Inner Temple's PASS, I examined in depth the factors motivating that intervention in the context of a deeply-traditional profession, and its likelihood of success. Through this it was possible to draw out key themes indicating whether other professional associations could be capable of instigating such a programme, and the likely impact of doing so.

Arguments evolved around four key themes, supported by existing literature and a case study. These are: the evolution of professionalism; individual stories; talent and meritocracy as recruitment criteria, and the diminished power of professional associations. Collectively they illustrated that substantive attributes of a professional association can provide a foundation upon which action to challenge manifestations of the central value system can be built. More nuanced matters such as the emotional ties between a profession and its members, and the leadership and importation of external practices by individuals, will influence the efficacy of a professional association's action. Furthermore, no professional association can be immune from societal concerns, and these may be reflected in attempts by external bodies to direct or constrain the professional association's action.

2.5.1 Evolution of professionalism

As would be expected of an embedded traditional professional association, Inner Temple has a strong attachment to the profession's central value system. At the Bar, aspects of this central value system have supported social closure. These aspects include attachment to elite status and potentially exclusionary ritualistic traditions, justified by the argument that it is necessary for the maintenance of high standards. Therefore, the decision by a professional association to take action which ostensibly challenges social closure as a tenet of the central value system through the implementation of an access scheme is worthy of exploration. The embedded nature of the professional association and its close attachment to the central value system mean that change can occur. For these changes to be as fundamental as they are portrayed to be, however, these developments will need to be (or be presented as) 'going with the grain' of existing values. I argue that in the case study such evolution 'went with the grain'; it was directed by societal concern with social mobility to which the professional association responded, and maintained existing structures focussed on retaining the Bar's elite status.

The theoretical underpinnings of the ways in which a professional association may act in an interventionist manner are assessed through the use of organisational change literature. These bring to the fore the second key theme: the role of the stories and experiences of individuals, both those who established the programme and those who participated in it.

2.5.2 Individual stories

Individual stories are under-valued in existing literature, partly resulting from the lack of literature on the Bar, meaning that its combination of public-service-focussed and self-employed attributes are not taken into account by existing analytical models. Such individual stories featured strongly in this book, and their role in mobilising a professional association towards change was clear. The presence of this theme also highlighted the relative neglect of the affective domain in professionalism; this was an important tool in individuals' motivations to be involved in professional association projects, especially those relating to access.

2.5.3 Talent and meritocracy as recruitment criteria

The Bar has historically utilised recruitment practices that favoured identifiers of traditional backgrounds, such as linear educational routes; familiarity with social norms of the Bar, and work experience. This meant that socio-economic circumstances contributed significantly to a person's likelihood of succeeding in recruitment processes. PASS was claimed by those who established and administered it to be intended to re-focus the recruitment process on 'raw' talent, and was believed by those students who participated in it as being able to do so. This emphasised not just non-academic skills, but transferable skills such as communication and analytical abilities. The motivation for doing this continued to focus, however, on maintaining the Bar's elite status – accessing 'non-conventional talent', as one participating student referred to it, so that the profession could continue to 'be the best'. The agenda promoting meritocracy could not be construed as straightforwardly altruistic (see Chapter 4); it also encompassed an element of self-interest, and a maintenance of the profession's elite status.

Furthermore, PASS itself contributed to maintaining the status quo through reinforcing the value placed on work experience. This led to it confirming the continued importance of historically-accepted markers of suitability for the Bar, and their perceived correlation with the raw skills needed for the Bar. I therefore argue that it is not the radical move away from the traditional construction of 'talent' that some participants in this research portrayed it as, as it does not disrupt existing structures of cultural reproduction.

2.5.4 Diminished power of professional associations

With increasing external constraints operating on professions, professional associations can no longer steer the development of the profession in the direction of their choosing. This loss of power has occurred through increased legislation and regulation, and pressure from external perceptions of the profession; it is observed in the evolution of professionalism discussed above tracking wider societal concerns. Not only will direct regulation constrain the actions of professional associations, so will less obvious and more general factors. For example, the efficacy of PASS was influenced by the life experiences of the participating students: their pre-existing individual stories could not be altered by the programme. Where a professional association does maintain power to influence the profession, however, individuals within the association will be key to exerting that power.

This academic interest in the actions of an Inn of Court also casts light on an area of the legal profession previously overlooked by research. Despite some research into the operation of the equivalent body in the solicitors' profession (the Law Society; Francis, 2004), no research has specifically focussed on the contemporary operation of the Inns of Court. Historical accounts of the Inns provide a helpful background (see Cocks, 1983; Polden, 2010), and a comparative element can be introduced through research into the workings of the Bar associations in America (e.g. Larson, 1977; Halliday, 1987). The relationship between the Bar and the Government in England has also been explored by Abel (2003). How an Inn of Court as a professional association may attempt to cause changes within the profession (in this case study, attempting to diversify demographics) is, however, previously unexplored, perhaps reflective of the Bar's general suspicion of research, as encountered by Rogers (2010: 48–9).

3 Conceptualising professional associations
Powerful or power-hungry?

A conceptual framework, heavily rooted in a neo-Weberian 'social closure' approach, was constructed from existing sociological literature. This was used to analyse data from the case study, creating a symbiosis of the literature and the case study. Through this, ideas are developed surrounding the ability and motivations of professional associations to intervene within the profession on divisive, politically-sensitive matters. It also brings to the fore the challenges of increasing social mobility at the Bar, and the experiences of participants in access programmes, as students or practitioners, aiming to achieve that. This chapter also introduces literature on how professional associations operate, as this research focusses on the crossover of what is known about social mobility and what is known about professional associations. To analyse how the latter may influence the former, their attributes and processes must be explored.

3.1 Conceptualising professional associations

Although often 'behind the scenes' players, professional associations may nonetheless hold significant influence over their profession. In many professions they perform representative, disciplinary and supportive functions for their members. For traditional and conservative professions such as law and medicine, they may act to maintain the profession's elite status. This research draws heavily on the work of Larson (1977), Abbott (1988) and Abel (2003), amongst others who have written on professions and their associations.

In controlling the actions of the professional associations, the powerful segments of the profession directed their endeavours (Bucher and Strauss, 1961: 331), sometimes leading to a break-away by those segments which had sufficient power to distance themselves from their professional association and then collaborate with it on their own terms (Francis, 2011: 144–160). More recent literature has depicted professional associations as less powerful than they used to be. The Law Society was depicted by Francis (2004) as declining in influence over the profession that perceived it as unable to pursue collective advancement. Various theoretical suggestions for this occurrence have been advanced. These are revisited towards the end of the chapter, considering whether professional associations are now, in fact, falling within those elements of professionalism that Nelson and Trubek described as 'formal structures rooted in symbolic processes rather than technical requirements for organisational practice' (1992: 212).

Freidson proposes professionalism as 'a logically distinct and theoretically significant alternative to currently received models for conceptualising the organisation and control of work' (1994: 8). He asserted that the essential elements of professionalism are continuing but in a new, hierarchical, form with everyday practitioners becoming subject to the control of professional elites who continue to exercise the technical, administrative and cultural authority that professions have had in the past. Francis notes that professionalism has, in specific areas of the concept, been redefined by the most powerful elements of the profession to further their own interests (2011: 137), as Flood (2011) had already recognised in relation to regulatory frameworks. The role of professional associations is now as the 'professional elite', exercising increased control within the profession itself, but not necessarily outside of it. It appears that this is an accurate representation of the Bar; within the professional associations, seniority remains key for mobilising projects. Outside of the professional associations, however, the influence of them seems diminished.

Although it is recognised that there has not been one specific path for each profession, and that prevailing cultural and political norms in each country have influenced the process (Freidson, 1994: 6), academic critiques divide roughly into those prioritising functionalism and those preferring a monopolistic approach. The functionalist approach, stemming from work by Durkheim (1957), emphasises the purpose of professions as embodying sociological desires for order, and possessing as defining qualities altruism (Marshall, 1963), autonomy, self-regulation, consumer control, community, specialist knowledge and their own culture. Functionalism provides a framework that 'gives internal coherence for the idea of a profession' (Kultgen, 1988: 72), and encouragement to strive for an ideal. The status enjoyed by professions is perceived as a reward for striving for this ideal, and professions as deserving of their elevated status as they perform an important function (1988: 73). Furthermore, professions are portrayed as helpful to the functioning of Western society (Semple, 2015: 187), contributing positively through their altruism and specialist knowledge.

Adopting an alternative perspective to functionalism are the process-based approaches, including power and action approaches. Power approaches prioritise how professions came to hold power which separates them from other occupations, and how, having secured this power base, they then move to expand it (MacDonald, 1995), with an emphasis on organisational change. Action approaches, meanwhile, prioritise the ways in which professions interact with other organisations, both positively and negatively (Abbott, 1988), and how they use their power to influence their operating environment, emphasising the impact of individual agency in shaping these changes.

This research does not subscribe wholly to one theory of the professions; rather it advances a picture of potentially evolving professionalism within a particular sector (the legal profession) and a smaller sub-sector (the Bar). This professionalism has developed through interplay between various aspects of the profession, including tradition, self-employment and relationships between individual members and professional associations. Therefore, elements of functionalist, power and action approaches are each brought into the theoretical framework to analyse the case study.

Functionalism allows the examination of what the professional association is trying to achieve; what ideal is it striving for in attempting to promote social mobility? A functionalist approach also emphasises altruism and community, two themes prevalent in this research. Power-based approaches, meanwhile, allow an examination of the ways in which the instigation of PASS may illustrate a professional association asserting power by demonstrating its ability to act in an innovative way. The use of organisational change literature enables an analysis of Inner Temple's actions as potentially demonstrating a desire for increased recognition, and potentially greater influence, than other professional associations within the profession. Finally, incorporating elements of an action-based approach is important in the context of the Bar, as the interaction between the different professional associations, and between the professional associations and individual members, is another key theme emerging. Such approaches also allow consideration of the potential effects of individual action, and how individual agency may operate within a professional association context, especially when it is aimed at changing previously-accepted attributes of the profession.

As elements of varied approaches are engaged to build an understanding of why a professional association may act to alter entrenched characteristics in the profession, a grounded theory approach was developed (see Chapter 2). As it became clear during the research that recourse to one theory of professions would not give the layers of nuance needed to fully engage with occurrences within the professional association in the case study, others were interwoven to allow full analysis.

3.1.1 Ideologies of the legal profession

How ideologies develop within a profession is key to this research. An ideology which includes elements that contribute to social closure has developed: can this ideology now be restructured so that it no longer indirectly supports social closure? As Nelson and Trubek note, many activities undertaken by professional associations are 'an event in the production and reproduction of ideology' (1992: 178).

Differences between the ideologies seen in different areas of practice at the Bar shed further light on matters relevant to increasing diversity. Bar Council figures show that in England and Wales there are more likely to be entrants from non-traditional Bar backgrounds in some practice areas than in others (Bar Council, 2014: 27, 105): The attitudes and working cultures prevalent in some practice areas may be less inclusive and welcoming to those from under-represented demographics than in other practice areas. Practices that reflected the ideology of earlier generations, once embedded in institutional structures may appear as given or inherent in the work or the organisation itself, and thus difficult to alter.

For example, ritualistic events such as Qualifying Sessions and Call in their traditional forms are not necessary to the practice of law as a barrister, but the underlying processes are required: education and admission. Qualifying Sessions could take the form of educational lectures without the traditional formal dinner afterwards, and Call could be replaced by a document which stated that the individual had been accepted by the Inn as a fit and proper person having passed all the required qualifications. However, these ritualistic traditions are perceived by many both inside and outside the profession as being integral to the profession. Their indirect effect, however, PASS participants confirmed, can be to dissuade aspirant entrants to whom such practices are unfamiliar and may be discomfiting.

In this way, ideological product becomes material reality (Nelson and Trubek, 1992: 212). Such embedded ideologies may obstruct access to the profession for those from non-traditional backgrounds who feel that those ideologies are necessary for practice as a lawyer, when they are not actually inherent in daily practice. The embedding of these ideologies is therefore undesirable, and propagates a homogeneous profession. A vicious circle then occurs whereby embedded traditional practices mean traditional entrants feel comfortable within the profession. Many non-traditional entrants are indirectly discouraged by the unfamiliarity of traditional practices and thus the profession remains largely homogenous. As the practices are embedded and accepted, and traditional entrants are comfortable with them (Bourdieu, 1984), such practices are not subjected to scrutiny which may identify them as separable from the profession's core function of legal services.

It is not, however, accepted by sociologists that the current demographic of a profession is its natural one: some theories emphasise the possibility of individuals following a path which has not previously been commonly associated with someone from their demographic. Contemporary social theory has stressed the potential for individuals to form an identity different from that which may be expected (Beck and Beck-Gernsheim, 2001). This explanatory model suggests that further democratising of professions is possible as individuals drawn from diverse social backgrounds begin to enter professions once almost exclusively occupied by white, middle-class males (Wilkins, 1998; 1999). As an organisation becomes more diverse so do applicants, as they recognise themselves within the organisation, and can identify with it. The emphasis on the possibility of change within an organisation, caused by individuals within it, implies a weakening of the social stratification of access to resources, both material and symbolic, and of the role of traditional ideologies in shaping individual trajectories (Sommerlad, 2007). As Nelson and Trubek (1992) note, it is easy for ingrained practices in a profession to appear crucial to the operation of the profession, when they could be abolished without harm to its *raison d'être*. Limited demographics fall within this category.

Some scholars suggest that these ideological processes are particularly significant for professional organisations, where professional education is 'providing members with a common culture, in the sense of shared definitions of problems and common repertoires for managing those problems' (Tolbert, 1988: 104). Yet workplace ideologies often serve the interests of some groups in the organisation more than others, and can legitimise practices that are arguably harmful to the larger society (Nelson and Trubek, 1992: 213), as seen in the maintenance of the status quo of recruitment practices for which traditional entrants are well equipped.

Nelson and Trubek's 'arenas' approach explicates the relationship between professional ideology and social power: lawyers' visions of their working life and working relationships are intimately related to the kinds of organisations they construct and the roles they play in political, social and economic exchange (1992: 213). Therefore, Nelson and Trubek argue, scholarship on the legal profession must examine the construction and deployment of professional ideology in the myriad of contexts in which lawyers appear, not just the arenas that are most visibly associated with the power of the professional group, to advance a broader understanding of how the practices of lawyers reflect, reproduce and alter the social order (1992: 214). This research therefore focusses on participants' accounts, including those of the internal processes that occur when a professional association decides to utilise its power to alter professional ideology, and how it may enact this (see Chapter 4).

One way in which the social order is maintained is social closure, and the discomfort that homogeneity arising from its operation can cause to those who enter the profession without the expected social norms and professional identity. Nonetheless, the deployment of professional ideology in this specific context has been neglected by research, and social mobility at the Bar has not previously been examined in relation to the behaviour of a professional association.

Nelson and Trubek's depiction of the profession as comprised of arenas is also useful in any attempt to explore how practices may permeate across professional borders. In the case study there was particular interest in whether the action taken by Inner Temple might have any effect on ideologies in other areas of the profession – other Inns of Court or the Bar Council, for example. Bucher and Strauss highlight that a smaller sub-group within one large organisation might be capable of acting separately from the larger organisation; within any group smaller sub-groups with different purposes and goals develop organically (1961: 332). A seemingly united action, Bucher and Strauss suggest, may be caused by the most powerful segments presenting their position as that of the whole profession (1961: 332). Underlying such a presentation will often be competition between segments with differing stances on which position should be presented as that subscribed to by the whole profession. This inspired the engagement in this research with interviewees from a variety of chambers and professional bodies, to capture where disagreements had occurred, even if they were 'swept under the carpet' in the final formulation of the intervention. Changes to the archetypes guiding the relationships between bodies within the profession may also facilitate such permeation (Greenwood and Hinings, 1993). Key to the theory of archetypes is a desire for common understanding, an interpretative scheme that applies across organisational boundaries to give coherence in the organisations' working relationships (Greenwood and Hinings, 1993: 1056). Through this common understanding there is arguably an increased possibility for the transfer of practices and values.

3.1.2 Occupational closure

As referenced in Chapter 2, occupational closure is the result of society's inherent tendency to stratify, manifested within occupations. A group formed predominantly of those of higher social strata will impose entry requirements which militate against access by those from lower strata to exclude them.

The usual method of such closure is by requiring aspirant entrants to have certain qualifications: a degree, a vocational qualification or a certain amount of experience in a specific field (Larson, 1977: 171). Such entry requirements 'screen out' people without those qualifications; those who, for whatever reason, are unable to obtain them, as well as those who are unwilling. At the Bar this is illustrated in part by the current requirement of a degree to be considered for entry (in all but the most exceptional cases where other educational routes have been followed, often by mature entrants). This need not be a Law degree due to the GDL, often referred to as 'the conversion course', which can be completed in a year by those with a degree in any discipline.

Social closure at the Bar is also supported indirectly by a central value system emphasising tradition and professionalism. At the heart of any cohesive group such as a professional association will be a central value system (Shils, 1975). This is likely to be defended rigorously by the profession collectively, and the more central a professional association is within its profession, the greater its attachment to the central value system is likely to be (Shils, 1975: 10), and therefore the more determined its defence and maintenance of those values. In the case study, therefore, Inner Temple would be expected to defend the central values.

Such a value system will not be tangible, and its content may not always be obvious or easily defined or discerned. It consists of notions, ideas and values to which members of the organisation subscribe. Such subscription will often be subconscious or automatic; central value systems will often be maintained through traditional and accepted practices within an organisation. For example, at the Bar, formal dining is a ritualistic practice which has occurred for many hundreds of years, and contributes to the maintenance of a central value system of collegiality and traditional values. For an individual to feel comfortable within an organisation they will need to (subconsciously) subscribe to at least some of the values all of the time, although which values are being subscribed to may vary by time and circumstance (Shils, 1975: 10).

Within the legal profession, and at the Bar specifically, the central value system incorporates many traditional practices. Whilst it is not suggested that social closure is itself a central value, this research argues that many seemingly neutral traditional practices propagate social closure by indirectly discouraging those who are not familiar with such tradition from applying to join the profession. Those from lower socio-economic backgrounds have usually been exposed to less traditional circumstances through their personal and educational experiences, meaning that they are unfamiliar.

Possessors of specialist knowledge, such as those who practice law or medicine, set about building up a monopoly of their knowledge, and are consequently able to develop a monopoly of the services deriving from it (MacDonald, 1995: 32). The concepts of 'exclusion' and 'social closure' are crucial to monopolies, as they act as mechanisms which help to achieve and maintain the social standing of the group. An illustration of this in the legal profession is the requirement of work experience, without which candidates are unlikely to be considered for training contracts with solicitors' firms, or pupillages in barristers' chambers (Francis and Sommerlad, 2009; see Chapter 6). This is a manifestation of a central value system; a pattern of behaviour focussed on supposedly maintaining quality services actually causing indirect social closure due to differential access to work experience. Professional associations, as outlined above, often act as the 'gatekeepers' regulating those who may join existing members, and maintaining the elite status of the profession. Nonetheless, despite their general conservatism and established central value systems, academic literature shows that professions are also capable of change.

3.1.3 Can professions and their associations adapt organisationally?

Despite the diverse conceptions of professionalism that may be operating simultaneously within any one profession (Nelson and Trubek, 1992; Bucher and Strauss, 1961), it is largely accepted by academics that professions as a whole struggle to adapt at any significant pace to changes of admission or composition. Kritzer suggests that legal professional associations have 'avoided coming to grips with this "brave new world"' of post-professionalism (1999: 732), and Francis explored structural problems constraining the Law Society's responses to this new environment (2004: 347). Kritzer's (1999) analysis of professional associations as 'avoiding' acclimatising to a changing professional environment demonstrates that it is opposition to change within an organisation that hampers development, as opposed to a fundamental inability to make those changes.

Kritzer (1999: 732) characterises the Anglo-American legal profession's response to change as 'try[ing] to hold onto an outmoded image of professionalism'. The developments to which he refers are those seen in the 1990s: roles carried out increasingly by specialised non-professionals; increased use by companies of competition between law firms to obtain favourable deals, and the accessibility to the general public of information previously only available through professionals.

Some theorists suggest that the professions no longer enjoy the levels of power and autonomy they previously had, which is key to the question of whether professions remain 'masters of their own destiny', or whether we see them now as significantly weakened since their 'glory days' of governmental influence, monopoly and self-regulating autonomy. Kritzer (1999: 725) identifies the West as having entered a period of 'post-professionalism'. This finds support in the English system: for example, under the LSA, it is possible for those who have not completed their legal training, but are supervised by a suitably qualified person, to undertake work in chambers in the County Courts. Some smaller barristers' chambers have merged with others to gain the size needed to benefit from opportunities to win contracted work (e.g. for contracted work in family and crime, KCH and Garden Square on the Midland and Oxford Circuit merged (*Nottingham Evening Post*, 2011)), and to benefit from economies of scale and consolidation by mergers of larger well-known sets with smaller ones (e.g. the merger between Atlas and 4–5 Gray's Inn Square).[1]

The increase in tasks done by those who are not fully legally-qualified has removed barriers to involvement with the law in an occupational capacity, but other research, as documented above, has suggested that professionalism and the barriers that it creates are still very much a live issue which the Bar needs to tackle to secure the best candidates.

Other writers have advanced similar arguments, differing in detail and label. The first is 'deprofessionalisation', as postulated by Haug (1973), in which attention is focussed on the reduced legitimacy of professions stemming from higher levels of education within the general population, making knowledge monopolies hard to justify. A less deferential society also means that the higher social status once afforded to the professions has dwindled. McKinlay and Arches (1985) suggest 'proletarianism': that an advanced capitalist society has had the effect of making all work equal due to the processes of bureaucratisation and corporatisation.

This research does not argue that the Bar has been particularly affected by deprofessionalisation or proletarianisation. Rather, it advances the argument that professions, and professional associations by proxy, are having to 'move with the times'. As society expects a commitment to meritocracy, so the Bar is required to at least appear to deliver. The extent to which an appearance of such movement reflects reality, what motivates this movement and the willingness with which it is done are all key matters previously unexplored that this research seeks to contribute to understanding. It is argued that these institutions, professions and professional associations can still be maintained, but for that to occur they must be seen to be moving in line with society's wider concerns, such as meritocracy and fair access. Going forward, Kritzer (1999) identifies the tension between increasing specialisation and multidisciplinary practice. Changing structures of, and demands upon, law firms arise through subcontracting, reduced regulatory autonomy and the increasing ability of potential clients to administer self-help through the ever-increasing availability in both printed and electronic forms of legal information. Sometimes individuals can manage without lawyers entirely, or come to them later in the process, having been able to conduct the litigation themselves in the earlier stages (Kritzer, 1999: 735–748).

To some extent this mirrors the analysis by Halliday (1987: 47–51) of the abilities – as opposed to simply the ideological willingness or reluctance identified by Kritzer – of larger or heterogeneous professional organisations to adapt

---

1 www.legalbusiness.co.uk/index.php/lb-blog-view/95-4-5-gray-s-inn-square-merges-with-public-lawspecialists-atlas-chambers [accessed 6th August 2017]

to change. Once again, such adaptation for those organisations is not an inherent impossibility, but the characteristics of those organisations make effecting change much harder, to the point that a de facto impossibility may be reached, as no course of action can be agreed upon.

Francis (2004) examined the changes to the conception of professionalism within the Law Society (the representative body of solicitors), and particularly the differences between the conceptualisation held by the Society and that held by solicitors' firms themselves. He perceived that the difficulties the Law Society was experiencing at that time in performing the roles which it had traditionally fulfilled were not simply due to contemporary issues which would pass; instead it was symptomatic of a more fundamental problem: that the Society's ability to 'serve as the fulcrum of the profession's collective advancement' was in decline. This was due to increasing divergence in the interests of City law firms (such as the 'Magic Circle' firms; Flood, 2011) and High Street firms. It has been suggested, however, that this has not been seen at the Bar. Amongst the solicitors' profession there were other indications of a lack of cohesion: for example, that some City firms could, and did, dictate the content of the LPC in favour of their predominant practice areas, causing areas such as probate, which were of importance to High Street firms, to be removed from the course (Francis, 2004: 334). They then went further, with eight City firms setting up their own LPC specialised to their training needs (Francis, 2004: 332) and this has been followed by an accelerated LPC which is completed in six months and favoured by Magic Circle firms such as Freshfields.

The Bar, however, has not seen such a shift, with all aspiring barristers still completing the same BPTC regardless of the area of law or geographical location in which they intend to practise. This continuing unity within the Bar, even if it is a 'facade of united action' (Abbott, 1988: 106), arguably strengthens the Bar's professional associations (including the Inns of Court) as organs of organisational change, as there have been fewer formalised divisions within the profession. This may mean that an Inn of Court finds it easier to exert influence over the rest of the profession. This may be partly due to the relatively small size of the Inn of Court itself (especially its decision-making body – the Benchers), increasing the likelihood of internal cohesion on a matter, making action aimed at the rest of the profession more likely to be effective (see Chapter 4).

The role of behaviour patterns, individual and collective, within the organisation itself is also important. Theories surrounding institutional logics, embedded agency and institutional entrepreneurship are consequently engaged in analysing how such change is begun within the organisation's social frameworks. Institutional theory recognises tensions between the power of an organisation and the power of individuals within it. As Ocasio (1997) highlights, every institution has a typical arrangement of institutional elements, within which it may have multiple institutional logics.

Institutional logics are the patterns which influence the thinking and action of individuals within the institution, and also organisational behaviour (Friedland

and Alford, 1991). Institutional theory has vacillated between emphasis on an institution as passively receiving influence from its wider context (DiMaggio and Powell, 1983), and emphasis on it as a leviathan determinedly resisting all attempts to influence it, within which any exercise of individual agency is 'entrepreneurial' due to its apparent difficulty (Lounsbury and Crumley, 2007: 993). This second position stemmed from DiMaggio (1988) arguing, in response to misinterpretations of an earlier paper (DiMaggio and Powell, 1983), that neo-institutionalism lacked an understanding of agency.

This research argues that neo-institutional theory, with its emphasis on the transformative nature of interactions between 'field and firm' and the organisation's context (DiMaggio and Powell, 1991) is not inherently incompatible with embedded agency. Instead, embedded agency can add another layer to the organisation's attributes affecting its interaction with external bodies. This research further argues that the actions of individuals within an organisation can influence an organisation in steering a middle course between the dichotomous positions of institutions portrayed as 'passive cultural dopes', or as 'hypermuscular supermen' (Suddaby, 2010: 15). Indeed, the experience of Inner Temple suggests that a 'happy medium' is attainable.

Ultimately Suddaby (2010: 15) suggests that institutional theory should be a paradigm aiming to explain why organisations often behave in ways that defy, or do not advance, economic logic, and do not seem aligned with rational behaviour in a certain circumstance (Thornton, 2004: 8). For the Bar, widening access will not increase profitability as it might in a corporate setting, and there is financial outlay involved in establishing programmes such as PASS, although it does not defy rationality. Nonetheless, institutional theory offers two contributions important to the current research. First, a way of analysing action by a professional association as an institution; and second, the importance of socialisation, an explanation advanced as contributing to why non-traditional aspirant entrants may struggle to access the profession (see 2.4.1 above).

3.1.4 Capacity of elite embedded professional associations to effect change

The importance of the distinction between embedded and non-embedded professional associations is that those that are embedded may find it harder to act independently from, and thus exert power over, their members, especially on divisive matters. For embedded professional associations, departure from established practices is harder, as it is likely to require either a distancing from the profession (which is almost impossible due to its embedded nature), or a move away from tradition by the profession as a whole (also unlikely in traditional professions, which are usually known for their conservatism; de Tocqueville (1899: trans. Reeve, 1946)).

Conversely, however, a wholly 'outsider' body is unlikely to be able to exert sufficient influence over a profession to instigate change (Halliday, 1987: 344). This research suggests that the key role of trust between members and their professional association helps to explain why such difficulties may be experienced by an outsider body. This supports Francis' observation that an actor may be able to balance central and peripheral traits to maximise its effectiveness in causing change (2011: 30).

Capacity to act may arise collectively or be created by individuals within the organisation. Greenwood, Suddaby and Hinings (2002: 61–2) identified three reasons why a professional association may retain influence over its related profession. First, that the professional association may act as an arena within which the profession interacts collectively; second, as a means through which interaction with other communities (and, specifically, other professions and the Government; Abel, 2003) is facilitated; and, third, as a compliance-monitoring mechanism of normatively or coercively sanctioned rules. However, this overlooks the internal mechanisms within the professional association which allow it to exercise this influence. For example, in the case study it is necessary to understand how PASS came about within the professional association before examining how it was presented externally. This requires some attention to individual-level effects.

Institutional logics (Friedland and Alford, 1991) help to explain the relative ease with which a professional body can exert pressure for change either within itself or on the wider profession, and thus provides one potential explanation for how change may be brought about within a traditional profession's embedded professional association. Friedland and Alford argue that it is impossible to understand an individual's behaviour, or that of an organisation, without locating it in a societal context (1991: 232). Such an assertion, whilst seeming simple, is attractive; an organisation is fundamentally a group of individuals and for any cohesion to occur it is necessary that the organisation forms patterns of human activity by which time and space are organised, and meaning attributed to them in a consistent fashion (1991: 243). Such patterns are social reproductive processes which are propagated within the organisation by their role as 'the rules of the game' (Jepperson, 1991: 143). Any person wishing to be subsumed into the organisation successfully will need to adapt to at least some of the institutional logics: certain ways of processing and relating to the world around them.

Institutional logics are products of human interaction; 'socially-constructed, routine-reproduced program or rule systems' (Jepperson, 1991: 149), and are therefore malleable, meaning that in a professional association they may alter and adapt as the profession itself prioritises different goals. Ritualised behaviours reproduce these principles of the organisation (Friedland and Alford, 1991: 250), but an individual entering the organisation from outside may resist full adoption of the institutional logics. In this way, institutional logics may gradually alter – a necessary corollary of the fact that even undesirable matters may become subsumed into them (Jepperson, 1991: 149). Such alterations were thought to occur in pursuit of increased profit or efficiency, though Thornton (2004: 5) acknowledges that institutional logics help to explain why corporate decisions may deviate from economic efficiency and instead pursue collective outcomes, such as greater social diversity, which will not directly increase profit or efficiency.

It has been noted in management literature that the (as was) 'Big Five' accountancy firms could straddle international and jurisdictional boundaries, thus seizing opportunities for growth in contradiction to prevailing institutional logics (Greenwood and Suddaby, 2006: 40). On a much smaller scale, it may be that the ability of Inner Temple to disrupt previous patterns of cultural reproduction both internally and at the Bar more widely is improved by its employment of staff familiar with other institutional logics as they have moved from the human resources field into the legal field. Their experience of other institutional logics influences their professional approach, and this was seen in the case study in how they approached social mobility matters. The use of other institutional logics by employees with experience in non-legal fields may cause a subtle shift in those prevailing within their current legal setting. These alterations may, over time, manifest more widely in the legal setting in interactions with other organisations, consequently altering the archetypes governing the wider field.

Battilana (2006) used Bourdieu's social field theory to identify which individual actors had the greatest likelihood of causing institutional change. This signalled a shift from an emphasis on the power of expected and constrained behaviour moulded by the habitus and doxa operating on actors to an emphasis on the actor's own position within the social field. She emphasised that the success of any project undertaken by embedded actors is likely to be related to their position within the field, not just their ability and willingness (2006: 659–660). Other factors will also be relevant, however, and some of these are specific to the legal profession. Braithwaite concluded that:

> the literature suggests that such [diversity] campaigns may be problematic as a driver of change in the large law firm context, not least because there is a lack of strict enforcement, blurred objectives and a failure to recognise the resilience of the law firm status quo.
>
> (2010: 143)

The recognition throughout Braithwaite's article of the resilience of the status quo is, possibly, of even greater significance for the Bar, as it continues to rest much more upon its historical roots. However, the Inn, as a professional organisation, occupies a different position to that of an internal department trying to exercise influence over the rest of the firm from its embedded position. Although the Inn is an embedded professional actor, in that it is placed both physically and ideologically within the profession with which it is associated, it has the advantage of employing separate staff to chambers, giving it a greater distance from those whom it is encouraging to act. It is not in such close proximity to those over whom it is trying to exert influence as internal diversity staff in a solicitors' firm.

This assertion can be applied by analogy to a professional association within a field as it was to an individual actor within an institution. Actors who were most likely to feel strongly about acting to increase access to the profession were often those on the outside of the profession, and therefore although they had the willingness and potentially the ability (Sommerlad, 2007: 216–7), they lacked the position within the field needed to be able to effect change (as identified by Battilana (2006)). Based on Shils' formulation of the central value system, Francis (2011: 29) states that it is often those at the periphery who have the capacity to drive forward changes, given that they have much less of an attachment to the central value systems than embedded actors or individuals. There is a fine line between those who are peripheral enough to not feel strongly attached to the 'inherent' (Nelson and Trubek, 1992: 212) central value system but who are sufficiently integrated into the profession to cause change (Battilana, 2006: 659–660). In this respect Inner Temple occupies a unique position: its embeddedness allows it to take meaningful action to promote change because it occupies an elevated position within the profession's 'social field', and has both the capacity and intra-profession respect as an elite actor.

Therefore, it can put into practical effect the feelings of a critical mass of individuals. The central value system will never be subscribed to wholly by every member of an institution; 'The central value system which legitimates the central institutional system is widely shared, but consensus is never perfect' (Shils, 1975: 10). Whilst many members will not wholly affirm it, most will affirm all of it some of the time, or some of it all the time. Consequently, there is opportunity for disagreement with a central value short of removing oneself from the institution. However, such disagreement may also found a desire to initiate a change in the central value system. Such a desire has been key in the case study, and its combination with a powerful field position allowed a potential challenge to the indirect effects of the central value system.

3.1.5 Motivators for change within a professional association

Motivators for change may come from various sources, internal or external. Even within one element of change there may be mixed and nuanced motivators experienced by different individuals within the professional association. For many organisations, the possibility of increased profit arising from being perceived to be diverse and inclusive is a significant driver (Kotter, 1995: 60). This includes within the legal profession, where the 'diversity approach' was used to convince senior partners in a solicitors' firm that investment in access programmes was financially worthwhile, as equality of opportunity can be 'sold' as good for the firm's reputation (Braithwaite, 2010: 141). Considering the lack of a profit-increase-based incentive at the Bar, it seems likely that other reasons take precedence in motivating a professional association.

This is not to say, however, that these motivations may not have an element of self-interest, with much of the data from interviewees revealing mixed motivations. Whilst many interviewees prioritised the perceived potential positive effect for non-traditional aspirant entrants, many also admitted that they were aware that gain for the profession was a likely concomitant. Some interviewees saw this as a 'side effect' that happened to be favourable, whilst others perceived it as an aim equal in importance to that of improving opportunities for non-traditional aspirant entrants.

Although at the Bar equality cannot be 'sold' as a profit-making attribute, Rogers (2012) suggests that it can be used to improve reputational profit. She found that the Inns of Court perceived 'inclusiveness' as an attitude which aspirant entrants wanted, so it sought to convince aspirant entrants at recruitment events that it held such values (Rogers, 2012: 212). Therefore, any programme aimed at increasing diversity at the Bar is likely to hinge around an ideological commitment to the potential of every individual, and the transformative nature of a group, albeit not a firm, being diverse to gather greater lived experience within its members (Sommerlad, 2008: 193).

Other literature addresses altruistic acts of non-governmental organisations (Fisher, 1997), as well as the symbolism of such programmes in a climate where 'inclusiveness' is seen as an important value by aspirant entrants (Rogers, 2012: 220–1). Where the motivation is portrayed as altruism, an inherent challenge is the subjectivity of what comprises an 'altruistic' act. Altruism, arising from Comte's work (1851: trans. Bridges, 1973), is the doing of things to further the welfare of others. Here this was claimed by some interviewees as the motivation for Inner Temple's introduction of PASS; an action by Inner Temple to further the (occupational) welfare of non-traditional aspirant entrants.

One interviewee went so far as to state that, without a commitment to meritocratic access and social diversity, the Bar would no longer be entitled to call itself a 'profession'; it would simply be an occupation. This belief illustrates the complex link between altruistic behaviour and gain for the profession itself which is likely to be a contested area in any access scheme, though this may not be articulated (see 4.4), and which was expressed by many participants. There was clear awareness in many that the inter-relation between self-interest and altruism made it hard to separate the objectives of opportunity for non-traditional aspirant entrants and a stronger recruitment pool and improved perception for the profession.

With any such action, questions can be raised about whether it objectively improves the position of the group in whose interests the action is supposedly being taken. This research, however, focusses instead on the subjective experience of those participating in an access programme. More probing angles of examination therefore are those exploring the perceptions of the action's 'recipient'. Research into organ donation, for example, has identified the deeper complications of 'gift practices' that underlie the 'gifting' of anything: there must be a giver and a recipient, a creditor and a debtor. Where a gift has been given, there may be an implicit expectation of reciprocation, albeit not in kind (Scheper-Hughes, 2007: 508), and unspoken attributions of value and self-worth (or lack thereof) to the parties (Kaufman, 2013: 58). Some PASS participants communicated levels of indebtedness that suggested the power imbalance already experienced by them as outsiders was exacerbated by their participation. This was particularly the case for those who did not perceive any benefit to the profession from PASS; their belief that PASS was wholly altruistic seemed to generate disproportionate feelings of gratitude (see 4.4.1.2). This is despite the characterisation in this research of any act as having both altruistic and self-interested motivations, so closely intertwined are the two that it is almost impossible for one to exist without the other (Mansbridge, 1990: 134).

A further consideration is that action is often developed subjectively by the organisation conducting the intervention. This creates a risk that the organisation projects onto the subject group particular needs or characteristics, and makes unfounded or misguided assumptions about what will assist the group (Fisher, 1997: 458). Conversely, a professional association may act in the pursuit of external recognition, but it is unlikely that this would be expressed as the justification for action.

As Dent and Whitehead (2002) note, there is a substantial body of work theorising the professions. However, there is much less which engages with how these theoretical aspects of professions and professional associations affect their operation in practical terms. Rogers' (2012) research addressed one such dimension in exploring how the profession marketed itself to aspirant entrants. This research addresses another dimension by exploring the relationship between the theorising of professional associations and the development of a programme aimed at contributing to an alteration of a longstanding characteristic of the profession.

3.1.6 Challenges to sustaining change within a professional association

Once a professional association has brought about change, the process does not come to a halt. The next challenge after instituting new practices is to maintain them. Researchers have attempted to formulate models which explicate the stages that an organisation will go through in incorporating changed values or practices into the profession's identity and routine interactions. The ways in which Inner Temple had brought about change and were making efforts to incorporate it into the profession's identity were examined through frameworks constructed to evaluate organisational change.

One challenge posed by the existing literature on sustaining organisational change is that it often presumes a profit-making entity. In the case of the Bar this is not an ideal model – the profession, in line with its claims to altruism (Carr-Saunders and Wilson, 1933), tends to construct its identity more closely aligned with a public service model than a business model. Such tensions, however, resonate with discussion in Chapter 7 surrounding changes to models of the legal profession. Not only does research need to account for evolution, but also for the different ways in which evolution may affect professions with less common structures.

As addressed above, the motivations may therefore be different. The non-profit measures of organisational change, however, remain relevant in the context of this research. Ferlie and Pettigrew (1988) note that differing models also pose different challenges of quantification of change. In their research into the National Health Service they considered different facets of change, each of which could be considered to give a holistic portrait of the change that had occurred within the organisation: speed, quantity, quality and processes experienced by the organisation's members. Kuipers et al. (2014) address the role of factors defining success or failure. They note, as I also argue, that it is impossible to assert success or failure when it is not agreed what changes would amount to success, or what would denote failure by its continued existence or occurrence (2014: 11). Definitions of success and failure are key to assessing whether a desired outcome has been achieved (Kuipers et al., 2014: 12).

Pettigrew et al. (2001) criticise the apparent lack of interest in the dynamic and holistic appreciation of both processes and outcomes (2001: 701), suggesting more attention be paid to how success in the management of change is defined, with potential focus on quantity, quality and pace of change, and how these three may interact or operate in conjunction (2001: 701). The factors suggested by Pettigrew when studying change – context, content, process and outcomes – are endorsed by Kuipers et al. (2014). They also suggest the addition of a fifth factor in the context of assessing change in public organisations which has been overlooked: leadership (2014: 2). This supports arguments advanced by Kotter (2008: vii) that leadership is wholly distinct from management, and that the two should not be confused (Kotter, 2013).

A further consideration when examining changes attempted by Inner Temple is how such changes have been directed. Kotter argues that leadership plays a key role in organisational change, stating that many organisations today do not have the type or level of leadership that they need to facilitate and secure a change process (1999: 1). Albeit on a smaller scale, this research attempts to engage with those issues in considering the likely longevity of the change, despite the methodological limitations discussed in Chapter 2.

3.2 Inns of Court as professional associations: inventor or agent?

As can be seen from the brief overview in the previous chapter, the Inns of Court are the main professional associations directly involved with practising barristers. The way in which professional associations affect the operation of a profession has been the focus of previous academic research, mainly based in the USA (e.g. Halliday, 1987; Nelson and Trubek, 1992). Professional associations also play an important role in the identity of a profession. Not only are the Inns practically important due to their 'gate-keeping' function, Larson notes that it is unclear how much community would exist without the 'institutional supports' of professional organisations and institutions of this kind (1977: x), and such significant organisations are crucial in the formation of a central value system (Shils, 1975: 4) and its exercise as a means of authority (1975: 24). This research illustrated the potential that an Inn of Court had to influence the profession into altering recruitment practices due to the high esteem in which practitioners held it. This potential was unfulfilled due to insufficient challenges to established practices within PASS, but the underlying mechanisms used to implement PASS could be used as a foundation for more radical action. The willingness of chambers to engage with Inner Temple on PASS is indicative of a recognition of leadership accepted through choice instead of coercion.

Although the role of legal professional organisations in England and Wales has been subjected to relatively little academic exploration, most notably by Francis (2011) and Rogers (2012; 2014), the role of Bar associations in America has been much more widely researched. Whilst the English legal system functions differently to that in America, it is still instructive to examine research on American Bar associations and their relationships with their members, as the human element remains regardless of geographical location.

Halliday (1987: xiii) highlights that, in general, the existence and operation of closely-knit professional associations (described by Halliday as 'collegial organisations') has scarcely been noted by either sociologists or the general public, and poses questions requiring exploration:

> Do they affect the policies and the administration of those institutions in which they have such a central role? Is their expertise deferred to by legislators and administrators? Do they effectively mould public policy – but out of the public eye? And what of the associations themselves. What kind of resources can they bring to bear on the objects of their collective action? Can they act cohesively? Or is the internal diversity of a profession such that forceful action is all but impossible? Do professionals mobilise their clients? Can the web of associations, comprehensive and specialised, state and national, act in concert?'

In the context of the English Bar, this research begins to unravel some of these questions. The most novel contribution to this unravelling comes from the exploration of the role of the affective domain and loyalty to the professional association, and how that itself can be framed as a resource that the professional association can utilise (Francis, 2011: 135). Since Halliday's writing in 1987, these issues remain largely untouched when it comes to the English legal profession. Although Rogers' (2012) research examines how the profession 'sells itself' at recruitment events organised by Inns of Court, it examined the message being communicated externally to aspirant entrants. This research explores not just the message being communicated externally, but the development, and practical enactment, of an access scheme internally.

Much existing research into the professions examines monopolistic theory (e.g. Larson, 1977): actions which the profession possesses the unique right to perform, and action it takes alone to preserve them. The capacities and motivations for professional collegial action – that by which a profession seeks to further general interests, or joins together with another organisation with similar aims and objectives to pursue such a matter – are therefore not explored. This constitutes a significant gap in existing scholarship that this research contributes to closing. In contrast with much of the existing research, I explore action taken by a traditional embedded professional association which is not intended to increase or preserve a monopoly power, but instead attempt to alter accepted practices and patterns of behaviour that may support social closure. This research engages with a professional association as interventionist actor, and analyses how a professional association may affect its own profession, and what motivates it to do so. Such attempts can variously be portrayed as self-interested, altruistic or symbolic; all motivations considered in this book. Motivations are especially a matter of interest where the intervention appears to address an indirect effect of traditional central values.

There currently exists little exploration of the motivations behind an organisation's actions. In Auerbach's (1976) research into education and practice at the American Bar, he undertook documentary analysis to explore motivations behind concerted actions, but only to the extent that it was recorded in those lawyers' papers seen by him. Therefore, as a non-monopolistic action, why a professional association has chosen to act in this way and how it then does so is of interest to the academic community, as existing research has largely focussed on action by the professional association aimed at outside bodies or individuals.

Halliday examined how the demographics of a professional association can affect its ability to act. He used the Chicago Bar Association as a study subject, using its internal documents to:

> explore interiors of elite decision making and also, more importantly, to examine the universe of professional action through that panoptic: it was a comprehensive record of professional collective activity, not edited for public inspection, but as it was recorded in internal files, giving a balanced perspective on professional associations.
>
> (1987: xv)

His research demonstrated that any organisation that falls short of complete representation of professionals in a state or a country can less convincingly persuade a government that it should have statutory powers of self-regulation and monopoly and can less authoritatively influence government (1987: 49). These are attributes that a profession maintaining occupational closure to preserve its elite character is likely to need, as detailed above. Inclusive associations command legitimacy by their representativeness, and tend to control substantial resources denied to their more exclusive counterparts. Due to their foundation based on shared attributes, such associations are likely to be able to secure consensus relatively easily, because of their homogeneity (1987: 312), but may also struggle to influence policy decision at a higher level due to their small size (1987: 137). This, however, conflicts with Larson (1977: xv) and Abel's (2003) respective analyses, which state that homogeneity within a profession is crucial to the professional project, as it allows agreement to be reached more easily on divisive matters, and is perceived as allowing maintenance of its elite status.

A substantial risk associated with failing to represent different views amongst practitioners, practice areas or seniorities within a profession is the establishment of organisations running in opposition. In the 1960s, young lawyers from the Chicago Bar Association formed a counter-Bar association, as they felt that their interests as young practitioners were not being acknowledged (Halliday, 1987: 133). A similar outcry occurred in England in 1985 when young barristers perceived the Bar Council as unrepresentative, and took this complaint to the Government (Abel, 1988: 130). Both incidents demonstrated the risk a professional association faces if it is, or is perceived to be, unrepresentative. Without members who feel that the professional association represents their interests, and are therefore willing to contribute to the work of the professional association, any meaningful action will be stymied. The field position, membership and form of a professional association thus has a significant effect on its ability to take collective action, and also influences the matters on which it chooses to take such action. For Inner Temple, its specific situation as an embedded professional association within an elite and historical profession affects its capacity to represent views and act in divisive matters. It does not restrict its capacity as far as might be expected, however, where there are key individuals who are willing to take action that may disrupt the status quo (although whether such action does in fact fulfil that mandate is explored in Chapter 6). This action needed to be combined with leadership at both elite and salaried levels in Inner Temple for mobilisation across the professional association to be effective.

3.3 Conclusion

This chapter brought together the main concepts upon which the rest of the book rests, grounding the key arguments in existing theory as is common when using a grounded theory approach. In combination with Chapters 1 and 2 it provides a foundation for the exploration of the complex issues of the actions of professional associations and access to the Bar, and the particular challenges at the meeting of those matters. Chapter 4 now moves to the substantive material with which this research is concerned, setting out the key nature of a central value system to any profession, and arguing that it is counter-intuitive for a professional association to act in contradiction to a long-held notion within that value system. Such counter-intuitive behaviour therefore requires an analysis of the motivations that may have caused a professional association to behave in this way; how such behaviour is perceived by a target audience, and whether the target audience's perceptions conflict with those of the professional association.

4 Values, attachment and professional associations

> If we don't continue to have altruistic motives then we won't be entitled to call ourselves a profession.
> (Interviewee 9, Inner, M, Bencher, other prof. assocs.)

This was the response of an interviewee, a highly successful QC and Deputy High Court Judge, when asked what he thought had motivated the establishment of PASS. This chapter argues that professionalism, as one element of the central value system subscribed to by the Bar and many other elite professions, can evolve. Due to the number of professional associations of the Bar, this research makes its arguments based on the professionalism articulated and espoused by one professional association within the field. It argues that the professionalism articulated by Inner Temple is shown in this research to be capable of evolution. Certain attributes of the professional association facilitate such evolution; specifically, in this research, the smaller size of the association's decision-making element (the 'elite', who hold significant influence), and the association's relative heterogeneity giving it the internal respect of its members. Furthermore, the field position and links to other sites of power gave Inner Temple the ability to bridge boundaries. Combined with the respect in which it was held, this made it a potentially powerful institutional entrepreneur.

This chapter also introduces a previously under-researched matter in professions: the affective domain (Francis, 2011: 135). In the case study the affective domain was engaged through practitioners' loyalty towards their Inn of Court, something Inner Temple capitalised on in developing PASS. This loyalty manifested itself as trust in the professional association to only pursue a change in the central value system through the evolution of professionalism where to do so would not cause harm to the profession. Emotional engagement also increased the human resources available to Inner Temple.

These resources were important. Practitioner involvement was key to the programmes' credibility both within the profession and amongst aspirant entrants. Both parties seemed to agree that only current practitioners could provide accurate information about the profession, and many aspirant entrants stated in questionnaires and focus groups how much they valued interaction with those in practice. Where these interactions were positive, links were fostered with aspirant entrants on an emotional level which suggested that, if they later entered the profession, they might also show such loyalty to the Inn, continuing a cycle of members willing to assist in efforts such as access programmes.

Finally, the chapter explores what might motivate a professional association to pursue such evolution. Such motivations may be manifold, conflicting and complicated. In the case study, it was possible to identify differing motivations perceived by different groups: participating students, chambers, Benchers of the Inn and salaried staff of the Inn. These included altruism and reputational gain for the profession. Notably, it is argued that evolution was 'going with the grain'. There are two dimensions to this notion. First, evolution occurring in accordance with existing professional values and priorities. Second, evolution also going with the grain in the context of wider societal and market changes. These two dimensions might be diametrically opposed, causing tension. Evolving professionalism is thus unlikely to challenge either prevailing trends in society or, perhaps paradoxically, more deeply-held values and ideas within professionalism. The structuring properties of these fields, possibly combined with pragmatism from those in leadership positions, shape the limits of what is possible, meaning the conservatism of professionalism continues.

4.1 Central value system of the Bar

Any profession has values that are central to its identity. These produce behaviour patterns that group members acknowledge and follow. In a traditional elite profession, such as the Bar, such values revolve around long-established ritualistic practices and professionalism. A 'side-effect' of traditional values has been social closure, as non-traditional aspirant entrants struggle to adopt a persona recognisable by the profession. This is partly due to their non-traditional educational pathways (Francis and MacDonald, 2009) and adherence to different social norms (Bourdieu, 1984), identifying them as 'different' from traditional entrants. They therefore struggle to demonstrate the social capital expected in both applications and interviews. For those that do enter the profession manifestations of a traditional central value system make some feel uncomfortable, dissuading them from continuing within the profession. This leads to a higher attrition rate and consequent socio-economic homogeneity in the higher reaches of the profession.

Similarly, 'professionalism', requiring high standards of the service provided by the profession's members (Larson, 1977: 145), may indirectly cause social closure. Here social closure results from the maintenance of standards being used as justification for higher entry requirements, including expensive professional qualifications that cannot be afforded by many non-traditional aspirant entrants from lower socio-economic groups (Witz, 1992). Even though social closure is not itself a central value, it is a product of central values which are portrayed by the profession as a necessary part of the professional project.

4.1.1 Impetus from the top: the role of the elite

As established in Chapter 3, the more tightly linked the professional association itself is to the profession's values, the more it is likely to defend those values. Due to the historical role of the Inns in creating much of the central value system through their control over admissions (see Chapter 2), their ideologically- and physically-embedded nature is likely to increase their attachment to the central value system.

The key group influencing a professional association's direction is its 'elite': those 'maintaining the organisation, controlling the conduct of its members and fulfilling its goals' (Shils, 1975: 4). Within an Inn of Court, the elite is the Benchers, those elected to office to govern the Inn, and who chair the committees that usually direct decisions on the Inn's interactions with the profession.[1] In this case study, this elite of senior practitioners, combined with specific attributes of Inner Temple explored in this chapter, give it significant power as an institutional entrepreneur (Garud, Hardy and Maguire, 2002: 958–961). An 'institutional entrepreneur' is defined by DiMaggio, who is credited with coining the term, as an individual or group who 'create a whole new system of meaning that ties the functioning of disparate sets of institutions together' (DiMaggio, 1988: 14).

This research illustrates that the elite's approval is key in any evolution of the central value system. In the case study, some members of the elite had gone further than mere approval, contributing to the very impetus to alter inherent practices that lead to social closure. At Inner Temple there are already Benchers who have themselves come from non-traditional backgrounds; even in the small sample used for this research, there were Benchers from state and grammar schools, as well as independent schools, and they were conscious of their duality as members of the elite with an understanding of the challenges faced by non-traditional aspirant entrants. This diversity and awareness permeating up the professional association's hierarchy increases the likelihood of decisions being made mindful of the needs and experiences of non-traditional aspirant entrants. This will arguably facilitate a challenge to the inherency of some exclusionary patterns of behaviour, as these Benchers remember their own experiences. The inherent role of the elite in constructing the central value system (Shils, 1975: 5) means that commitment amongst the elite to furthering social mobility is more likely to be reflected within the institution's core operations and aims than if that commitment was held only by those in less powerful positions. Therefore, a combination of position within the professional association's elite and diversity of the Benchers involved in PASS promotes an understanding of the challenges faced by non-traditional aspirant entrants which could come to be reflected in evolutions of the central value system (though I argue in later chapters that this does not occur for other reasons).

---

1 www.innertemple.org.uk/component/content/article/103-history/itad/319-memberships-of-the-innsof-the-court [accessed 2nd August 2017].

Practising barristers represent a more diverse group than previously, and aspirant entrants are likewise representative of many different ethnicities, socio-economic and educational backgrounds (Bar Council, 2014a). A professional association wishing to cause change must innovate towards a central value system better reflecting this. Ideologies of previous generations that are irrelevant and unnecessary need to be acknowledged as anachronistic, and their inherency challenged. Traditional patterns of behaviour from these ideologies have become subsumed into the habitus of the social field, thus appearing to be inextricably embedded. However, many student participants, and a number of interviewees, recognised that they can be removed or modified (Bourdieu and Wacquant, 1992: 133) to reflect modern society and respond to concerns about the lack of social diversity within the Bar. They further recognised that such alteration could make the profession more accessible to entrants unfamiliar with social conventions which represent the traditional past but have little functional purpose. Such a process is likely to be slower within an embedded historical professional association, but the leverage that such a professional association has over its own members, and the wider profession, is likely to be crucial to effecting change.

4.1.2 Tradition and professionalism: two central values contributing to social closure

Professionalism is prioritised over management ideas and procedures at the Bar (Muzio and Ackroyd, 2005: 641) as the key basis for professional practice (2005: 620). Its construction varies (Francis, 2011: 53) but all arenas recognise the notion and its basic components (Nelson and Trubek, 1992). Professionalism has a very traditional form at the Bar, so whilst professionalism survives social closure continues. However, this research illustrated that it is propagated at the earliest stage at chambers-level in selection for mini-pupillages, instead of by the profession on an occupational basis, illustrating that Muzio and Ackroyd's findings in the solicitors' profession (2005: 618–9) apply equally to the Bar.

At the Bar, I argue that such closure can occur at two stages. First, if a non-traditional aspirant entrant cannot afford the BPTC fees and does not secure a scholarship; or second, if they complete the BPTC but do not get pupillage. At the BPTC-entry stage, private providers exacerbate closure through the exorbitant cost of the course (see Chapter 7). The Inns of Court also feature at this stage because they award financial scholarships for the BPTC, with the highest exceeding the full cost of the course, through a process of application forms and interviews. As is discussed later, the ways in which a candidate presents themselves both on paper and in person will be influenced by their socio-economic background and life experiences (see Chapter 7). Therefore, although it is outside of the scope of this research, it is suggested that the scholarship stage poses similar challenges and faces similar criticisms to those seen in the application for and allocation of work experience; the system favours traditional intellectual achievements through a recognised educational path (Francis and Sommerlad, 2009). The two stages at which closure may operate also illustrate two different sites of occupational power, as Muzio and Ackroyd identify in the solicitors' profession (2005: 618–9), both using patterns of behaviour contributing to social closure.

Professionalism, therefore, despite being defended as the maintenance of standards to ensure that unwitting consumers do not receive sub-standard service (Abel, 2003: 96) is shown in this research to result in social closure at the Bar. Participants in the current research had mixed views about the role of traditions and professionalism in social closure at the Bar; particularly interesting was a lively debate in the Pathways focus group. The researcher asked the students how they felt about some of the more obviously 'traditional' elements of practice at the Bar, and used as an example the wearing of wigs and gowns by Criminal counsel, eliciting responses such as:

> Tradition and culture is good, sometimes it's good, but you don't, it's not really needed as long as you can fight the case, and I think that's what's important.
> (Pathways FG Participant 3, F)

> It's what makes a barrister a barrister . . . it gives identity to the community.
> (Pathways FG Participant 9, M)

> I don't think tradition puts people off anything.
> (Pathways FG Participant 7, F)

> I think what you wear doesn't really matter; what you do and your actions matter more than what you wear.
> (Pathways FG Participant 6, M)

> But what about culture, tradition? Culture and tradition is good, but in some parts it's not. For example, the wig – what's the point in wearing the wig?
> (Pathways FG Participant 1, M)

This illustrates that even within a small group of non-traditional aspirant entrants (nine students) reactions to manifestations of tradition are very different. Whilst some students could not see the practical utility to such traditions and therefore dismissed them as unjustified (such as participant 6), others perceived them as vital to the sense of belonging within the profession (such as participant 9).

4.1.2.1 Closure and community

Such a sense of belonging and community as articulated by the Pathways students was a key theme in this research.[2] Another student in that focus group commented insightfully on the dichotomy between the perceptions of individuals

---

2 The role of loyalty to the professional association is returned to later in this chapter at 4.3.1.

internal and external to the profession, highlighting that some determined aspirant entrants may 'see through' manifestations of tradition that discourage others:

> I would never ever say it was a bad thing, but the tradition, the idea of going in and wearing a wig and . . . it's by no means a bad thing but it gives off the impression that you have to be a Lord's son or something to go into it, or have God-knows-how-many connections within the actual area and that's just the way it is. It's the prestige it has, and as I say, that's not a bad thing at all and I think it's just one of those things that, if you are interested in becoming a barrister you will realise that that's not always the case.
> (Pathways FG Participant 2, F)

The variety of reactions illustrates the tensions that a traditional profession might experience in attempting to reduce social closure through removing practices not necessary to the provision of legal services. Whilst to some students the profession's mystique, partly consisting of unfamiliar traditions and practices, is alluring, to others it is intimidating. Even those who found it intimidating, said that it denoted community. For those enticed by its mystique this gave them something for which to aim; they saw the Bar as a community, recognised their position outside of it, and used their desire to join the community to motivate themselves to pursue entry. Those participants who described it as intimidating, meanwhile, found the community aspect symbolised closed-ness and separation, emphasising their difference. Amongst the Pathways students, the first view was not so common, and where held was more likely to be expressed by male participants than female. The second view was more common, especially amongst female participants. Amongst the PASS students, however, the first view was more common amongst both genders. This may be partly attributable to the PASS participants' position closer to entry to the profession, compared with some Pathways students still undecided whether to pursue legal careers.

As non-traditional aspirant entrants as a group are less likely than traditional entrants to have encountered traditional organisations before, they may feel more intimidated than attracted. Any access effort must therefore seek to balance the removal of traditions propagating social closure with maintaining the sense of community valued by both existing members and aspirant entrants alike. Many practitioners were also aware that the profession's outward manifestations of tradition could be off-putting to non-traditional aspirant entrants:

> We do present, if we don't do something about it, a sort of rather formidable face to the outside world of exclusivity which makes it quite difficult for people from non-privileged backgrounds to even contemplate walking through the gate.
> (Interviewee 9, Inner, M, Bencher, other prof. assocs.)

Opinion was divided on the solution to this. Two commonly-cited options were demystifying the profession through better public engagement, or reappraising whether some traditional practices were necessary. Reappraisal was particularly recommended where interviewees felt that such practices were neither necessary nor in keeping with the Bar's desire to present itself as 'inclusive' (Rogers, 2012: 220) and meritocratic. Some interviewees supported more radical changes, acknowledging that a central value system may require updating. It is argued that professionalism is an evolving concept that is likely to develop reflecting societal sensitivity to topical issues. Academic analyses of professions need to account for such societal changes (Kritzer, 1999). It is therefore theoretically possible that professionalism at the Bar could develop to enshrine the pursuit of meritocracy as a social justice ideal. Although the doxa of the Bar is already well-established, this research argues that an entrenched value can theoretically be removed or modified. Whether this can be done by a professional association depends upon the interplay of complex factors in both theory and practice.

Therefore, it appears that a close attachment to the central value system can actually facilitate a professional association in causing change within a profession. This may seem unexpected, yet Inner Temple's commitment to the central value system, and status as a traditional professional association, appears to have bolstered its leadership. Members of the profession felt it a trustworthy body that would only seek a re-evaluation of central values if prudent and necessary. Nonetheless, to cause change a professional association will also need other attributes.

Any group will have a central value system. At the Bar, this consists of traditional historic practices. Whilst these are not necessarily intended to exclude those from certain socio-economic backgrounds, they often have that effect. In the formation and potential evolution of a central value system, the elite will be a key group in influencing the direction of such development. In the case study, adaptation of the central value system has been led by Benchers – Inner Temple's elite.

4.2 Initiating organisational change

In the case study, Inner Temple was regarded by interviewees as more likely to succeed in initiating organisational change than other professional associations of the Bar. The key attributes explored in existing literature as facilitating or hindering the initiation of change are size and heterogeneity. This research also advances the importance of the affective domain (Krathwohl, Bloom and Masia, 1964; Francis, 2011: 135), embodied in the case study in the role of loyalty, a matter mentioned somewhat unexpectedly by a majority of interviewees and student participants. It is argued that, due to the predominantly self-employed structure of the Bar, loyalty is important in any consideration of (non-disciplinary) professional association action due to professional associations' relative lack of coercive power.

4.2.1 Size (isn't everything)

Of the professional associations of the Bar (see Chapter 2), the Bar Council is the smaller organisation, with 115 members comprising the Council at any one time,[3] but with the ambit of representing the whole profession. Although not explicitly stated by any participants, one perception supported by academic literature is that the Bar Council struggles to take any decisive action because although its membership at decision-making level is relatively small, by the time of appointment, those members may have further professional goals in mind. Such goals, for example, being appointed a judge, may make them less willing to support bold steps:

> By the time that people get to the top they have got appointments being dangled over them historically, so they all behave.
> (Interviewee 7, Inner, M, Bencher, other prof. assocs.)

Meanwhile, the Inns are much larger organisations, but represent only the approximate quarter of the profession within their membership. Despite their overall size, decisions are usually made by smaller committees, giving opportunities for active membership and thus greater representativeness. This may be another contributory factor to practitioners' generally favourable feelings towards Inns, and closer working relationships with them, facilitating support for even potentially controversial moves, such as challenging the central value system.

It is argued that this combination of a smaller decision-making body but membership of approximately one-quarter of the profession allows an Inn to benefit from aspects of both attributes. The size of a professional association has been identified as crucial to its ability to gather sufficient agreement to make an alteration to the status quo within the profession (Halliday, 1987: 136). Smaller numbers are more likely to lead to consensus, and where an organisation is smaller, communicating with all members is more straightforward. At the Bar the dispersed nature of members posed a challenge in the past. However, the embrace by professions of technology in the post-professional era (Kritzer, 1999: 728) means that communication both within and outside the professional association is much easier; email, social media and websites being especially useful. This allows the association to engage with members offering support en masse, even if they cannot be physically present. Membership is not so large, however, that this task is impossible.

In PASS dispersed membership helped the functioning of the programme, with Inn members often 'selling' the scheme to their chambers, encouraging it to participate. As members are dispersed across chambers, this was regarded by most interviewees as effective publicity; the fragmentation of the profession helping, not hindering, increasing participation in programmes such as PASS. This research therefore supports earlier research on the effect of size on the mobilisation of professional associations. It does suggest further nuance, though; that a smaller decision-making group within a professional association may ameliorate potential challenges arising from large overall membership.

---

3 www.barcouncil.org.uk/about-us/constitution-and-structure [accessed 2nd August 2017].

4.2.2 Heterogeneity

Size alone will not be decisive; composition is also important. Previous academic literature has demonstrated that the authority of representativeness can be subverted internally by the inability of the representative body to mobilise quickly and consensually on many of the most critical questions either for the profession or for the state. Thus, inclusiveness may cause stalemate, as it brings inside the organisation the full range of conflicts and polarities that divide and segment a profession (Halliday, 1987: 123). The most controversial questions are also likely to be furthest-reaching, and it is those on which a representative organisation will struggle to act. The tension is aptly summarised by Halliday: 'wealth of inclusiveness is at once its poverty. The weakness of strong associations comes precisely because at the point of its maximal inclusiveness an association has internalised the complete range of diversity within a profession' (1987: 136).

Due to the relatively small size of the Bar Council, there is arguably less opportunity for dissenting voices to infiltrate and make themselves heard, especially in the wider context of the career stage of many. It is therefore argued that the Inns of Court are able, and Inner Temple has succeeded, in 'negotiat[ing] the fine line between the stalemate of inclusiveness and co-ordination through oligarchy' (Halliday, 1987: 310). The use of committees, whereby members can discuss potentially divisive matters in small groups, before deciding how to advance them to the Inn at large, may allow the presentation of ideas in a more considered way within a smaller group. Feedback can be given, the idea nuanced and developed, meaning that when it is presented to the professional association's whole membership at large there is an increased likelihood of wider agreement.

Although decision-making occurs in the same way at the Bar Council, it was perceived by practitioners as being removed from their professional concerns and interests, and with a decision-making body that was not representative. It was also implicit in some interviews that practitioners felt that the Bar Council could not be relied upon to prioritise the profession's best interests, although no substantive reasons were given for this. An apparent vicious circle occurred: because practitioners were reluctant to engage with the Bar Council, it could not increase the human resources at its disposal through willingness of practitioners to assist in running programmes, for example. However, because it ran few programmes, it was perceived as ineffective and blasé to the concerns of the profession. Practitioners felt more involved and included by Inns of Court (see 4.3.1 below) suggesting that a combination of small size at decision-making level and reduced ambit facilitated action by Inner Temple. Such action was respected by members as although the elite were small in number they were viewed as diverse and therefore decisions were more likely to be 'for the greater good' of the profession. It could gain consensus and then mobilise effectively as practitioners were willing to assist.

One interviewee suggested (see 4.2.1), and indeed this is often an insult used within the profession more widely, that a cause of the Bar Council's impotence was that its members were often aiming to hold significant offices, and this discouraged them from pursuing politically difficult topics at Bar Council level.[4] This may explain, partly at least, why the Bar Council struggles to gain the respect of some practitioners, and why it is not perceived as able to make significant contributions on controversial matters. A recent illustration of a perceived (by practitioners) failure of the Bar Council was its lack of intervention when the Government announced plans to further cut the legal aid budget, with serious ramifications for the Criminal Bar and criminal justice more widely. Some unity was regained as walk-outs were staged, and eventually a joint response was issued by the Criminal Bar Association and the Bar Council.[5]

This research suggests that an analogy may be drawn between the Inns of Court and the voluntary work organisations of the early 20th century, where men (as they invariably were) could shape their organisations 'into instruments for the fulfilment of their purposes . . . [t]he professions would become the exemplars and bulwarks of social stability' (de Tocqueville, quoted by Halliday, 1987: 18). In the past, members have shaped the Inns themselves into such instruments, preventing entry by those whom the majority did not feel 'suitable candidates'. The 'social stability' resulting from its homogeneity eased the tensions associated with trying to take collective action when membership is diverse, as described by Halliday (1987, see above), so the Inns historically favoured homogeneity as would be expected from a conservative traditional body. Nonetheless, as demonstrated here, a combination of organisational and individual factors is instigating the pursuit of greater heterogeneity. This suggests that de Tocqueville's assertion may no longer hold the power that it once did, with a greater recognition that any professional association will need to balance the ability to reach consensus with diversity to ensure that the majority of members feel that their interests are being represented.

A perceived lack of this combination seemed to be a key factor compromising trust in the Bar Council and supporting the Inns of Court. This internal collaboration facilitated within an Inn also extends to external collaboration, or at least the potential thereof, between the Inns of Court. The four Inns liaise, allowing agreement and collaboration on a much greater scale than could be

---

4 Very recent Bar Council Chairs have gone on to be High Court Judges soon after the conclusion of their time as Chair: Nicholas Lavender QC (2014 Chair) www.judiciary.gov.uk/announcements/high-court-judge-appointment-queens-bench-division-lavender [accessed 21st August 2017] and Maura McGowan QC (2013 Chair) www.judiciary.gov.uk/announcements/appointment-of-a-high-court-judge-mcgowan [accessed 21st August 2017].

5 www.barcouncil.org.uk/media-centre/news-and-press-releases/2014/july/joint-statement-by-the-bar-council,-the-criminal-bar-association,-the-circuit-leaders-and-the-ministry-of-justice [accessed 2nd August 2017].

facilitated between individual barristers or sets of chambers, albeit that the level of co-operation between Inns was not agreed upon by interviewees:

> It's very difficult sometimes to work out what the other Inns are doing. [Other Inn]: sometimes I think they are a bit like a secret society, I will probably get told off for saying that, but you just don't seem to be aware of what they are doing. When you ask for information, when [the] Bar Council asks, 'What are you doing in these areas?', they may well be doing something, but they are not prepared to tell us about it or they don't publicise it.
>
> (Interviewee 10, Inner, F, Bencher, other prof. assocs.)

> I really wouldn't want to speak for them, but I think the other Inns are happy that we do it and they often say things like, 'Oh, Inner's doing that', and it's almost a delegated responsibility at this stage, so I think they are absolutely fine with doing that.
>
> (Interviewee 11, Inner, M, salaried)

These interviewees had different modes of connection to the Inn, possibly explaining their different opinions on collaboration; there may be a greater level of co-operation between the salaried staff of the Inns than between Benchers. Furthermore, the first quotation may be an illustration of antagonism towards the Bar Council as much as a general reluctance to co-operate between multiple sites of professional power at the Bar.

4.2.3 Multiple sites of power within a profession

Whilst the previous section addressed heterogeneity within one professional association, this section addresses relationships between different professional associations and other bodies at the Bar. These relationships between the Bar Council, the Bar Standards Board, the Inns of Court, and chambers are significantly shaped by the unusual way in which the Bar operates: relatively small groups of self-employed practitioners joining together to form chambers, whilst also being members of Inns of Court, with the Bar Council as the overarching representative body. These sites of power may sometimes conflict when trying to act in relation to the same issue, such as social mobility, especially as it is a sensitive issue.

Relationships between these bodies were a recurring theme in interviews. Many practitioners had strong views on the utility or lack thereof of the Bar Council, and all apart from one were much more positive about the contribution of the Inns to the life and evolution of the profession than they were about the Bar Council's contribution. Many interviewees acknowledged tensions between the Bar Council and the Inns, and this was especially well known to interviewees who held, or had held, both Inn and Bar Council positions (of whom there were two). Of those two interviewees, one denounced the utility of the Bar Council, whilst the other took a more balanced view.

Salaried staff were more frank about the complications associated with the multiplicity of sites of power. They were straightforward in their admissions of the challenges faced due to a history of complicated relationships between the Inns and the Bar Council, but without attributing blame. In contrast, practitioners tended to be either more circumspect about the existence of challenges, or keener to attribute blame for the complexity of the relationship. What was widely agreed, however, was that there remains significant separation between the sites of professional power, potentially leading to duplication of effort, and a lack of cohesiveness of approach:

> I think if there was more cohesion, more targeting, then perhaps we could work together to achieve more together, but then when the profession is made up of different institutions, some have different amounts of resources, different agendas and it's very difficult to try and bring all that together.
> (Interviewee 8, Inner, F, salaried)

What was shared by both parties, however, was an awareness that interventions were likely to be much more effective when run by an organisation that was more 'in touch' with those practising in the profession:

> I am under no illusions that the Bar Council is not held in high regard by a lot of people in the profession. The Inns, however, have much more [idea of the] reality of day-to-day life of practitioners, so I would imagine that is why the take-up on the Pegasus Access Scheme has been much quicker than the Bar Placement Week was when it started.
> (Interviewee 6, non-Inner, M, salaried, other prof. assoc.)

This interviewee's unprompted and direct comparison between Inn-run and Bar Council-run access schemes illustrates the duplication of effort suggested by Interviewee 8 above, and also the awareness within the profession of the limitations of the Bar Council. Thus, it is argued in this research that the perception by practitioners of Inner Temple as active and involved in the life of the profession, as opposed to the more detached Bar Council, contributed to their willingness to support the programme. It is further argued, however, that this may lead to a vicious circle for other professional associations. As Inner Temple cultivates loyalty through its engagement with its members, this loyalty leads to an increased willingness for engagement. Where this then empowers the professional association to instigate and run programmes such as PASS, the eventual result may be a side-lining of other professional associations. This could include the other Inns if they are not so successfully cultivating involvement by their practitioners. The value of collaboration and cohesion between organisations is that it can overcome individual shortfalls.

Co-operation between Inner Temple and chambers seemed much less fraught. On the scale of PASS, it appears that internal coalitions were successful and sufficient (and the small scale of these coalitions is not necessarily a barrier to success;

Kotter, 1995: 62). These coalitions had allowed the programme to be promoted amongst chambers 'on the grapevine'. However, it seemed that forming wider coalitions would be a challenge, largely because the next sensible tactical coalition to form was likely to be with the Bar Council, but due to the historical conflicts this seemed unlikely to be a well-received option (the effect of the structuring properties of a field on professional association action are explored in more detail in Chapter 7). This suggests that any increase in the size and reach of PASS may be dependent at least in part on the historical relationship between these different sites of power.

4.2.3.1 Links between sites of power within the profession and the role of archetypes

Due to the tri-furcation of power of the BSB, Bar Council and Inns of Court in this research the archetypes that guide the interactions between these bodies are important, as they provide an interpretative scheme transcending organisational boundaries to give coherence in the organisations' working relationships (Greenwood and Hinings, 1993: 1056).

As all sites of power influence the archetypes guiding the relationship, institutional logics in one institution may affect those operating in another institutional site of power. Similarly, conceptions of professionalism operating in one area might affect another (Nelson and Trubek, 1992). These lower-level changes by one association (due to alterations within institutional logics or ideologies, for example) may alter the interplay with others, and consequently the archetypes in operation across the profession. Historically, acceptance of social closure would likely have been within the interpretative framework shaping relations amongst the professional associations, and between the professional associations and chambers. An alteration by Inner Temple to its approach to social closure may therefore influence other professional associations' awareness of, and action on, it.

It is argued that the case study suggests that archetypes within a profession can evolve over time. This is especially so if the profession is seeking to adapt to market changes, or other interactions are affecting its self-identity, as such adaptation is likely to involve interplay with other organisations within the field. Inner Temple is potentially altering the archetypes operating within the Bar by introducing social mobility as an additional new value underpinning its approach to its role as a professional association which may affect its interaction with other professional associations. Furthermore, by creating a scheme that requires interaction and agreement with chambers, there is support for Kirkpatrick and Ackroyd's observation that relationships between bodies often provide a catalyst or form of assistance to change (2003: 735). As a professional association in a profession consisting largely of autonomous chambers which select from the pool of aspirant entrants, it would be very difficult for Inner Temple to take any significant action that did not involve another party within the profession. The challenges posed by this, however, have been explored above.

To some extent the increase in managerialism and adaptation away from traditional professional archetypes in solicitors' firms (Pinnington and Morris, 2003: 86; Hanlon, 1997: 123–63) has been reflected at the Bar, but only by certain chambers. A group of progressive, large chambers have already adopted business-like structures, often including some Human Resources staff, such as the Chief Executive at this chambers:

> If you were thinking of [this chambers] as being a small business, I run the business . . . I organise the training, I organise the recruitment, I do business development, I manage the finances, I manage the business, I do quite a lot of coaching and mentoring of barristers from very early when they are trainees all the way through to becoming new members, maybe taking sabbaticals, maybe changing the areas they want to work in, maybe becoming a Silk or becoming a judge, so I do quite a lot of training and mentoring through that.
> (Interviewee 12, non-Inner, F, chambers' rep.)

This illustrates that even within a traditional profession some groups are already departing from archetypical behaviour, although at the Bar these are a tiny minority. Other chambers occupied a middle ground; whilst maintaining a largely traditional structure, they nonetheless integrated some elements of a more business-based model, such as more extensive administrative teams.

Such chambers tended not to participate in the case study programme, either because they felt that they were already sufficiently addressing social mobility within their own structure, or because they had decided to try a different approach, which meant that it was not logistically possible to subscribe to a programme based on mini-pupillage provision. This reflected their wider commitment to less traditional models of practice manifested in various ways, such as the removal of traditional labels unique to the Bar, such as 'pupillage' and 'door tenant':

> We don't do [mini-pupillages]. We made an active decision not to do it when we set up. We decided not to do it because they traditionally were, and I think they have changed now with things like the Pegasus system and some other schemes and systems that people put in place, but they were traditionally unpaid work experience . . . and it seemed to us to be very unfair to people who didn't have anyone that they knew and also that they were unpaid we thought was awful . . . so we have just never done it.
> (Interviewee 12, non-Inner, F, chambers' rep.)

Those chambers had the size and resources to initiate an alteration of archetypes, but these seemed not to have spread beyond a certain small subset of large and progressive chambers practising mainly in human rights and international law. For most chambers, archetype changes require instigation and assistance from a professional association (Greenwood and Hinings, 1996: 1027). Kirkpatrick and Ackroyd argue that archetypes cannot be generalised past the legal and accountancy contexts, and are especially ill-suited to analysing public services in the United Kingdom because of the lack of power held by professional groups (2003: 740). However, an unusual aspect of the Bar in many Commonwealth countries is the lack of coercive power held over members and chambers due to the predominantly self-employed structure of the profession. Even in America, where many attorneys are employed, the American Bar Association describes itself as:

> one of the world's largest voluntary professional organizations, with over 400,000 members and more than 3,500 entities. It is committed to doing what only a national association of attorneys can do: serving our members, improving the legal profession, eliminating bias and enhancing diversity, and advancing the rule of law throughout the United States and around the world.[6]

The very terms in which this is couched acknowledge that lack of coercion in even the biggest example of a professional association of the Bar. Similar voluntary membership also underpins the Australian Bar Association.[7] Although in England and Wales membership of an Inn is compulsory, there is an absence of coercive power (see 2.2). Therefore, what is usually levelled as a criticism of archetype theory, that it ignores the dynamics of more coercive change (Kirkpatrick and Ackroyd, 2003: 739), actually makes it especially well-suited to analysis of the Bar. Kirkpatrick and Ackroyd concede that archetype theory offers a satisfactory method of analysis for traditional professions in which professional associations hold significant power, as they are likely to be the origins of change in those professions (2003: 744). As observed, through PASS Inner Temple is challenging the archetypes of the profession in conjunction with chambers, illustrating the often-collaborative nature of such change (Kirkpatrick and Ackroyd, 2003: 735).

Inner Temple was observed to be moving into a site of power previously largely untouched by professional associations of the Bar. This site is interaction with aspirant entrants earlier and more intensely than Inns have done previously, with students participating in PASS before either formal (Call) or practical (pupillage) entry to the profession. Pathways to Law and the Bar Placement Week are run in conjunction between the Inn and the Sutton Trust, and the Bar Council and the Social Mobility Foundation respectively. Middle Temple runs the Access to the Bar Awards, but these are on a much smaller scale.[8] Thus there exists no other programme run solely by a professional association, and targeting students so close to the time when they will seek entry to the profession. Movement into an unoccupied area gave Inner Temple the opportunity to define the archetypes there, and consequently to direct the interactional pattern.

6 www.americanbar.org/about_the_aba.html [accessed 19th July 2017].
7 http://austbar.asn.au/about-the-aba/about-us [accessed 20th July 2017].
8 www.middletemple.org.uk/members/special-interest-groups/access-to-the-bar [accessed 2nd August 2017].

There is little suggestion that the power now being capitalised on by Inner Temple has ever lain anywhere else, albeit that the Bar Council, as the representative body, is arguably intended to lead the professional associations of the Bar. A number of interviewees claimed that the Bar Council was no more or less effective now than it had been previously, although some suggested that its role had become less clear since the removal of its disciplinary function to the BSB:

> It's effectively a trade union which is just so limp it's unbelievable.
> (Interviewee 7, Inner, M, Bencher other prof. assocs.)

This interviewee had held a Bar Council position and was consistently scathing about the organisation throughout his interview. He characterised the organisation as generally powerless, in direct contrast to his appraisal of the Inns. His reference to it as a trade union evokes images of unpopularity, divisiveness and politicisation. Although the Bar Council participates in the Social Mobility Foundation's Bar Placement Week scheme run in London, Birmingham, Leeds and Manchester,[9] despite having been established for some time this did not seem well-known in the profession. A number of interviewees who were not linked to the Bar Council had not heard of it, and most who had only mentioned it when directly questioned about other programmes. Inner Temple appears to be capitalising on a perceived gap left in the profession for both general leadership on divisive issues (see Chapter 7), and especially social mobility access programmes (see Chapter 6). In doing so it is arguably increasing its own power within the profession. This view, however, was not universal, with one interviewee, a member of both Inner Temple and the Bar Council, stating:

> I think [Inner Temple staff member]'s view is that the Bar Council should be just co-ordinating what's going on across the profession and not trying to run programmes as well, but we just took the view that unless the Bar Council did it, and we don't have massive resources to be honest, but unless we did it there were a whole host of young students that were going to miss out on the experience, we felt and I feel that there is a very strong argument for [the] Bar Council having to run programmes if there is no other resource to provide it.
> (Interviewee 10, Inner, F, Bencher, other prof. assocs.)

This provides an illustration of what interviewees perceived as a significant challenge within a profession with multiple sites of power. Not only may different sites of power not agree on what each should do, but what is done may be perceived differently, if it is known about at all. Interviewee 10's opinion was that the Bar Council needed to fill a gap in access programme provision, and acted effectively to do so. As a member of the committee which did that, this brought her

---

9 www.barcouncil.org.uk/media-centre/news-and-press-releases/2015/july/bar-council-holds-eighth-annual-bar-placement-week-in-london [accessed 2nd August 2017].

into what she perceived as conflict with a member of Inner Temple's Education and Training Department who perceived the Bar Council's role differently. That member of staff perceived a co-ordinated oversight role for the Bar Council with the creation and administration of specific programmes undertaken by the Inns. It is suggested that this approach could help capitalise on the closer links that other interviewees observed between the Inns and practitioners. This difference in perception compromises the possibility of programmes amalgamating for greater effectiveness and economies of scale, and one interviewee suggested that programmes may be perceived by their providers as 'in competition':

> I think there's one programme in particular, Middle Temple's Access to the Bar, which is only eight people but it offers people a mini-pupillage and a week of marshalling, and they also get a small bursary to help them cover the expenses, and I think there could be more co-ordination with that and there was potentially a bit of . . . between the two just because they were launched at similar times and obviously PASS has expanded exponentially since that and has potentially taken off more quickly.
> (Interviewee 11, Inner, M, salaried).

For student participants 'competition' between access programmes was absent from their analysis: barely any had heard of Bar Placement Week or the Middle Temple Access to the Bar Awards. However, there was unanimity that the provision of a programme such as PASS significantly increased the positivity felt by non-traditional aspirant entrants towards the Inn. This meant that it took precedence over the other Inns of Court and professional associations in the eyes of those who may be within the next generation of the profession, with one focus group participant saying, 'My loyalty lies with Inner', whilst another said, 'In terms of membership in the future I definitely wouldn't want to be a member of any other Inn.'

Fostering such early attachment through positive recognition of its access work by non-traditional aspirant entrants may further increase the Inn's power, as discussed later in this chapter (see 4.3.1). In addition to these attributes, the field position of an association will be key to its efficacy in implementing such changes, affecting as it does both the absolute power of the association and its power relative to others in the field (Battilana, 2006; Sommerlad, 2007).

Where organisational change is desired in an organisation with a very strong attachment to a central value system, certain conditions are likely to be needed before change can be sought. In keeping with earlier research, Inner Temple's nature as a mid-sized association seems to have assisted it in having sufficient support to mobilise, without being so big as to be unwieldy and unable to reach consensus. This research suggests that the role of smaller decision-making bodies is especially helpful in this. Compositionally Inner Temple is, relative to the profession, heterogeneous. This research suggests that there is a mid-point between complete heterogeneity and complete homogeneity at which mobilisation on divisive matters is relatively straightforward, and the resulting decisions are regarded as representing the wishes of the general membership. It is suggested that this occurs because different opinions and positions can be considered and incorporated through committee discussions, without being so numerous and diverse that any action is stymied by disagreement.

4.3 Field position of embedded professional associations

Inner Temple occupies a unique position: whilst many of its members want an end to social closure within the profession, its embedded position allows it to take meaningful action to promote change because it occupies an elevated position within the profession, and has both the capacity and intra-profession respect of an elite actor. Therefore, the combination of Inner Temple's field position and the support of its members for initiatives that aim to disrupt social closure give it capacity to cause change not seen in the Bar Council.

Inner Temple is sufficiently central to access necessary resources to gain respect (Battilana, 2006: 656). Through its members, it also seems to have the strength of feeling that Sommerlad suggests is more commonly found outside of the profession in those seeking entry (2007: 216–7). This strength of feeling comes from individuals (see Chapter 5), and it is argued that the ability of Inner Temple to disrupt previous patterns of cultural reproduction both internally and in the Bar more widely is improved by its employment of staff who are familiar with other institutional logics (see Chapter 5). These staff have come from the human resources field into the legal field, and brought with them institutional logics from their previous settings.

Meanwhile, many chambers are comprised solely of barristers and clerks; there is little scope within a chambers' setting for someone to come in from another type of organisation with different institutional logics and use those to innovate within chambers. Relatedly, often barristers and a skeleton support staff are so busy that they struggle to manage basic sifting of mini-pupillage applications (as Flood and Whyte (2009) recognise, the chambers' structure of clerks and minimal administrative staff can markedly affect how certain tasks, such as marketing direct access availability, are undertaken). As stated by one interviewee, this encourages the use of 'shorthand' measures of success that privilege students who have followed a traditional entry route, a significant challenge to non-traditional aspirant entrants. Another interviewee supported this assertion by himself setting out how, as the mini-pupillage co-ordinator, he did apply such measures, albeit in an effort to propagate fairness (see 6.3.1). Already identified in existing literature on the solicitors' profession (e.g. Sommerlad, 2007: 209; Francis and MacDonald, 2009: 222), interviewees confirmed that, in their experience, they are also used at the Bar:

> I think that chambers still use shorthand measures for how good a student is going to be, such as which university they went to, what degree awards they got. They don't look at the ... contextual data, say work experience, other competencies that have been developed. They don't attach enough importance to it.
>
> (Interviewee 6, non-Inner, M, salaried, other prof. assoc.)

84 *Values, attachment and associations*

The Inner Temple's strong links with individual barristers, chambers and the Bar Council and BSB mean it straddles professional 'jurisdictions', allowing it to act against prevailing institutional logics (as seen in the 'Big Four' in Greenwood and Suddaby's research (2006: 40), albeit for different reasons). Inner Temple appeared to be successfully bridging boundaries within the profession (similar to some members of the Society of Trustee and Estates Practitioners; Francis, 2011: 117), and this was partly attributed by interviewees to any chambers having members from all four Inns, making all chambers susceptible to influence from any of the four Inns:

> You see the chambers and the Pegasus Scheme, well chambers don't have an allegiance to an Inn. They pay their rent to an Inn, [but] there is no chambers allegiance.
> (Interviewee 7, Inner, M, Bencher other prof. assocs.)

Such a strong field position, being embedded yet perceived as broadly neutral, combined with elite status, is not occupied by any other professional association of the Bar (see 2.1 and 4.2.1). This dichotomy of embeddedness, yet removed from chambers, seemed to facilitate Inner Temple's channelling of practitioners' desires to assist in access schemes towards a collective effort in launching PASS. As explored above, its role as a non-partisan organisation allowed it to introduce a programme aimed purely at improving diversity at the Bar. It has also assisted it to secure participation of autonomous chambers through utilising links both between the Inn and chambers, and between individuals within different chambers. Its ability to liaise with the Bar Council, and to marshal willingness and experience though specialist salaried staff (see Chapter 5), has maximised the effect of the programme by preventing duplication and introducing those who have experience of specific issues being addressed, overcoming to some extent the difficulties caused by the profession's structure:

> The Bar is very fragmented. We have the Bar Council, which is notionally the top layer but actually is quite poorly resourced. You then have the four Inns which actually have the money, because they have scholarships and endowments, but vary enormously in terms of their commitment to social mobility and their willingness to change due to historical reasons, and then you also have as a separate stream, if you like, the specialist Bar associations like the Chancery Bar Association, the Criminal Bar Association. They don't have very much by [way] of administrative or cash resources at all but they quite often have really good contacts with their members and so really good ability to communicate with [members] and they will come forward. Then you have chambers . . . Even the largest chambers are quite small organisations compared with the big city firms so marshalling that through all these different organisations is one of the real challenges for the Bar.
> (Interviewee 2, non-Inner, F, other prof. assocs.)

Running programmes to combat social closure requires knowledge of access and education. Furthermore, it requires human resources: scrutinising each application to check eligibility, then considering aptitude displayed in potentially non-traditional ways. To participate in PASS, however, all that is required from chambers is a willingness to be involved; additional administrative burdens were borne by staff at Inner Temple with specialist knowledge of access issues (see Chapter 5).

4.3.1 Barrister loyalty to Inns of Court

Most interviewees referred to some form of emotional attachment felt by barristers towards their Inn of Court. This often manifested itself as identifying themselves with their Inn, and loyalty towards it. Many described willingness to participate in Inn-organised events, and to respond positively to requests for assistance such as advertising PASS. The Inn was portrayed by one interviewee as an organisation being shaped by its members to be an instrument for the fulfilment of a purpose (as described by Carr-Saunders and Wilson, 1933); in this case, improving access. In discussing this, he used the phrase, 'But I think we see ourselves as an Inn'. Such self-identification with one's Inn was a recurrent interview theme, and, even at a much earlier stage, with PASS participants. This self-identification seemed to found a strong sense of loyalty by practitioners to their Inns, which in turn motivated their involvement in, and support of, programmes that the Inn established. One interviewee admitted 'off the record' that they preferred Inner Temple to their own Inn, partly because Inner Temple was making a greater effort on social mobility, with which they personally identified, and they were consequently supporting PASS within their chambers.

This emotional connection suggests that the affective domain of professionalism (Krathwohl et al., 1964) is involved in how barristers regard the Inns of Court. The role of this, developed from Bloom et al.'s taxonomy of the cognitive domain (1956), has been previously underestimated when considering how legal professional associations mobilise with the practical support of their members (as noted also by Francis (2011: 135) regarding the attachment of Society of Trust and Estate Planning (STEP) professionals to their originating professions). In the next chapter close attention is paid to the role of individuals; however, the affective domain concerns that meeting point of the self with the organisation, and how that emotional connection is built and utilised.

A member of salaried staff suggested that some loyalty was generated through the scholarship scheme – 'Another factor may be that they feel they want to give back to their Inn because they have been given a scholarship, for example' – whilst another interviewee recounted visiting the Inn as an aspirant entrant himself and finding the staff helpful. Salaried staff also recognised that the relationship between practitioners and their Inn of Court was stronger than might be expected, and, it is argued, stronger than it is between members and most other professional associations:

> Members of the profession do feel a strong tie in loyalty to the Inns and their Inn in particular. They trust the Inns, perhaps it was because they got a scholarship from the Inn, or training, or they remember certain events, or because they walk around the Inn most of the day when they are based in London . . . You don't see that reflected in the same way in maybe other institutions at the Bar where they don't have the same loyalty or connection or history.
>
> (Interviewee 11, Inner, M, salaried)

As detailed above, almost all students in the focus group and questionnaire responses stated that if they did pursue a career at the Bar, they would only consider joining Inner Temple. Many expressly stated that the Inn's commitment to social mobility influenced this decision heavily (albeit that some may not have felt comfortable saying otherwise in research being conducted on behalf of Inner Temple). This suggests that it is possible to engage with aspirant entrants on an affective level early on, and that doing so may foster a loyalty which benefits the Inn by perpetuating a membership who support its schemes. For one participant, regardless of the motivation for establishing an access scheme, its very existence made her feel an ideological connection; that the Inn valued the same things that she did:

> The fact that they are putting the resources and the time into doing something like this shows that they value . . . diversity more than the other Inns do, and for me that's really important so in terms of membership in the future I definitely wouldn't want to be a member of any other Inn.
>
> (PASS FG1 Participant 1, F)

Both existing loyalty, and the ability to engage with aspirant entrants in a way creating loyalty in the next generation, gave Inner Temple added human 'resources' beyond those accessible by other professional associations: people to support its programmes practically through giving their time, knowledge and connections.

As discussed above, whilst specialist Bar associations benefitted from some of the loyalty shown to Inns of Court, and therefore were another professional association that could potentially establish such a programme, they were stymied by insufficient funding. This research suggests that the affective domain plays an important role at the Bar in the relationship between practitioners and professional associations, particularly the Inns of Court, and specifically Inner Temple. It is utilised by practitioners to give them a sense of community and belonging (see 4.1.2.1 above) and this is fostered by the Inns of Court. The Inns then capitalise upon this emotional connection, using it to engage with practitioners. Such engagement can take a variety of forms, but one is providing human resources and other practical support for endeavours by the professional association such as access programmes. The professional association, however, needs to provide underlying financial support, which specialist Bar associations were not able to do.

The role of the affective domain cannot be fully understood due to a lack of existing research, yet it appears to have potentially significant influence on the ability of a professional association to marshal support for initiatives representing a change from long-established practices (see Chapter 6). Such support is crucial for any traditional organisation seeking to implement practices aimed at increasing socio-economic diversity. The role of emotions features in another dimension as well: it is suggested that the affective domain plays a role, albeit in a different way, in explaining the importance of mini-pupillages as socialisation. Some practice areas require high levels of emotional labour (Harris, 2002), and a new or increased awareness of this was something referred to in post-programme questionnaires by some who undertook mini-pupillages.[10]

4.3.1.1 How does Inner Temple capitalise on this loyalty?

Inner Temple could capitalise on the loyalty of members spread across chambers and geographical locations because it had fostered a strong network. This meant those members fundamental in establishing and running programmes often had links with Inn members in other chambers, and supported formal requests for participation with informal friendly persuasion:

> The way it works is the senior people within Inner ring their contacts in the Inn – it doesn't matter where they physically are, they could be in Gray's, Lincoln's or wherever – and there is the arm-twisting over lunch to say, 'Come on, this is a jolly good idea, you know, we want your chambers signed up for it.' That's how it works.
> (Interviewee 7, Inner, M, Bencher, other prof. assocs.)

In this the Inn was assisted by a relevantly experienced member of salaried staff who harnessed and directed this willingness to assist into programmes designed to address salient issues (see Chapter 5). Most importantly, however, Inner Temple commanded a respect that the Bar Council, technically a higher-level professional association, had been unable to foster, with one interviewee saying that the Bar Council should cease to be involved in matters such as promoting access: 'I think the Bar Council should go and the Inns should carry on [running access programmes], the Inns should do it'. One of the reasons given by this interviewee was that the Inns of Court had greater resources through loyalty from members, and were therefore better placed to run such programmes.

Salaried staff showed keen awareness of the need for members' involvement in access programmes. It was re-iterated many times that human resources in the form of practising members were as necessary as finance, as only those practising

---

10 There was insufficient relevant data to expand a discussion in this book. However, this is an area where further research could advance our understanding both of work experience as socialisation and of the psychological resilience of practitioners.

could give non-traditional entrants a genuine account of the Bar as a profession; this was expertise that could not be 'bought in':

> All the activities that we do we very much rely on them for involvement.
> (Interviewee 8, Inner, F, salaried)

Disagreement arose, however, about the degree to which the source of a programme affected its likelihood of success. One interviewee stated that its Inn foundation was crucial to PASS's success, although he was not able to pinpoint why:

> For whatever reason they very much trust the four and I think the Inns having ownership over PASS in particular did very much help in that case.
> (Interviewee 11, Inner, M, salaried)

In this quotation the conflation of the four Inns is notable; another interviewee referred to Inner Temple's access activities as being done 'on behalf of all the Inns', as an acceptance of an implicitly 'delegated responsibility'. It was not universally agreed, however, that Inner Temple was charting new territory in this respect by acting ahead of the other professional associations. A dissenting interviewee suggested that, in fact, it was the Bar Council which had taken the lead on access schemes, and PASS represented the Inns seeking to keep up, not innovating. This interviewee also dismissed the importance of 'scheme ownership' – focussed on by many interviewees – instead focussing on the programme's quality:

> The scheme either sells itself or it doesn't. I think most sets of chambers wouldn't give a stuff whether it was from the Bar Council or the Inns. I mean they would just want a good scheme. I think sometimes because the Inns have been so slow generally, on some issues like this it gives it a novelty that the Bar Council is recognised to have done quite a lot of work in this area, whereas some of the Inns hadn't.
> (Interviewee 4, Inner, M, Bencher)

Of the professional associations of the Bar, Inns of Court are best placed to initiate an innovative intervention. This section has addressed the specific attributes of Inner Temple, and its relationship to its members, which have facilitated it as an embedded professional association to embark on an innovative project. A combination of size, heterogeneity and member loyalty has been key to the launching of PASS. It is argued, however, that the role of loyalty has been overlooked by existing research into professional associations. Data collected suggests that cultivating an emotional link with members could be very valuable to a professional association that wants to take an active role in shaping the direction of the profession. Examining more deeply how this emotional link can be cultivated, and those factors affecting both its development and its maintenance, could enable professional associations to better understand how to engage with their members.

A key question for this research is *why* a professional association, especially within a conservative traditional profession, is responding to societal pressures to ameliorate manifestations of its central value system that lead to social closure. From social closure as crucial to the professional project, it is argued that there has been a significant shift leading instead to an apparent focus on social mobility. This reflects a wider societal shift from valuing closure to valuing mobility (see Chapter 7 on the role of external factors). Besides societal pressure, however, it is argued that there are additional and more complex motivations for Inner Temple's actions.

4.4 Motivations for increasing diversity

In a profession with a long history there will be strong attachment to a central value system, meaning greater drivers will be needed for change. It is argued in this research that key individuals were present at every stage of developing and introducing PASS, and they recruited others to make the group more effective and influential.

Motivations driving participation differed between groups, however, and even amongst individuals within those groups. Some focussed on perceived gains for the profession, others for the Inn, others for wider society or lay clients, and others for non-traditional aspirant entrants themselves. This desire for social mobility, it is argued, is an example of tension between different elements of traditional professionalism. Professionalism has been portrayed as valuing altruism (Carr-Saunders and Wilson, 1933), which is one driver for increasing social mobility, and yet it has also pursued social closure for self-interested reasons (Larson, 1977: 74). Can this seemingly direct conflict be reconciled?

Practitioners and salaried staff interviewed all expressed a belief that the profession would be better for selecting entrants from the widest possible candidate pool, a possibility prevented by social closure. A salaried staff member cited this as the driving force behind many individuals' commitments to efforts to increase social mobility, and thus the diversity of the Bar, and, perhaps even more importantly, as a genuine ideological commitment of participating practitioners:

> I just think they really believe in the aims . . . in the overall aim of trying to have a profession which is diverse and which reflects the society it's representing. So in the overall theme I think that's why they are still enthusiastic and committed to the project . . . I think a lot of members of the profession do feel that way and perhaps we are giving them a vehicle for being able to contribute to that.
>
> (Interviewee 8, Inner, F, salaried)

Practitioners were particularly keen to emphasise that they did not see the role of access programmes as lowering the standard of entry, but of opening up the possibility of a career at the Bar to academically-able young people who, due to their background, may not have previously considered it. It was important to enlighten chambers about the diverse backgrounds of very able aspirant entrants:

> Particularly in terms of PASS, I think because of the criteria they apply, it's exposure I suppose to people from different backgrounds. It also ensures that as well as the people that we might see through conventional routes, members of chambers are being exposed to people from a completely different route and see how able they are, and I think that helps to keep . . . when you are recruiting people . . . to keep in mind, 'I remember so and so and actually they didn't do all these things but they are a really good candidate', and I think also a lot of us in terms of our own different routes are really keen to promote social mobility in the profession, and it's important for us to support and make a contribution generally.
>
> (Interviewee 1, non-Inner, M, chambers' rep.)

Many of the students also interpreted the role of access programmes as aimed at replacing an emphasis on aristocracy with an emphasis on meritocracy:

> I think that one of the most important things that a programme like Pathways does is just discard wholly the idea of minorities. And it's all about talent, because, realistically, talent is what you have that determines where you will end up, and, as the judges and barristers and people you mentioned, what they're looking for is talent rather than where you're from or what your status is. Bit by bit that idea is being banished and it's not . . . it's all about ability.
>
> (Pathways FG Participant 4, F)

To establish the participants' perceptions of the motivations behind this intervention, PASS students were invited to speculate on why Inner Temple had decided to establish such a programme:

> I can think of a lot of good reasons why they might be motivated to, though, and they involve perhaps widening the Bar to people who have encountered disadvantage. It might be a realisation that you get a lot of similar students, similar types of Oxbridge, public-school people who end up at the Bar. That isn't representative of people who have genuine talent, so there may be this sort of self-searching going on.
>
> (PASS FG2 Participant 2, M)

> The very fact that the Inner Temple has created the scheme, and I think forty or so chambers have signed up to it . . . just indicates the fact that this is something that they want to happen. They understand that there are people who may not fit the archetypal sort of barrister set-up . . . mould. They know that there are people out there who are just as capable, just not necessarily fitting in the mould, and they want to expose themselves to those people.
>
> (PASS FG2 Participant 1, M)

These references to talent seemed to refer to an inherent quality within a person – something that they had or did not have. I suggest that this is a reference to specific skills and traits that vary across individuals by nature. They have an innate-ness and cannot be taught 'from scratch'; some people are naturally good at them or possess them, and others do not. Examples include problem-solving, analysis and emotional intelligence. Participants (both students and interviewees) described such 'talent' or 'ability' as something which could not be taught, nor could it be removed by circumstances. It could, however, be constrained or obscured by them. All agreed that a combination of such abilities was necessary for practice at the Bar. Talent was innate, and Inner Temple was perceived as trying to remove the overlay of disadvantage that might hide such talent from the sight of recruiters.

Most students seemed to agree that the Inn had altruistic motives: it wanted to provide opportunities for non-traditional aspirant entrants to demonstrate their aptitude for the profession. Some articulated the possibility that the programmes were run for institutional gain, but student participants did not seem to think that this had been a significant aim:

> It may be purely to appear quite connected with the modern world, to satisfy the non-legal sector, to satisfy the politicians, this kind of thing, and discharge their duty. I mean, that's a slightly more cynical take but, y'know, possible. But I think the fact that so many barristers' chambers have sort of got involved is indicative of a concern that resounds in the context more generally. Whether that concern is of substance or just to try and appear well-connected and trying to help people who have got more obstacles doesn't really matter. The fact that they are doing it and that, it seems, they are going to continue to do it is the greatest support and they've definitely taken the initiative on this. That looks very good for the Inner Temple: they are *the* Inn that has pioneered this scheme.
>
> (PASS FG2 Participant 2, M)

Securing the best entrants, as some interviewees characterised PASS's aim, is not just aimed at fairness towards aspirant entrants; the profession will benefit from recruiting the most able. Existing literature on motivations behind programmes aimed to assist a particular section of society (e.g. Fisher, 1997) identifies various potential underlying theories. It is notable that there was not one agreed motivation, aim or objective behind PASS. Although all groups' answers incorporated similar key themes, there was not a consensus, even amongst members of the same group (e.g. students or participating chambers). This causes two challenges: first, it makes it difficult to identify what type of motivation is most likely to result in action by a professional association. Second, a lack of clear aims and objectives is a potential challenge to the effectiveness and sustainability of the programme (e.g. Kotter, 1995; Kuipers et al., 2014).

92 *Values, attachment and associations*

4.4.1 Sources of motivation

To develop a nuanced understanding of why a professional association acts to alter the central value system and increase socio-economic diversity within a profession, it is necessary to examine both the publicly-claimed motivations for actions and those underlying and undeclared. For this purpose, interviews with stakeholders were crucial; they were involved with a professional association's intervention, and provided different interpretations of motivations for the existence of the case study programmes. Student participants offered another viewpoint: their perceptions of a professional association's motivation to undertake such activities. Predominant themes arising were the symbolism of access programmes, and the extent to which such programmes could be characterised as altruistic.

4.4.1.1 Depiction and perception of access programmes

The PASS website describes the programme as a 'work experience programme that aims to support those from diverse backgrounds to consider a career at the Bar', and as 'part of the Inns of Court's work to encourage and support diversity and social mobility in the profession'.[11]

What emerged from interviews, however, was that the true motivations were not so straightforward. Whilst this official and publicly declared statement on the programme's dedicated website (which is wholly separate to Inner Temple's main website) emphasises as the motivations encouragement and support for non-traditional aspirant entrants, the perceptions of both interviewees and students varied greatly.

Despite potentially limited effects on demographic change (see Chapter 6), there are collateral benefits that a professional association may gain by running access programmes, such as awareness and improved perceptions. There was a deeper significance and symbolism attributed by some participants to the willingness of Inner Temple and chambers to participate in an access programme. For the students, it was notable that a professional organisation within an elite profession was investing resources in assisting them; it made the profession seem approachable, modern and engaged with social mobility issues. The following quotation reflects sentiments expressed in each of the three focus groups and many questionnaire responses:

> I think it makes them seem a lot more approachable and attainable to people who are from less privileged backgrounds . . . You think of Law and you just think, it's impossible to get into; you need to be the son of a Lord and have twelve million in your bank and stuff like that; you know, it's just . . . it's silly but it has somewhat a degree of truth to it, and I think today was quite good at . . . It shows that they are trying to build bridges to avoid that.
>
> (Pathways FG Participant 2, F)

11 www.pegasus.me [accessed 2nd August 2017].

Therefore, not only can such programmes demystify a profession to those who participate, they also serve a more general purpose by demonstrating that the profession is interested in being more accessible, and taking practical steps to make this a reality. Narratives such as this are similarly seen underpinning corporate social responsibility projects, with individual morality working both with and against collective responsibility where an organisation strives to be perceived as a 'good citizen' (Rajak, 2011: 64).

This is likely to cultivate good publicity for the organisation involved, as it will be perceived as socially aware, an increasing concern (e.g. Braithwaite, 2010: 153). Evidence of publicity in legal magazines such as *The Lawyer*[12] and *Legal Week*[13] suggests that such initiatives are regarded as promoting the Bar to the wider public as believing in fairness of access.[14] By being open about its role and work, it is perceived as taking positive action to further this aim. This is a practical step towards a more general dissemination of information, and a move away from the Bar as a secretive bastion of archaic practices characterised by 'demographic rigidity' (Abbott, 1988: 130).

The older students recognised potential gain for the profession in offering access programmes, and suggested that with widened university access, the spotlight had moved from education to occupations and now rested on professions. This spotlight had exposed the Bar as lagging behind:

> I think there's a lot of scrutiny on the Inns to make sure they're doing as much as they can [to] balance things out and to make sure things are on as even a keel as they possibly can be, and give those that have got less of a chance so to speak that little bit of an extra helping hand, because the Bar has got this awful reputation for being an old boys' club that hasn't evolved in the last 500 years ... and I think it's about what Inn can do the most to make sure it's really getting the most people to the Bar across all ranges, not just [the] crème de la crème.
>
> (PASS FG 1, Participant 2, F)

This quotation exposes the relationship (and potential tension) between two goals. First, a genuine desire to develop a programme that will make a meaningful alteration to exclusionary manifestations of the central value system, and second, the need, driven by external pressures, to be seen to be doing something to improve the Bar's reputation. Whilst these goals need not conflict, some students perceived a tension, constructing the first goal as pursued for the benefit

---

12 www.thelawyer.com/chambers-follow-prime-example/1011745.article [accessed 2nd August 2017].
13 www.legalweek.com/legal-week/analysis/2166242/pegasus-slaying-bars-beast-diversity [accessed 2nd August 2017].
14 When the author's free-standing evaluation report into PASS was published, the scheme received further attention on social media and sites aimed at aspirant entrants; www.legalcheek.com/2016/04/a-pupil-barrister-did-a-phd-about-social-mobility-at-the-bar-and-it-makes-for-uncomfortable-reading [accessed 20th April 2017].

of non-traditional aspirant entrants and the second as pursued for the profession's reputational gain. Some student participants portrayed these as conflicting because the second goal could be achieved by vacuous programmes and public-facing displays which did not actually improve access.

Despite this tension being recognised by the older students in focus groups and questionnaires, most seemed satisfied that, predominantly, access interventions were based on an ideological commitment to diversity. In questionnaire responses, a number of participants alluded to advantages that a professional association may gain, especially in improved public perception, from such activities. For example, a response to the question 'Why do you think chambers participate in PASS?' in the post-PASS questionnaire stated, 'To try and make their firms appear diverse and modern.' This respondent made no mention of whether participating in PASS represented a genuine desire for, or simply a desire for the appearance of, equality. Such questioning has accompanied some corporate social responsibility projects (Rajak, 2011: 12), but Rajak cautions against regarding such programmes as merely a 'smokescreen', as to do so fails to acknowledge the potential created for discourse and change within a value set. PASS's potential for creating interaction between the profession and non-traditional aspirant entrants may be much more significant than an alteration in demographics per se (see Chapters 6 and 8).

Some stakeholders, both lawyers and salaried staff, conceded that potential gains for the profession influenced decisions about such interventions. This supports the suggestion that, unsurprisingly, professional associations will also consider the potential for reputational gain resulting from these programmes:

> I suppose another measure of success for us would be for . . . I suppose could be quite selfish, but to see our profile increase as an institution that is aware of the situation for people trying to come to the Bar, and be seen as trying to improve that.
>
> (Interviewee 8, F, Inner, salaried)

Five interviewees hoped not just for improved public perception on a superficial basis, but a greater public understanding of what the Inns of Court actually did, especially relating to access, and recognition for that:

> For the Inns of Court to be seen as actors of diversity. Who would have thought that fourteenth-century institutions would be an arch actor of diversity? I certainly think more generally the public is seeing, at least starting to understand what the Inns do through some of this work.
>
> (Interviewee 11, Inner, M, salaried)

It is argued that the underlying drivers behind the intervention are genuinely mixed, a contention supported by inconsistency in the measures of success applied. Whilst there may be consensus on establishing a programme, this consensus may rest on different hopes and intentions for different individuals or groups within the organisation (Halliday, 1987: 139) creating uncertainty about what aims, objectives and measures of success should be applied. However, this research suggests that unity within the professional association may not be crucial to effecting transformative change, as the structure of the Bar means that various chambers may nevertheless differently interpret a programme administered by a professional association (unlike in other structures where a clear, agreed motivation and coherent implementation structures are needed; Suddaby and Hinings (2010)). The effects of such difference in structure are similarly illustrated by the differences seen in Braithwaite's research between organisations with and without shareholders (2010: 152) (see Chapter 7).

4.4.1.2 Altruism

A profession may be intent on 'reaching out' to an under-represented group; indeed, Carr-Saunders and Wilson (1933) uncritically ascribed altruism as a defining attribute of the professions. However, research has recognised tensions between characterisations of professional associations as alternately monopolistic (Larson argues that maintaining monopoly is key to the professional project; 1977: 79) or altruistic (Paterson, 1996), with Halliday preferring a sociological construction of the professions that highlights the juxtapositions between the profession as a narcissistic monopolist or benign altruist (1987: 3). Whilst non-governmental organisations are idealised as apolitical, motivated by altruism (Fisher, 1997: 442, 444), it could be argued that professional associations are more likely to be perceived as acting for reasons rooted in self-interest. Although apolitical insofar as not supporting political parties, they will not be apolitical within their profession, meaning interventions are unlikely to be characterised as neutral or wholly altruistic. It might be expected that a professional association would act for the good of others only when to do so will also confer a benefit on the profession. It is argued, however, that tensions between monopolistic and altruistic drivers cannot easily be resolved; indeed, they may exist as an accurate representation of a recurring struggle within professions.

Altruism and self-interest have been recognised as inextricably intertwined, such that their separation is impossible (Mansbridge, 1990: 134), and it has been acknowledged that social and institutional arrangements making unselfish behaviour less costly make altruistic behaviour more likely (Mansbridge, 1990: 137). In creating PASS, a possible interpretation is that Inner Temple has made behaviour perceived as contributing towards increasing diversity (the offering of work experience to non-traditional aspirant entrants) less costly to chambers. By absorbing the workload of constructing a more equitable application form, sifting the applications and interviewing where necessary, Inner Temple is taking the time-consuming and effortful procedures away from chambers.

Many interviewees highlighted this as a significant factor for chambers in deciding to participate in PASS. The construction of PASS, however, leads to a conclusion that it cannot instigate long-term change. Indeed, it is argued in Chapter 6 that for alteration to the provision of mini-pupillage that is sustainable without PASS, chambers will need to reconceive their mini-pupillage selection processes to take into account socio-economic disadvantage.

The inherent subjectivity of such interventions raises further debate. Friedman (1962: 2) states that 'what one man regards as good, another may regard as harm'. It is not suggested that, in this context, an access scheme per se could be regarded as harm. However, the way in which such a programme is delivered could, potentially, reinforce a non-traditional aspirant entrant's 'otherness'. This could be harmful both to that individual and to relations between the profession and non-traditional aspirant entrants if such occurrences are related more widely. One PASS student mounted an ardent defence of his placement chambers having mini-pupils from its direct application process in chambers at the same as himself. His comment reveals discomfort (see Chapter 6), illustrating that some may perceive altruism as being used within an existing power imbalance to further disempower the students:

> That obviously isn't the fault of the chambers, though, this is the thing: they just took mini-pupils as they would normally, and they were kind enough to take me as well.
>
> (PASS FG2, Participant 1, M)

The use of the word 'kind' in this context carries connotations of the benevolent bestowing of a gift; something which the recipient does not feel worthy to receive. It also suggests that, contrary to the comments of some other participants, this student did not feel that PASS offered mutual benefit to chambers and students through the mutual exposure detailed above. Arguably, this is more likely to create discomfort, and potentially impact on a student's perception of the profession as a meritocracy, although such language was not used by other participants.

Such problems with 'gifting' are well-identified by sociologists. Rajak (2011: 177–8) highlights potential difficulties when a corporate body 'gifts' assistance or resources to a community through corporate social responsibility programmes. The reciprocity inherent in gift-giving (Mauss, 1967: 63) causes difficulties for non-traditional aspirant entrants to the Bar and South African platinum miners alike by undercutting apparent empowerment with an implicit dependency.[15] Such dependency arises from the inability of the gift's recipient to reciprocate, further reinforcing their relative powerlessness (Kaufman, 2013: 58). Whilst this research raises the possibility that some reciprocity may occur through loyalty demonstrated to the Inn (see 4.3.1), there remains a power imbalance between access programme provider and participant that the nature of PASS may reinforce, hampering its ability to make meaningful changes, and an aspect which those formulating such programmes must carefully consider.

---

15 Viewers of the TV sitcom *The Big Bang Theory* may be familiar with the character Sheldon Cooper's similar views on gift-giving from the episode 'The Bath Item Gift Hypothesis', where he accuses Penny of giving him an obligation instead of a gift, because gift-giving is founded on reciprocity.

Whatever a professional association's intentions in instigating an access programme, it may do so in a way that nonetheless maintains the status quo (see Chapter 6). This may happen intentionally, or it may not be recognised that a programme is tackling issues superficially and not underlying assumptions. Indeed, such an implicit maintenance may be why a profession accepts the programme at all (Braithwaite, 2010: 161). However, as the Bar is formed of autonomous chambers, each their own 'arena' (Nelson and Trubek, 1992), there is likely to be variation in the ways in which different chambers respond to, and present, those participating in an access programme. Therefore, there is likely to be variation in how truly transformative PASS is across different chambers, depending on the extent to which each genuinely alters its approach to recruitment and non-traditional applicants as a result.

Considering the strong attachment to the central value system felt by traditional professional associations, what has prompted Inner Temple to try to alter an indirect effect of these values is an interesting question. There is not one single motivation that can be identified; instead there are many inter-linking and nuanced reasons why a professional association may take such action. Within the professional association, there may also be different perceptions on why the action was taken, as seen in Inner Temple. Whilst a broad consensus on the main themes prompting action emerged, examination of the details revealed a variety of other contributory factors perceived by both stakeholders and participating students.

4.5 Conclusion

This chapter has argued that exclusionary manifestations of the central value system at the Bar are being challenged by Inner Temple. This is possible because attributes of Inner Temple suggest that efficacy is influenced by more nuanced factors than simply size and homogeneity. The size and composition of the decision-making body, as well as the field position of the organisation acting, may mediate disadvantages in size or composition of the organisation overall.

Substantive attributes alone are not decisive, however. This research highlighted the role of the affective domain, with Inner Temple capitalising on feelings of loyalty. Practitioner co-operation attributed to this loyalty was key to establishing an access programme challenging the central value system, as it provided both human resources and ideological support.

Examining the motivations, both publicly declared and privately perceived by stakeholders and participants, gives a rich insight into difficulties surrounding gift practices, altruism and self-interest when professional associations take action surrounding access issues. The interplay between these motivations and the experiences of participants are explored in Chapter 7. Particularly notable is the potential reinforcement of power imbalances between the two parties when participants feel that they are rendered more powerless by an organisation 'reaching out' to them.

5 The importance of individuals within professional associations

Eventually I came to be doing pupillage with Robin Potts QC ... Robin was an important character in my life ... because Robin saw, or thought he saw, that there was something in what I could achieve. I didn't see it myself but he thought there was.

So said Michael Todd QC, former Chair of the Bar Council, in his speech at Keele University's graduation ceremony in 2015. It clearly conveys the lasting impact on him, both professionally and personally, of one member of the profession whom he encountered.

When there is an attempt to alter a profession's central value system by a professional association through a specific programme there needs to be individuals to initiate, administer and oversee it, as a professional association is otherwise a nebulous group potentially lacking in cohesion. In this chapter I argue that individual stories, such as that recounted by Michael Todd QC, cannot be overlooked despite their relatively obscured status in existing research into professional associations. To ignore the interplay between individuals' previous experiences and their present actions leaves untold an important part of the story of change initiated or participated in by human agents.

Separate from the role of individual stories is the role of individual agency: a person's actions and their ability to perform them. Although individuals' stories and agency are not the same, it is argued that the two are often connected, with stories motivating an individual's demonstration of agency. Neglecting the importance of individuals leads to overlooking how individuals within large and powerful organisations can innovate; acting as agents despite constraints imposed by the organisation (Battilana and D'Aunno, 2009: 31). This is referred to as the 'paradox of embedded agency' (Battilana, 2006).

Whilst occupational attributes of these individuals are relevant to the introduction and maintenance of change, so are their personal stories. This chapter draws on institutional theory literature, particularly institutional logics, to support the argument advanced at the end of the previous chapter that individuals within the professional association play a key role in that process. It is argued that where a professional association is seeking to cause change, the professional and personal backgrounds of individuals within it increase their ability to demonstrate agency and provide leadership. Leadership here is identified as distinct from management (Kotter, 2013), incorporating an ability to inspire linked to the affective domain (see 4.3.1), as opposed to merely hierarchical superiority.

At Inner Temple, leadership arose from a combination of salaried staff and Benchers, who between them had access expertise, different institutional logics, and influence within the profession through their elite status.

There were broadly three sets of individual stories: those of non-traditional aspirant entrants, practitioners, and salaried staff. Their stories influenced their perceptions of access at the Bar, and what could and should be done to improve it. For salaried staff, their stories were of professional involvement with education and access. They had previously been employed outside of the legal profession and consequently brought into Inner Temple (and other professional associations) institutional logics from other areas. Others within the profession often perceived them as inspirational or visionary.

Importing this experience from human resources backgrounds, or professional experience of the 'target matter' that the professional association is pursuing (in the case study, education and access matters), gave these individuals a basis from which to innovate. It also helped them present convincing arguments for innovations with the potential to alter practices resulting from the central value system which contributed to closure, as detailed in Chapter 4. They did this despite being within the professional association; they demonstrated 'embedded agency'. This chapter argues that such agency, bolstered by the hierarchical power and access to resources of the Benchers involved, was vital to bringing about change at Inner Temple.

Amongst practitioner interviewees, many recalled parts of their own professional journey. Five of the seven practitioner interviewees identified themselves as coming from non-traditional backgrounds, and a further one recalled feeling that he 'didn't fit in', despite his traditional attributes. For those most active in access matters, it seemed that a combination of loyalty (see 4.3.1) and their own stories had influenced both their general involvement and their work with PASS particularly (see below). For others, it was an awareness of the challenges to entry for non-traditional aspirant entrants caused by prevailing social norms within the profession. I argue that these stories have influenced which practitioners become involved with access programmes; the evolution of such programmes, and personal responses to non-traditional aspirant entrants.

For the students, their personal stories were not yet inextricably linked to the Bar. However, the effects of their home and educational experiences on their perception of the Bar and their participation in PASS are explored in Chapter 6, and analysed as one source of constraint on the efficacy of professional association action in Chapter 7. The present chapter concludes by arguing that the importance of individual stories is illustrated in the possibility of the transfer of innovation. It becomes clear that without individuals in an organisation who will commit both ideologically and professionally to making such a change, entrenchment of practices seems likely to defeat change efforts. Consequently, it is not possible to state that a model such as PASS could simply be transferred to another organisation (see Chapter 8). Tangible and human resources available to an organisation must be assessed. One element of such human resources might be individual stories.

Methodologically, the current research also responds to criticisms made by Suddaby (2010: 16). He noted that research concerned with institutional theory largely neglects motivations and subjective experiences of the actors involved. This research addresses this absence by particularly attending to the role actors' experiences play in their engagement with access initiatives in this chapter, in addition to the consideration of the motivations of the actors (see 4.4). Qualitative research methods allowed exploration of the subjective experience of those actors. Interviews with key actors in the case study engaged with the nuances of institutional action, facilitating an effort 'to understand how institutions operate through the influence and agency of individuals' (2010: 17).

5.1 'When I came to the Bar . . .': the importance of individual stories

Despite being neglected in previous research into professions, the importance of individual stories came to the fore in this research in a way I had not expected. Due to qualitative data collection, many interviews elicited stories of interviewees' own journeys to the Bar. Of the seven practitioners interviewed, five self-identified as being from non-traditional backgrounds. Three of those were Benchers, and all made clear the influence of their professional journeys on their involvement in access initiatives. Not only had their individual experiences influenced them, interactions with other people along the way were crucial, especially where those interactions had been the very thing that enabled them to enter the profession:

> The reason I joined Inner all those years ago was because I had no connection with the law at all and I went round all the Inns and spoke to the Education and Training departments. I am not sure it was even called 'Education and Training' then. I remember her name: Miss Geddes, who used to run what is now the Education and Training as a one-woman band, and because she was the most open and welcoming and supportive and sorted out a mini-pupillage on the telephone there and then – a mini-pupillage which then translated into a full pupillage – is a reason (a) I was able to come to the Bar and (b) the reason I chose Inner.
> (Interviewee 7, Inner, M, Bencher, other prof. assocs.)

Their awareness of pivotal moments in their careers provided by other individuals inspired a number of them to contribute to access programmes. For others, their experiences led them to form strong views about factual challenges to access, both past and present. This sometimes led them to categorically dismiss questions of perception which this research argues are important (see Chapter 7), as they believed their experience represented a sole reality:

> When I came to the law I was told, as a matter of history, when I decided I wanted to be a barrister, 'You have to be able to speak Latin', which is of course rubbish; 'you had to know French' because of legal French, which is of course rubbish; and 'you had to have family in the law' – rubbish, we have none.
> (Interviewee 4, Inner, M, Bencher)

What was striking was that some interviewees seemed unaware that their own routes into the profession had not been through formal processes. At the relevant times, however, the way in which they obtained their pupillages was the only way; no formal application systems existed, and entry to the Bar was always on an informal basis (these practitioners had been Called in the 1980s). All that was required was convincing a practising barrister to take you as his pupil (albeit that the pupil had to pay their pupil-master for the privilege until this was abolished in 1975; Pirie and Rogers, 2012: 146). Indeed, one interviewee suggested that formal processes had inhibited social mobility, as all aspirant entrants were reduced to pieces of paper, requiring the application of inflexible criteria to make the process of paper-sifting manageable for the busy junior tenant undertaking it (see 6.3):

> I was able to come to the Bar because it wasn't constrained with rules and regulations and that's why social mobility has gone backwards . . . I walked into Jean Geddes' office and I said I wanted to be a barrister, and obviously she took a view that it was certainly possible and picked up the phone and said, 'Look, I have got somebody here who is very keen, can they come and do a week's work experience?' and the barrister at the end, who is a very eminent family Silk now, Christopher Lockhart, he said yes. He couldn't care less where I came from. He didn't say, 'Which school did you go to? Which university did you go to?' He said, 'Of course he can. He can start in three weeks; I am doing a long planning enquiry, come and do it', so I went and did work experience for a week and ultimately I got a pupillage in those chambers.
> (Interviewee 7, Inner, M, Bencher, other prof. assocs.)

This interviewee believed that a strength of PASS was that it re-introduced this level of nuance – this possibility to look past the presence or absence of traditional identifiers, and consider candidates' drive and raw skills:

> Compare that to the Pegasus Access Scheme where, and there couldn't be a better person doing it, [X] sits down and reads all the forms and then rings people up and has an interview. It's Mrs Geddes!
> (Interviewee 7, Inner, M, Bencher, other prof. assocs.)

Indeed, both this individual and another explicitly stated that having joined the Bar, the profession could be the ultimate meritocracy because of its unusual structure (see 7.3), with solicitors only instructing counsel who proved themselves competent:

> It is an absolute meritocracy, in fact it's probably the perfect market in the sense that if you were good you get work, if you're not you don't . . . I was Called in 1987, and there was very little, 'Oh, he's known as and she's known as', that anyone got work. It was the perfect meritocracy in that

respect and much better I think than any other profession. The weakness as with all professions is who actually gets to be Called to the Bar and have that opportunity.

(Interviewee 4, Inner, M, Bencher)

The other theme arising from interviews apparent in this quotation is the difference in the perception of practitioners of how they accessed the profession as compared to current entrants. In some interviews there was allusion to feelings of a lack of willingness to try, a lack of resilience and a lack of drive to keep trying. These were innate attributes regarded as key to success at the Bar (see 4.4), and interviewees did not seem to consider that lower self-confidence, and consequent reticence to 'aim high', may itself result from socio-economic disadvantage (see 7.4):

> Yes, we have to give the message that if you want to come to the Bar, wherever you come from you can, but there is an aspect of self-selection. There is no point in going out and recruiting people to the Bar; it's hopeless. You have got to have that something in you.
>
> (Interviewee 7, Inner, M, Bencher, other prof. assocs.)

A member of salaried staff also noted this, similarly suggesting that it illustrated a lack of innate 'talents' that aspirant entrants, regardless of their backgrounds, needed if they were to enter the profession:

> I am noticing more and more that the number one skill or attribute that they need, I am finding strangely is diminishing, is resilience. They're knocked down once and simply can't pick themselves up again. I've had really shocking e-mails from some students who were on PASS, they didn't get an Inns scholarship, and I can understand that if it is for financial reasons they will come back [and try again the next year] and various things, but instead I just get vitriol, anger.
>
> (Interviewee 11, Inner, M, salaried)

The importance of individual stories in driving involvement in access programmes and the journeys of those within professional associations raises the question of whether non-traditional practitioners will drive forward change, or re-enact the closure that they themselves faced as entrants. In general, interviewees who had experienced such closure seemed keen to ensure that it was not reproduced, but were also quick to emphasise that there was no circumnavigating the need for 'talent'. Even though schemes such as PASS allowed circumnavigation of a part of the process that currently does not appropriately respond to disadvantage (mini-pupillage selection), 'talent' was a non-negotiable requirement. Those practitioners who had not faced closure themselves took more varied stances. Some, whilst sympathetic to the general cause, seemed to lack the depth of understanding of particular challenges facing non-traditional aspirant entrants.

Others displayed an equally nuanced understanding of the challenges as their non-traditional counterparts. Such understanding often affected individual action, the focus of the next section.

5.2 Individual power within powerful organisations: embedded agency

Individual agency was portrayed by most interviewees as crucially important at Inner Temple, emphasising the ability of individual actors to perform institutional work (Lawrence and Suddaby, 2006) as embedded agents (Greenwood and Suddaby, 2006). There was clear evidence that the 'paradox of embedded agency' (Battilana, 2006), based on the assumption that it is impossible for an actor to alter the institution conditioning their actions (Battilana and D'Aunno, 2009: 31), was engaged. Actors involved in PASS were involved in a clear attempt to alter institutional logics.

Two groups of actors demonstrated embedded agency in Inner Temple: salaried staff and Benchers. Both groups would be expected to be constrained by the organisational norms of social closure, and thus unwilling to challenge it. In doing so, therefore, they are demonstrating embedded agency. In these respective demonstrations differences were observed. These were due, at least partly, to hierarchical differences between the two groups; factors affecting Benchers as the elite (see 4.1.1) differed from those affecting salaried staff.

A common theme in interviews with both groups was that the Bar's nature meant that individual action alone could only be the spark, providing inspiration and initial ideas. Additional individuals were then needed to develop the idea into a meaningful plan and enact it. For example, whilst Michael Todd QC was acknowledged by interviewees as the 'spark' that had encouraged the profession to improve socio-economic diversity, others within the profession had been important in progressing that objective. The fragmented structure of the Bar could prove challenging, but such difficulties were reduced when action was taken by a professional association with access to many members, enabling like-minded members to be brought together, whatever their own individual stories (see 7.3).

Committees were the main structure by which salaried staff at Inner Temple accessed the greater influence of elite members (see 7.3 and 5.3 below). They felt supported in promoting actions with potential to disrupt previously entrenched characteristics of the profession by those with whom they were in close professional contact. These were often members of the Outreach Committee, supporting arguments made about the role of committees in ameliorating other structural constraints (see 7.3). The Outreach Committee consists of around twenty people: practitioners and Benchers, as well as the Outreach Manager (a salaried member of Inner Temple staff). Its responsibility is directing the Inn's outreach activities, advised by the Outreach Manager.

Within this setting, ideas could be considered in a small group before putting them to the wider membership, and all interviewees seemed to regard it as a 'safe space' for strategy discussion. Convincing the whole professional association's membership could be more difficult, and the profession at large even harder still. When advanced by a committee, however, ideas seemed to be regarded as more authoritative. A picture is therefore painted of two notions of embedded agency. First, of individual embedded agency as widely recognised in the literature (Greenwood and Suddaby, 2006: 26), often providing the 'new idea' in a controversial area, or a novel approach to an existing challenge. Second, collective embedded agency, whereby a small group engaged in entrepreneurial behaviour to advance an individual's idea.

The role of the elite, as already highlighted (see 4.1.1) continues to be of interest in examining mechanisms of innovation within a professional association. Due to their central position and consequent attachment to the central value system (Shils, 1975) the elite would be expected to conform with accepted practices, not to demonstrate institutional entrepreneurship or seek to disrupt existing institutional logics. Not only were personal stories important for some in their decision to make these challenges, but the elite could combine institutional entrepreneurship and embedded agency to form the preconditions for institutional change caused by individuals (Battilana, 2006: 664–5). Many other variables, such as individuals' formal positions in the organisation's hierarchy and informal positions in internal networks, were also important, further supporting Battilana's findings.

In keeping with earlier findings in this research on the importance of the social field position of the professional association (see 4.3), individuals' social field positions within the organisation affected their ability to act as institutional entrepreneurs. This is expected from Bourdieu's analysis of social fields (Battilana, 2006: 654). Salaried staff and Benchers acted in developing PASS on behalf of a group with no field position (non-traditional aspirant entrants), and used their own position to pursue institutional change for the under-represented group that could not secure such change itself.

Although external impetus came from the 'Entry to the Bar' Report into social mobility at the Bar (Neuberger, 2007), and the LSA (see 4.4 and 7.1.1), for change to occur it was necessary for individuals inside the professional association to commit to the cause. Such a change came about through an initial action by one key Bencher:

> Basically, when Michael Todd QC was Chairman of the Bar Council he was very keen that we should be more aware on the social mobility side and so he asked [A – Bencher] to form a committee.
> (Interviewee 10, Inner, F, Bencher, other prof. assocs.)

This was then built upon by the recruitment of a salaried staff member with specialist knowledge of access and diversity. In analysing the success of these individuals in establishing PASS, their social field position within Inner Temple is key. Bourdieu (1984) postulated that social fields consisted of two main concepts: 'habitus' and 'doxa' (see 2.4.1.1); someone with an implicit understanding of the habitus and doxa of a field will feel more comfortable within it. Benchers had this advantage, and used it to the benefit of the newly-recruited member of salaried staff, who had been brought in from a non-legal organisation and was unfamiliar with the Inns of Court. This allowed that individual to establish a stronger field position for themselves within the professional association (potentially a 'segment' with part of its identity as a concern with social mobility; Bucher and Strauss, 1961: 330), and thus increase their chance of success in promoting social mobility-advancing interventions such as PASS. In turn, PASS is aimed at promoting a change in ideology away from social closure, which could facilitate the entry to the profession of those who have no position in the field. This data provides illustrations of the significant powers of individuals in certain circumstances, and in conjunction with other groups both internal and external to their organisation. This research also casts doubt on claims by some scholars who argue that individual agency within large organisations is not powerful enough to have a notable effect (DiMaggio and Powell, 1983).

To perceive an institution such as a professional association as a product of human agency as opposed to a constraint upon human agency (as suggested by DiMaggio and Powell, 1991) allows far greater recognition of the ability of the association to be transformed by the will of those within it. There is significant opportunity for entrepreneurial behaviour within professional associations, even if it is initiated by a small group of members. For the current research, the promotion of social mobility and access on the scale seen in PASS is unique to Inner Temple amongst the Inns of Court, although Middle Temple runs a smaller programme with a similar aim (see 4.2.3.1). On a micro-level, not every member of Inner Temple is involved in the promotion of access through the Inn's programmes. However, drawing on Battilana's analysis (2006: 664–6), and that of Bucher and Strauss (1961: 332) this is not an obstruction to the programme's success; it is only necessary that those acting occupy a position and hold views which facilitate their effective intervention. These include personal ideological views, political views and those views developed from personal experience of other institutional logics, all of which affect the way individuals within the organisation contribute to the endeavour to remove social closure from the definition of professionalism at the Bar (see 4.1.2 and 5.1).

Further interacting with the personal stories of individuals, and deeply intertwined with their ability to display embedded agency, are the institutional logics of their immediate environment. The institutional logics of the Bar overall, and Inner Temple more narrowly, therefore exert influence on those involved in PASS. The institutional logics at the Bar have long operated to the disadvantage of those from non-traditional backgrounds – not unexpectedly as they are an under-represented group.

5.3 Challenging prevailing institutional logics

A reconceptualisation of the prevailing institutional logics could reduce this disadvantage, but would be expected to be difficult to achieve in a traditional profession. Those with the most interest in challenging prevailing institutional logics are those for whom those institutional logics cause discomfort or difficulty

(Battilana, 2006: 661). Such individuals usually have neither the field position nor access to resources (see 4.3) needed to alter these logics. In the case study, however, it was not just non-traditional aspirant entrants who wished to challenge the prevailing institutional logics to assist their entry. So did members of the profession, albeit with different aims (see 4.4). Members of the profession articulated the aim of access for all 'able' aspirant entrants to provide a more competitive pool from which to recruit to maintain the profession's elite nature. Salaried staff focussed on the social justice imperative.

This parallel interest in challenging the institutional logics held by members of the elite and salaried staff, albeit directed by differing motivations, meant that they were willing to use their influence within Inner Temple to initiate a challenge to the existing institutional logics of closure. The taking of action by those with an elevated field position within the organisation counteracted the relatively low levels of power and influence held by non-traditional aspirant entrants. This relative powerlessness was addressed by members of the elite acting, partly through appointing specialist staff, in an attempt to alter the institutional logics: a powerful group challenging institutional logics on behalf of a group for whom they are not favourable. Action by the elite on behalf of a powerless group still requires an examination of how the elite were not constrained by existing institutional logics, however.

Inner Temple took clear steps with the intention of promoting social mobility. For reasons explored in Chapter 6, it is argued that this falls short of a fundamental remodelling of professionalism at the Bar. However, it is argued that it does amount to at least an attempt to alter the institutional logics within the professional association, in the hope that such an alteration will spread outwards to chambers and potentially other Inns. Through developing a programme which, regardless of uncertainties over the measurement of success (see 8.1.3), brings non-traditional aspirant entrants into contact with the profession, and which seeks to promote the general notion of social mobility, Inner Temple appears to be attempting such an alteration. It is argued in the next chapter that it is doing so, to the extent of providing information to non-traditional aspirant entrants and mutual exposure between them and the profession. A gradual move towards a more socially-inclusive profession may therefore occur. This would happen through the introduction and institutionalisation (Jepperson, 1991: 148) of new institutional logics which did not support manifestations of the central value system that were exclusionary on socio-economic background.

This research illustrates the importance of both positional and relational power within an organisation, affecting its institutional logics (from Thornton's typology; 2004: 16). Individuals who possessed power in one category formed alliances with those holding power in the other. This reinforced PASS with both the requisite specialist knowledge and the necessary seniority and influence within Inner Temple. The implementation of PASS in an organisation where social closure historically occurs illustrates that whilst the role of socialisation is important (see 6.3.2.2), it neglects to explain how behaviour can nonetheless be changed for strategic reasons (Thornton, 2004: 38–9).

However, the possibility exists that organisational structures differentially emphasise elements of socialisation and logics according to the organisation's intentions or desires at a particular time (Thornton, 2004: 39). Realising that elements of its existing logics may be incompatible with social mobility, in 2009 Inner Temple appointed a salaried individual from a non-legal background with responsibility for directing the organisation's 'outreach activities' (itself a potentially loaded term). This employee ('X') was well known by all interviewees, as he was central to the Inn's outreach activities. He brought from his previous employment institutional logics providing him with frames of reference that precondition choices and vocabularies, and contribute to the formation of a sense of identity (Friedland and Alford, 1991). It appeared that he had then partly adapted these existing logics to the legal profession, giving him a new 'global' logic (Jones and Livne-Tarandach, 2008: 1078, 1080). He had also maintained fragments of his previous occupational identity, which gave him a greater repertoire of competing logics to draw upon, facilitating adaption of behaviour (Meyer and Hammerschmid, 2006: 1012). Social mobility and promoting access remained at the core of his professional actions, but were explained and interpreted differently depending upon the audience (similarly witnessed in Magic Circle firms; Braithwaite, 2010: 173).

A marked alteration in institutional logics is unlikely to result from one individual as different groups (referred to as 'social orders' by Friedland and Alford (1991)) within an organisation have different institutional logics. Institutional logics can therefore inform three levels of analysis: the role of individuals within the Inn; the Inn as an organisation itself, and its connection with non-traditional aspirant entrants. Every interviewee was exposed to multiple institutional logics. They moved in a variety of institutions: at least two or more of the Bar Council, the Inn, individual committees within the Inn and/or the Bar Council, specialist Bar associations, their chambers and other smaller special-interest groups (e.g. Young Legal Aid Lawyers). Each of these, regardless of its relative size or influence, will have different institutional logics. It was particularly notable within the salaried staff, and especially the member of staff who was key in creating PASS, that they had been influenced by their experiences in previous employment, to the extent of bringing existing access programme links with them. One salaried employee had worked with the Pathways programme whilst at a higher education organisation, and had negotiated Inner Temple providing the Bar-based part of the programme.

Some interviewees suggested that organic change had been gradually occurring, with the Bar becoming more diverse and lessening its reliance on recruitment through old-boys' networks. Specific individuals were credited with advancing the cause at a faster pace than would have occurred organically. However, institutional logics play a key role in determining the actions open to actors within an organisation, as detailed in the next section. This research also illustrates that they will shape collective behaviour, meeting Lounsbury and Crumley's criticism (2007: 993) that individual actions have become celebrated at the expense of an awareness of the multi-level nature of change, and that the notion of performativity is preferable. Within performativity change is construed as constant and innovation ongoing, but contributed to, and steered by, individuals and small groups (2007: 996).

5.3.1 Individual and collective challenges to institutional logics

Actors do not simply reproduce existing institutional logics; some also have the capacity to adjust or alter them. This may happen through mechanisms such as theorisation and transposition. As discussed above, institutional logics may be portrayed as a 'tool kit': they are malleable, and applied differentially across social situations (Thornton, 2004: 40). Where individuals form a group, collectively they have a greater array of tools. Specifically, they may benefit from an elevated social field position which research suggests will increase both their willingness and ability to alter a dominant institutional logic (institutional entrepreneurship; Battilana, 2006: 659). Therefore, it is argued that it is not necessary for all the properties to meet in one individual for institutional change to occur.

At Inner Temple, X was a key institutional entrepreneur identified by all interviewees. This individual was not a practitioner; they had a professional background in organisations focussed on higher education, and within those positions relating specifically to increasing access and improving social mobility. Similarly to the salaried human resources staff in Braithwaite's (2010) research, therefore, this individual brought in ideas and practices from other spheres and applied them to challenges at the Bar. They were also able to marshal people who shared the 'unique mission' (Bucher and Strauss, 1961: 330) of increasing social mobility, through their administrative powers and links to members of the organisation at all levels.

Their individual entrepreneurship was supported by their ability to bolster their own relatively low position in the organisational hierarchy by being perceived as a legitimate actor by stakeholders at all relevant levels, and the ability to build bridges between those stakeholders and their diverse interests and aims, allowing access to a variety of both human and financial resources (Battilana, 2006: 660). This individual does not fit neatly into either of Battilana's 'incumbent' or 'challenger' categories (2006: 661). It is argued that this is at least partly attributable to this individual having been head-hunted for the express purpose of bringing their specialist knowledge on access matters into Inner Temple. They therefore occupied a harder-to-define position, whereby although in hierarchical terms they were relatively low, they nonetheless wielded significant power in respect of access projects. This seemed to stem from having been brought in by the organisation specifically to develop access programmes due to their specialist knowledge, which seemed to contribute further to their relative lack of constraint by institutional logics. Consequently, their very purpose was perceived, partly, as challenging existing exclusionary practices and logics.

This research illustrates that the Bar's structure causes significant challenges to the alteration of institutional logics, as compared even to the solicitors' profession (e.g. Braithwaite, 2010). Whilst a very small number of the largest and more progressive chambers employ staff with backgrounds in other institutional logics, this is not possible for most chambers; financial constraints mean minimal administrative staff. This precludes opportunities to introduce members of staff with other institutional logics which they may use to assist institutional entrepreneurship. Professional association involvement addresses part of this challenge as it can employ staff who can co-ordinate larger-scale initiatives not restricted to one chambers but ranging across the profession (see Chapter 4).

As discussed above, two groups were especially important to the establishment of PASS: Benchers and salaried staff, and within those members of the Education and Training Department and the Outreach Committee. The Education and Training Department is an administrative department staffed entirely by salaried employees, many from non-legal backgrounds, who were instrumental in setting up PASS and other outreach activities. Two such employees were interviewed. The Bar Council similarly had salaried employees from higher education and the not-for-profit sector who collaborated on social mobility projects, of whom one was interviewed. These staff had operated in different institutional logics in previous roles, which seemed to have a significant effect: they brought new ideas and alternative ways of enacting them, as well as a passion for, and knowledge of, their specialist area. Their expertise and its importance were recognised by others within the professional association as key to establishing PASS:

> It's been entirely driven by Education and Training, which is fantastic in Inner Temple. We then recruited [X], who has driven this forward with great skill and passion.
> (Interviewee 7, Inner, M, Bencher, other prof. assocs.)

> We have an Education Department, we have a Recruitment and Outreach Manager, so all those sides of it mean that there are people who can deal with that because barristers can try and conceive the schemes, get guidance from someone who is as expert as [X] and recommend it and persuade others to join, but I am afraid you need someone day-to-day administering it.
> (Interviewee 4, Inner, M, Bencher)

Although constraints from the institutional logics of the Bar will operate on salaried staff coming into Bar organisations, these constraints seemed to be ameliorated by the importation of elements of previous institutional logics. Furthermore, by having colleagues also from non-legal backgrounds in similar posts in other organisations, there was more opportunity for collaboration between sites of power (see 4.2.3) that could capitalise on organisations being stronger together, despite the historical inclination against this, as discussed in the previous chapter. Salaried staff who worked for different professional associations of the Bar, but had broadly shared professional backgrounds, did not seem to feel so constrained by inter-organisational antagonism detailed by some practitioner participants (especially between the Bar Council and the Inns of Court). In these circumstances, strong working relationships between individuals were seen as the best way to overcome such difficulties:

110 *The importance of individuals*

> I have to say that [Y] and the Bar Council has been fantastic and [Z] before him has been absolutely fantastic about representing the work that the Inns do in this respect, but there always has been some wariness, I think.
>
> (Interviewee 11, Inner, M, salaried)

Salaried staff also implicitly confirmed that they brought in outside logics:

> I had had experience with Pathways from [when I was at] the Russell Group [university organisation]. It was lauded as one of the most successful ... and all the research showed it having a very positive impact on students and access to higher education and access to professions thereafter. So I brought them in and started to run all the Bar-related activities.
>
> (Interviewee 11, Inner, M, salaried)

Research on the effects on individual actors of contradictions or complementarities between logics which they experience across different institutional settings has disclosed varying results. The degree of malleability of institutional logics varies between organisations and individuals. However, actors often tailor institutional logics to fit practical activity, creating pluralism in institutional logics in specific local settings such as corporations and organisational fields (Lounsbury and Crumley, 2007: 996). Such pluralism at the Bar is illustrated by the varying approaches to social mobility of different chambers and Inns; even within one broad 'institution' (the Bar) and smaller sub-institutions (one Inn) there will be differing institutional logics influencing differing approaches to those matters within that institution.

It was therefore clear that, in attempting to incorporate social mobility into Inner Temple's conception of professionalism, individuals accustomed to other institutional logics were key in initiating the project. They brought with them a level of innovative thinking which may be harder to access internally within an embedded professional association of a traditional profession such as an Inn, or which once accessed needs expertise to utilise. PASS demonstrates innovative action is possible when a mixture of individuals from the established logic, and other logics, come together with individuals from the professional association's elite, and are numerous enough to form their own segment, based on their values and ideas, within the organisation.

Many participants singled out X as the 'driving force' behind many of the Inn's achievements in promoting social mobility and setting up suitable projects to further that aim:

> [X] will probably be very modest about it but I think that is very much largely down to him and his efforts and the way he views things ... I might be wrong but I do think it is [X], because I do think he is very progressive and forward-thinking in the way he does things.
>
> (Interviewee 10, Inner, F, Bencher, other prof. assocs.)

Nonetheless, it was emphasised by others that this individual, although playing a crucial role, nonetheless relied on the enthusiasm of others to participate in access schemes, which could be channelled through the Inn's organisational and administrative facilities as a professional organisation:

> A lot of that is down to having a very enthusiastic Outreach Manager, but it's something that this Inn, we are very proud that we are involved in those activities and we think it is important, and obviously with any project that you set up, if you want it to keep going, you have got to keep the enthusiasm going and our members are very enthusiastic about the whole thing.
> (Interviewee 8, Inner, F, salaried)

X was a clear example of the potential power of individual agency. Prior to Pathways, Inner Temple undertook very limited social mobility activities, and it was the targeted recruitment of X that led to a drastic increase in the Inn's involvement in social mobility initiatives. In interviewing X, the qualities that other interviewees attributed to him were apparent. In combination with his charisma, he was perceived as having a powerful mix of professional skill and ideological commitment to access issues. This combination of skills and personality meant that he had demonstrated agency and succeeded in driving progress in an historically controversial area.

The previous chapter established that attachment to the central value system need not be a hindrance to innovative action by a professional association. This chapter therefore focusses on the role for individuals and particularly, in the case study, on the potential influence that a small group of individuals can have on a large organisation. Addressing the paradigm of embedded agency, it suggests that when wider conditions within the organisation are right, it is possible for individuals to behave in ways which appear not to be constrained by existing norms and institutional logics. However, this is often easier for individuals brought into the organisation from other professional environments, due to their experience of other institutional logics informing their approach to the matter being addressed in their present employment.

5.4 Can a professional association alter the conception of professionalism within its segment or arena?

On the basis of the attributes of Inner Temple as a professional association portrayed in Chapter 3, and the roles played by individuals as detailed so far in this chapter, it is argued that Inner Temple has the power and field position required to effect changes within the profession, resulting from internal changes. These are largely attributable to the actions and knowledge of those from other professional backgrounds importing different institutional logics into the professional association. Whilst it is argued that it is too early in the life of PASS to be able to assess whether the conception of professionalism held within the 'arena' of the Bar has been altered by Inner Temple to include a commitment to social mobility, it is argued that changes in the central value system on an institutional level appear to be occurring.

This research argues that not only might a profession recognise societal changes requiring it to adapt to maintain its elite status, it may also try to adapt to those changes, although a number of factors will influence the success of its attempts. Any attempt altering the dynamics or practices of the profession, or a segment thereof (Bucher and Strauss, 1961), could be considered as the concept of professionalism evolving, albeit incrementally or slowly. The notion of an evolving conception of professionalism was particularly strikingly articulated by one interviewee:

> Because I believe that the Bar will be significantly under greater threat as a profession if we don't improve the access for all groups in society to a career at the Bar, because I think we need to be more representative of the society we serve than we probably are.
> (Interviewee 9, Inner, M, Bencher, other prof. assocs.)

This suggests that some members of the profession believe that, to continue its claim to be a profession, the Bar must ensure that it is diverse, and representative of those whom it serves. However, on the basis of Kritzer's assertion that a profession may struggle to come to terms with changes which are significant for its self-identity (for example, less complex services no longer provided by the profession), the idea that diversity is now an integral criterion for a profession to so call itself is likely to be controversial. Changes to the conception of professionalism within the highly traditional legal profession would not be acceded to so easily.

Kritzer states that in the Anglo-American legal profession, 'The response by the legal profession to these and other developments has been to try to hold onto an outmoded image of professionalism' (1999: 732). Some movement has already been seen – for example, the requirement that those applying for Silk demonstrate 'diversity' as a 'competence'.[1] Inner Temple's actions in seeking to promote social mobility through PASS suggest that that statement may not hold true across an entire profession and all of its professional associations. Indeed, by creating and developing PASS, one could argue that Inner Temple is attempting to update the image of professionalism, by portraying social mobility and diversity as an integral part of a new 'professional project' whereby entry is solely determined by ability and determination:

> In all this the message is not that we are going to lower the standards to get wider access. What we are saying is that the standards are high; they will

---

1 www.qcappointments.org/wp-content/uploads/2017/02/The-Competency-Framework-2017.pdf [accessed 30th August 2017].

become increasingly higher as the numbers go down because it's competition. All we are saying is, do not be put off going for the challenge simply by virtue of what your parents did, where you went to school or where you went to university, but you still have to be the best.

(Interviewee 7, Inner, M, Bencher, other prof. assocs.)

This message was also being successfully communicated to non-traditional entrants, as evidenced by comments from Pathways students that such programmes were not about making entry easier, but fairer in practice and not merely for appearance's sake (cf. comments explored under 4.4):

There are certain pervasive ideas of the Bar to the effect that it is a middle-class profession dominated by airs and decorum, which excludes those who don't comply with a certain manner of behaviour, a members' club masquerading as a profession. I never believed that, but some aspects of it seemed to ring true. But this perception was totally undermined by my experience at [chambers]. Instead of class or background, the primary criteria for entry actually seemed to be intellectual ability, flair for advocacy, alacrity, industry and wit. So in other words, the meritocratic rhetoric of government and Inn of Court pamphlets was shown to bear some resemblance to reality.

(Inner Temple post-PASS feedback questionnaire, Cohort 1)

Therefore, it is argued that although Inner Temple's promotion of social mobility through PASS is not sufficient to amount to an alteration of the profession's conception of professionalism, it does nonetheless reflect a potential change in both the central value system, and the institutional logics of the professional association. Arguably the latter is needed before the former can occur. For change in the central value system action will be necessary in the professional association's quotidian operation. Therefore, removal of institutional logics supporting social closure could contribute to a removal of manifestations of the central value system that support closure. Such presence will occur when it is incorporated into the 'rules of the game' (Jepperson, 1991: 143) used by actors within the professional association in their decision-making processes and systems of understanding that they apply to their daily life within the organisation.

It seems that Inner Temple may be building foundations for an alteration within the Inn of its manifestation of the central value of professionalism to one promoting social mobility and equal access. This change within Inner Temple's 'arena' (Nelson and Trubek, 1992) may extend externally to other Inns over time, although the degree and rate of this will be dependent upon various matters. Specifically, whether Inner Temple manages to consolidate the changes made in such a way that they are sustainable in the long term within Inner Temple itself. If so they may be able to permeate to other arenas (see 5.5). A second matter upon which it will depend is the attributes of other professional associations to which permeation could occur, as the attributes of a professional association play a significant role in whether that organisation can initiate, maintain and consolidate new practices. Any organisation hoping to facilitate such change would need to have attributes supporting these processes; it would not be enough that the attributes were present in the originating organisation. Each subsequent organisation would then need to institutionalise the process and values, as described above.

5.5 Challenges to transfer of values in the case study

Building upon the idea that there may be a new conceptualisation of the central value of professionalism at Inner Temple by reference to existing literature, Paterson (1996: 139) conceives professionalism as a contract between profession and state which can be under constant renegotiation. He states that despite extensive renegotiation, many core values relating to professionalism will survive, with more uniting the profession than dividing it. Francis (2004: 324) suggests that the value of Paterson's model is as a 'recognition of the evolutionary nature of professionalism'. This is the most helpful interpretation in relation to this current research, focussing as it does in detail on a programme run by the Inner Temple which has amongst its aims the incorporation into the arena of professionalism operated by the Inns a commitment to social mobility of aspiring entrants.

This research highlights that a profession may be divided into 'segments', which compete to impose a dominant profession-wide conception of legal professionalism (Bucher and Strauss, 1961: 330). Although, as stated by Nelson and Trubek (1992: 186), professionalism's form is contingent upon the particular arena in which it is being exercised, its production and form in one arena may influence its production and form in other arenas. Due to the fragmented structure there are a greater number of arenas than in most professions, many with crossover of membership (e.g. chambers, specialist Bar associations, Inns of Court, the Bar Council). Furthermore, each of these arenas has significant autonomy. For example, on 11th July 2014, COMBAR, the Commercial Bar Association, was announced as a partner to the rebranded PASS[2] – a move by one specialist segment independently from others.

The production and form of professionalism in a particularly strong segment/arena may exert significant influence over smaller or less stable segments/arenas within the same profession. When there is one professional organisation presiding over the whole profession, this may cause discord: Bucher and Strauss (1961: 330) stated that no professional association could be wholly representative; it could only ever represent a segment within a profession. However, at the Bar, for

---

2 www.pegasus.me/?page_id=162 [accessed 1st August 2017].

example, where there are four Inns of Court, it is theoretically possible that each Inn may construe and pursue professionalism slightly differently without any significant impact upon the profession as a whole. Compared to chambers and the Bar Council, it appears that the Inns are the most important arena for effecting change within the profession, due to their combination of size, loyalty and heterogeneity (see 4.2). Furthermore, if part of the profession develops an institutional logic which values social mobility, this may permeate into other parts.

Due to the less rigid hierarchy and membership overlap between segments within the profession, changes within one segment may permeate into others more so than in other professions, an advantageous situation when trying to implement access initiatives. On the views of those interviewed for this research, it would appear that, within Inner Temple's 'segment', actors perceive diversity and access as sufficiently important to attempt to alter both the prevailing institutional logics and the interpretation of the central value system, with PASS being one example of a mechanism by which this is occurring. However, only time will tell whether other organisations of the Bar will incorporate this into their segments, as all have different attributes affecting both their ability and willingness to effect change.

A notable challenge to such permeation is a lack of collaboration between sites of power. The individual X worked closely with a colleague, 'Y', in a similar job at another professional organisation within the Bar (not an Inn of Court), who had a similar background in access matters and policy, and was also lauded by other participants as being a significant influence in achievements at the Bar in promoting the social mobility agenda:

> With the current chair of the Social Mobility Committee [of the Bar Council] and the current policy officer, I don't know if you have met Y? He's very dynamic ... I think there's a much broader sense and we can't do everything but we need to have as broader approach as is consistent with being effective, really.
> (Interviewee 2, non-Inner, F, other prof. assocs.)

However, this cohesiveness was not universal:

> It's very difficult sometimes to work out what the other Inns are doing. Inn X, sometimes I think they are a bit like a secret society. I will probably get told off for saying that, but you just don't seem to be aware of what they are doing.
> (Interviewee 10, Inner, F, Bencher, other prof. assocs.)

Some participants were rather more pragmatic:

> I would say that we are all very much in close contact with the other Inns so anything we do in terms of, particularly with the schools, we are doing very much very much on behalf of the other Inns as well.
> (Interviewee 8, Inner, F, salaried)

The first quotation illustrates a distrust and unwillingness to share new ideas and best practice. This may hinder transfer into other arenas of a professionalism committed to equality of opportunity, and consequently the ability of the Bar to strive for greater social mobility. However, due to the trust and loyalty displayed between practitioners and the Inns (see 4.3.1), the Inns of Court nonetheless seem best-placed to drive such changes to the widest audience, although the extent of this within any particular Inn would be limited by those attributes explored above. Cohesiveness (or a lack thereof) between the Inns is partly a further symptom of the unusual structure of the Bar, as many participants discussed. In the context of a question about how the Inn would measure the success of PASS, one participant stated:

> I would say they [the Bar as a whole] are sharing a view on what would be a measure of success but they may not . . . The Bar isn't exactly cohesive in its approach to trying to achieve that success.
> (Interviewee 8, Inner, F, salaried)

This supports the observation that confusion and a lack of clarity surround the aims and objectives of PASS (see Chapter 6), which hampers an access programme in fulfilling its potential. The lack of a cohesive approach may be symptomatic of a lack of shared vision across the profession on what outcome amounts to 'success' in access programmes. Whilst a general agreement on a desire for greater diversity of the Bar was articulated, quantifying that was far more complex. All interviewees were asked what they would regard as a measure of success for PASS, and many articulated very different potential measures (see 6.4.2).

It is argued that one barrier to a transfer across professional associations was the structure of the profession (see 6.4.2), as it seemed a recurring theme that the professional structure of the Bar did not lend itself well to concerted efforts in any sphere of difficulty, such as access and social mobility. However, other facets of its unusual structure also prevented it from tackling that lack of cohesion:

> I think if there was more cohesion, more targeting, then perhaps we could work together to achieve more together, but then when the profession is made up of different institutions, some have different amounts of resources, different agendas, and it's very difficult to try and bring all that together.
> (Interviewee 8, Inner, F, salaried)

There seemed to be a greater degree of cohesion between the Inns (albeit that some comments suggest this was not so with all four Inns), and between Inns and practitioners, than there was between practitioners and the Bar Council. This was admitted even by those who had held Bar Council posts. One such interviewee stated that the Bar Council was, and always had been, 'absolutely hopeless', characterising it as a 'limp trade union' whose existence had previously been justified by the regulatory function, now removed to the BSB.

Others who had similarly sat on Bar Council committees were less scathing about their experiences, with one stating that the Bar Council acted to fill perceived gaps in access provision, despite financial constraints. Apart from one, those who had sat on Bar Council committees were generally more favourable towards its efforts than those who had not:

> I think [X] gets quite cross with me because I am quite keen for all the Bar Placement Weeks to be rolled out onto the circuit and that is quite a tall order, and I think X's view is that the Bar Council should be just co-ordinating what's going on across the profession and not trying to run programmes as well. But we just took the view that unless the Bar Council did it – and we don't have massive resources to be honest – but unless we did it there were a whole host of young students that were going to miss out on the experience. We felt and I feel that there is a very strong argument for [the] Bar Council having to run programmes if there is no other resource to provide it.
> (Interviewee 10, Inner, F, Bencher, other prof. assocs.).

The lack of cohesiveness amongst the Inns, and between the Inns and the Bar Council, it was suggested by one interviewee, diluted the human resources available for such projects, and consequently made it seem that, in some practice areas particularly, there was not much enthusiasm for such projects:

> Given the way the Bar is structured, although chancery work has a greater problem than the Bar as a whole in terms of attracting students and supporting and promoting and recruiting students from less privileged backgrounds, it's still really quite a hard topic. There is quite a lot of enthusiasm out there and every time we put a plea out for support for one of our schemes we get a huge amount of volunteers. So it's harnessing it that's the difficulty.
> (Interviewee 2, non-Inner, F, other prof. assocs.)

One interviewee suggested that programmes run by Inner Temple were 'being done on behalf of the Inns as a unit', but this attitude was not one expressed by other participants, and neither was it interpreted as such by the recipients of the intervention (see below). However, some practitioner participants thought that if the programme could be a genuine joint effort and presented as such, this would be for the good of the programme:

> I do think that schemes like this would probably be stronger if they were run jointly by all the Inns but for that to work it would have to be run jointly by all Inns in a way that Inner Temple runs the Pegasus scheme.
> (Interviewee 9, Inner, M, Bencher, other prof. assocs.)

Such cohesiveness and collaboration would be necessary for a spread of altered institutional logics within professional associations, and altered archetypes shaping the relationships between professional associations (Kirkpatrick and Ackroyd, 2003). The unusual professional structure of the Bar makes this an area in which more research could contribute to the exploration begun here of the effect of one site of power on another in a complex professional structure (see 4.2.3).

This tension regarding the extent to which the actions of one Inn can be, or are perceived to be, on behalf of all Inns of Court could not be explored due to the lack of availability of any Benchers or staff from the other Inns approached for interview. However, when it was put to interviewees that Inner Temple was forging ahead in this area in a way that did not seem to be occurring at the other Inns, their reactions were mixed:

> I can't really speak for other Inns and I'm actually not one of those that feels comfortable with the idea that we do things better than other people, partly because I have got no evidence based on it.
> (Interviewee 9, Inner, M, Bencher, other prof. assocs.)

> I have to say I am very lucky to be in Inner Temple, but Inner Temple are at the forefront of [social mobility work].
> (Interviewee 10, Inner, F, Bencher, other prof. assocs.)

Where participants conceded that Inner Temple was breaking new ground in this area, its ability to do so was normally attributed to the individual who had specific responsibility for the outreach activities undertaken by the Inn, again emphasising the importance of individuals explored above:

> I think at the moment, so far as other Inns are concerned, Inner is ahead in terms of these projects, partly because we set up a Recruitment and Outreach Committee and partly because we were lucky enough to get someone as excellent as X.
> (Interviewee 4, Inner, M, Bencher)

A shift in the construction of the central value of professionalism to include a commitment to social mobility appears to have occurred within Inner Temple. Any possible spread of this, however, is likely to be constrained by the prevailing norms and the individuals in other organisations. As this research has established, it is a complex interplay of circumstances that may give rise to the ability to attempt innovative action. This research suggests that these circumstances include size, composition, human resources such as loyalty, and the presence of motivations both within and external to the professional association. Therefore, it is not a simple case of sharing best practice; there need to be circumstances integral to the organisation for such innovation to spread. Even were it to do so, it might be interpreted differently by other organisations.

5.6 Conclusion

Despite criticism that Bourdieu's social field theory ignores the role of human agency which this research argues is crucial, Bourdieu responds that 'habitus is not the fate that some people read into it . . . it is an open system of dispositions that is constantly subjected to experiences' (Bourdieu and Wacquant, 1992: 133). Thus, it is the experiences that a person has that play a significant role in shaping their habitus, with every experience having the potential to alter it. Therefore, actions by individuals can have significant effects on the habitus of others, and this can include the habitus of an organisation.

This chapter has argued that the stories of individuals, and their roles within an organisation, are extremely important to an understanding of professional association action, especially in a matter of human interest, such as social mobility. How these personal stories affect the actions of those individuals is further shaped by the prevailing institutional logics, which require alteration if a truly meritocratic recruitment agenda is to be pursued.

Inner Temple as an organisation, through the work of individual actors and groups of actors, is seeking to change the habitus of the field from one with attributes which propagate social closure to a new habitus of professionalism where only ability, demonstrated through traditional or non-traditional methods, is valued. A particular challenge to this aim is that Inner Temple is an embedded professional organisation within a very traditional profession, and both it as an organisation, and the profession at large, are steeped in archaic practices and methods with established doxa and habitus.

These are demonstrated in social closure resulting from the central value system, and longstanding institutional logics implicitly supporting social closure. Challenges are now being made to the central value system's indirect support of social closure, and the institutional logics supporting that, within the professional association. This, coupled with the field position of Inner Temple within the wider profession, means that as a professional association it is well placed to behave innovatively, and such that that innovation may spread to other professional associations within the field.

PASS demonstrates institutional entrepreneurship by Inner Temple in a clear attempt to shift tacit, unexamined and accepted assumptions within the field, perceived by many outside of the profession, even though some within argued that this shift had already begun:

> I went to a state school and didn't tick any of the boxes really that I should have ticked if I had wanted to become a barrister, and I think in many ways we get an unfair press. I think there is a lot of media hype about the Bar: they like to portray us in the press as middle-aged, middle-class white males who are all fat cats and it really isn't made up of that anymore and hasn't been for twenty years . . . So I think slowly we are getting through all that.
> (Interviewee 10, Inner, F, Bencher, other prof. assocs.)

However, this is by no means the end of the story. It is not enough for abstract changes to occur, for a shift in the central value system and institutional logics developing if no real change is felt in concrete efforts in outward interactions.

Such outward interactions and perceptions will be particularly important where recruitment matters are concerned, as they may encourage or deter certain groups of people from applying. The next chapter therefore moves on to examine the case study programme in much more detail. It looks specifically at whether PASS is in fact challenging the status quo of social closure through its provision of mini-pupillage for non-traditional aspirant entrants, or whether it is propagating traditional notions of skill valuation which disadvantage non-traditional aspirant entrants. It considers whether the changes discussed so far are being converted into meaningful action by a professional association to pursue change in the promotion of social mobility, and the experience of those students participating in the programme. Although the intervention does represent an attempt to address social mobility issues, it is argued that its likelihood of doing so on any noticeable scale, in the short term at least, is low.

6 Transformative action for social mobility

Radical innovation or maintenance of status quo?[1]

It has been argued in the preceding chapters that social closure remains a defining feature of the Bar, resulting from central values which indirectly privilege entrants from traditional backgrounds. Although it may be possible to identify the articulation by and within Inner Temple of a model of professionalism containing an explicit commitment to social mobility (see Chapter 4), the capacity of this professional actor to affect models of professionalism in other arenas (Nelson and Trubek, 1992), or the profession overall, is far less clear. This chapter argues that an intervention by a professional association may not be as radical as it first appears if it reinforces the status quo by creating opportunities for an 'outsider' group to conform to the 'accepted' norms of the profession. Work experience at the Bar is used as an illustration; a programme offering legal work experience opportunities to non-traditional aspirant entrants, it is argued, reinforces the privileged status of legal work experience over other methods of skill acquisition, consequently failing to tackle deeper causes of social closure.[2] As noted by Ashley et al. (2015), society should be wary of programmes aimed at altering the characteristics of candidates ('supply'), instead of the preconceptions of professions ('demand').

This chapter focusses on the role of work experience in establishing and propagating social closure at the Bar, and explores how a professional association may undermine this. Work experience may fulfil many roles: experiencing the daily life of a barrister; gaining helpful knowledge from contact with practitioners; experiencing specialisms outside degree syllabi and fulfilling a formal requirement for many pupillage applications. It has therefore been identified as offering a unique opportunity for identity formation (Francis and Sommerlad, 2009: 65), as it exposes students to the profession's social norms and behaviours. These consist of

---

1 I am grateful for helpful comments on this chapter's analysis from attendees at the 2015 Socio-Legal Studies Association Warwick conference, and the Legal Education Research Network/Sheffield Law School workshop in 2016.
2 Throughout this chapter, reference to legal work experience, unless explicitly stated, refers to mini-pupillages specifically. Whilst legal work experience more generally, for example in a solicitors' firm, was favoured above no work experience, mini-pupillages were particularly privileged in the process of gaining full pupillage.

unspoken and assumed rules ('doxa') which direct social interaction and behaviour ('habitus') within the social field of the profession, and are known to those within it (Bourdieu, 1984). For those from non-traditional backgrounds, often without informal contacts within the profession, securing such exposure is harder than for their counterparts from traditional backgrounds, reducing opportunities to assimilate norms and practices of the Bar.

Work experience has been a crucial method of 'gate-keeping'. How it is obtained, and the experience of the mini-pupillage itself, commonly disadvantage students from non-traditional backgrounds, making it a key dimension of social closure at the Bar. For a professional association hoping to improve access, increasing opportunities for non-traditional aspirant entrants to undertake mini-pupillages makes this 'moment of identity formation' more widely available, allowing them to make informed choices about careers in the legal profession and present themselves as serious candidates. For traditional applicants, social capital (Bourdieu, 1984: 69) and their recognisable educational paths make them more likely to secure mini-pupillage through chambers' direct application processes, accessing this mutual exposure.

Identifying students as encountering the profession through an access scheme can be problematic, contributing to their feelings of being 'outsiders'. In the case study it must be questioned how significant an effect such a small-scale programme can have on a large and traditional profession. Whilst PASS may be a significant and useful experience for its participants, its potential to cause a genuine demographic shift should not be over-estimated due to both its small scale and its neglect of more fundamental issues underlying the challenges experienced by non-traditional aspirant entrants. This chapter illustrates how a seemingly radical intervention may not drastically affect the status quo, instead subtly propagating social closure by leaving unchallenged the privileging of experiences more easily accessible to a particular group.

Indeed, whether a demographic shift is even desired may be questioned (Braithwaite, 2010: 150), and discerning this was difficult due to the opaque aims and motivations. There were disagreements between stakeholders as to whether a demographic shift was indeed one of PASS's aims, or its sole aim.

It is argued that until a measure of success is well-defined and agreed upon, it will not be possible to quantify the success of such schemes at all (see 8.1.3). Such quantification is hampered by the innate subjectivity associated with initiatives aimed at 'helping' or 'doing good' (Fisher, 1997). Even numerical analysis does not necessarily reflect meaningful change within the profession; Braithwaite (2010: 150) cautions that 'defining diversity by reference to numbers risks tokenism and ultimately leaving the status quo unchanged'. Furthermore, any change may be confined within the 'arena' of the specific professional association running the programme (Nelson and Trubek, 1992), not causing a demographic shift across the profession unless the relevant association wields significant influence through size and cohesiveness (Halliday, 1987: 133). Even a programme run by a professional association in a strong field position and with attributes indicative of potential wider influence within the profession will be reduced if it maintains the status quo.

Ostensibly, using work experience as an entry criterion is a way of securing the best candidates, something clearly in the profession's best interests. Evidence suggests that direct legal work experience is an attribute perceived by the profession as possessed by the best candidates. However, due to the barriers identified in this chapter, the importance of work experience to those making recruitment decisions may be unjustified. Whilst a profession would be expected to set its entry criteria such that the best candidates succeed, the importance attached to mini-pupillage is only delivering the best candidates from a certain subset: those from traditional backgrounds. Those from non-traditional backgrounds, who may in all material ways be equally good, are disadvantaged. Consequently, the profession does not access the best candidates overall whilst it continues to privilege direct legal work experience in the form of mini-pupillages.

6.1 The Bar as a social class, or the Bar as a series of social norms

Various explanations have been offered for limited demographic diversity at the Bar. Some writers suggest that the Bar is a wholly separate social class (de Tocqueville; ed. Stone, 1980), whilst others prefer an analysis of the Bar as transcending class (Larson, 1977: 169), but with strong links to the 'ruling' classes to preserve monopolistic privileges (1977: 81). Whilst such transcendence may be superficially achieved by a commitment to an ostensibly 'value-free' identity (Lee, 2000; Wilkins, 1998), this identity itself may be easier to attain for those from higher socio-economic groups.

Whilst notions of the Bar as a separate class, or existing outside of the class hierarchy altogether, have been advanced, it is argued that Bourdieu's theory of social capital (1984) offers a more cohesive explanation for access barriers experienced by non-traditional aspirant entrants. Body language, speech patterns and dress, for example, will denote whether an individual has assimilated the habitus of a higher social class (e.g. language; Bourdieu, 1984: 58) expected by the profession (e.g. Sommerlad, 2007: 200). A student who has not assimilated these traits may both struggle to access the profession, and if they do so, not feel comfortable. Practitioner interviewees identified that non-traditional aspirant entrants may struggle to impress at both the paper application stage and interview, for these reasons:

> But I think it [lack of familial links in professions] is a disadvantage only probably in the way that they conduct themselves in an interview and the way they might present their information on paper.
> (Interviewee 10, Inner, F, Bencher, other prof. assocs.)

A profession which attaches such significance to history and tradition may be especially difficult to penetrate due to its idiosyncrasies, but those with existing links through family members or friends, and those familiar with other professions, will integrate more easily. Those who have no such links may struggle to obtain the knowledge and guidance that they need from within the profession whilst seeking to enter it. They therefore cannot display familiarity with social norms and accepted conduct expected within the profession. One way of gaining this knowledge is through mini-pupillages. Non-traditional applicants may struggle to obtain work experience (Francis and MacDonald (2009); Sommerlad (2008). Why work experience holds such importance will now be explored.

6.2 Work experience: an opportunity for identity formation

Work experience is important for three reasons: first, it is often a criterion found in pupillage and training contract applications; second, and relatedly, it allows firms and chambers to assess potential applicants; third, it is one way in which students can assimilate the behaviours expected by the profession, as they can observe and experience occupational facets and how members of the profession conduct themselves. Student participants described their difficulty obtaining mini-pupillages, reflecting official observations on the small number of places available compared to applicants (Neuberger, 2007: 40). Not only had most of the students experienced difficulties in obtaining mini-pupillage, they believed that their non-traditional status contributed to this.

Whilst the Legal Education and Training Review (LETR) highlighted the difficulties posed by the profession requiring work experience, and particularly difficulties non-traditional aspirant entrants faced in accessing work experience (2013: 239), it made few recommendations. Instead it highlighted that the success of access schemes had yet to be successfully measured (2013: 240), and the only recommendation relevant to this research was a more cohesive system advertising work experience opportunities (2013: 19). Although desirable, this chapter illustrates that cohesive advertising is unlikely to make much impression on the challenges facing non-traditional aspirant entrants in obtaining and participating in mini-pupillages.[3]

Mini-pupillage application processes vary between chambers. Most commonly, applications are made either on chambers-constructed application forms, or by curriculum vitae and covering letter. A barrister (usually) paper-sifts; an unpopular job as it is time-consuming, so it often falls to a junior tenant:

> It tends to be the most junior tenant . . . When I arrived here it was 'suggested' that I might like to take on [the role].
>
> (Interviewee 5, non-Inner, M, chambers' rep.)

---

3 And in such an attempt being made, its lack of effect has been clear, with only thirty-one chambers even listing themselves on the 'Mini-pupillage Hub', the Bar Council's response to this element of the LETR: www.barcouncil.org.uk/careers/mini-pupillages [accessed 2nd May 2017].

Implicit in the allocation of this task to a junior tenant is that it is undesirable. More troubling, given the importance of mini-pupillages established in this research, is the implication that it is unimportant: not worth the time of a senior member of chambers. Similarly, at most chambers it is not deemed worthwhile having the applications read by more than one member of chambers, although one chambers participating in PASS had panels of three barristers of varying seniority appraise the forms. This was in keeping with that chambers' general reputation for a progressive ethos.

The application process is entirely paper-based, with no interviews.[4] Mini-pupillages can last from one day to a working week, and structure varies greatly. All chambers' representatives interviewed for this research stated that most chambers were inundated with applications and often unable to respond to unsuccessful applicants. As an initial filter, many will not take students before their second year of university. Throughout this chapter, obtaining mini-pupillage in this way is referred to as obtaining it by 'direct' or 'external' application.

Traditional students may use familial links to secure such mini-pupillages without having to apply in this way, thereby circumventing sifting. For self-employed barristers there are no obstacles to being accompanied by individuals who have not been selected by chambers, meaning that 'informal mini-pupillages', as they are referred to here, are a regular feature. By simply approaching social contacts at the Bar and asking if they may accompany them about their work, these aspirant entrants can add another traditional identifier to their applications, further advantaging them in accessing the profession. They also avoid comparison with external applicants.

For any student, regardless of their background, to present themselves as a serious candidate within the legal profession they need to have undertaken work experience (Young Legal Aid Lawyers, 2013: 22). Often legal work experience will be a criterion for passing a paper-sift, or at least valuable evidence towards fulfilling other criteria.[5] Some chambers require a student to have undertaken a mini-pupillage with those chambers before they will be considered for pupillage.[6] However, at a more nuanced level it allows aspirant entrants to assimilate behaviours comprising the identity expected of a legal professional (Carbado and Gulati, 2000: 1260). Many students from traditional backgrounds have already formed fractions of this 'appropriate identity' from familial or educational settings, whilst

---

4 The exception being where chambers requires an assessed mini-pupillage to be undertaken as part of the application process for pupillage, when an interview may be undertaken before or after the mini-pupillage.
5 For example, Wilberforce Chambers' Pupillage Policy states that selectors will primarily focus on, amongst other things, a potential pupil's 'motivation to do chancery/commercial work as demonstrated, for example, by mini-pupillages' (Wilberforce Chambers, 2013: 5, para 4, available at www.wilberforce.co.uk/join/pupillage [accessed 31st July 2017]).
6 For example, Brick Court Chambers; www.brickcourt.co.uk/pupillage-and-tenancy [accessed 31st July 2017].

non-traditional students may have had less opportunity, and formed fewer or none of the traits identified as desirable by the profession. Such traits are necessary to secure work experience, and often also operate as a formal credential sought by application panels and interviewers.

Whilst existing research (e.g. Francis and Sommerlad, 2009; Francis and MacDonald, 2009; Ashley et al., 2015) focusses heavily on students pursuing the solicitor route, not only is work experience equally crucial for those aiming for the Bar, it can be even harder to secure, and the social norms requiring assimilation even more opaque, as the Bar has clung more determinedly to historical practices. In her Report as Chair of the Committee of Inquiry into Equal Opportunities at the Inns of Court School of Law (1994), Dame Jocelyn Barrow referred to the Bar as 'an alien environment for those who are not used to Chapel, Grace and drinks'; an effective summary of the rituals that prospective students face (cited in Abel, 2003: 124). This was reinforced in the current research, with one practitioner interviewee stating:

> Somebody who's done three or four mini-pupillages may be better able to represent themselves better than someone who is on their first one and they're just learning the etiquette and everything else.
> (Interviewee 1, non-Inner, M, chambers' rep.)

The cultures created by value-imbued constructions and organisations may shift in content over time. However, they often make non-traditional entrants feel unwelcome, required to either leave the profession or assimilate the majority's characteristics to smooth their continuation within the profession (Wilkins, 1998). Thus, the lack of a recognisable professional identity can hamper not only access but also progression and retention. Therefore, the opportunity which mini-pupillage affords to a non-traditional entrant to develop the behaviours expected within the profession is important beyond initial access.

Recruiters in firms or chambers expect aspirant entrants to display legal work experience on application forms, and manifest it in their presence and conduct; it is a step on the 'typical path' (Francis, 2011: 38). Combined with a familiarity with the norms of the field, traditional aspirant entrants are more likely to fit in seamlessly by already displaying behaviours and preferences demonstrated by those around them, making joining the profession more comfortable (Bourdieu, 1984: 255–6). Non-traditional aspirant entrants may experience cognitive dissonance as they try to reconcile their professional surroundings with earlier experiences (Costello, 2005: 3–4).

Interviewees identified the legal profession's preference for a traditional educational route and potential indirect discrimination against those coming through other routes. Regardless of other attributes, and transferable skills gained through other activities, they were disadvantaged by a lack of familiarity with the profession's norms, contributed to by their lack of opportunity to secure legal work experience due to other responsibilities outside of studying (Francis and MacDonald, 2009: 225, 239):

It's often geared towards traditional routes in. I can see quite a number of mature students who find it very, very difficult, not just to get mini-pupillages under their belt . . . A Levels were quite some time ago and actually those grades meant something very different back in that time, or they are looking after a small child so they didn't perform as well in their undergraduate degree, or they can show quite a lot of experience in many other things but maybe those don't always relate quite as clearly or as neatly.

(Interviewee 11, Inner, M, salaried)

The partiality of most chambers towards traditional educational routes was identified by interviewees as particularly challenging to non-traditional students:

Actually drilling down to the sort of information that might be on a form relating to someone's educational disadvantage, I am sure in some cases they just don't even get that far – if they haven't got a 2:1 then they are already in the 'no' pile. Yeah, it's difficult and I think education of chambers is something that we need to look into as well.

(Interviewee 8, Inner, F, salaried)

Some disagreed with this, citing that their chambers was much more concerned with the candidate's actual skills, and their interest in a career at the Bar:

Sometimes if a candidate isn't as able academically but has a lot of life experience and practical experience that can balance it out, and conversely . . . everybody in these chambers so far has had different kind of backgrounds and stuff, and I think because of that . . . we all recognise and draw on that and try and make sure people who really understand and have a commitment make that sort of journey, that progress, and understand what the job is about, and they deserve an opportunity to go and they usually make quite good barristers . . . What kind of educational path they have taken is irrelevant.

(Interviewee 1, non-Inner, M, chambers' rep.)

This illustrates that the approach by chambers to non-traditional aspirant entrants seeking mini-pupillages remains varied. Due to the structure of the profession, it is hard to enforce a uniform approach, as chambers have little coercive power over barristers, and in turn the professional associations have little coercive power over chambers. This has been demonstrated in the Bar Council issuing a 'good practice guide' for mini-pupillages (Bar Council, 2016). Aside from criticisms that it does not go far enough in encouraging new practices to truly challenge practices disadvantaging non-traditional students,[7] the guidance has no force. There is no carrot, nor stick, for compliance or a lack thereof.

---

7 As I wrote in an article for *Counsel Magazine*: Freer, E. (2017) 'Maximising mini-pupillage', *Counsel Magazine*, March, London: LexisNexis.

For these reasons, it is argued that the provision of work experience, and the difficulty experienced disproportionately by non-traditional applicants in securing it (as previously evidenced in Francis and MacDonald (2006)), is one way in which social closure at the Bar has continued. Questionnaire responses illustrated the challenges faced by non-traditional aspirant entrants applying for mini-pupillages through direct application. This left them unable to fulfil the objective, factual criterion of having legal work experience in its own right. Of the forty-one PASS students in the 2013/14 cohort, thirty-three answered a questionnaire on their previous work experience. Four had not been able to secure any work experience, despite extensive applications. Of those that had secured it, twelve had done so through a programme such as the Social Mobility Foundation or Pathways, and a further three had had it arranged through school or college. Whilst appearing to be an objective criterion, the requirement of legal work experience may operate as an indirectly discriminatory recruitment criterion which non-traditional applicants are less likely to be able to meet. Furthermore, they have not had an opportunity to market themselves to the profession, and are less likely to be able to demonstrate the social norms expected within the legal profession, as they have not had an opportunity to assimilate them.

6.3 Challenges in securing and participating in work experience

6.3.1 'They're like gold dust': securing work experience

For many traditional applicants, accessing work experience within a profession is straightforward: due to their recognisable educational path they often succeed through direct application. Where they do not, they can often utilise familial or social links to secure informal work experience. Less recognisable educational paths and lack of informal contacts disadvantaged non-traditional aspirant entrants in securing work experience, and this challenge of access to mini-pupillages was the key hurdle that PASS sought to address. One interviewee regularly experienced approaches from social contacts seeking work experience for young relations:

> I have had requests from solicitor clients to have their son or daughter for work experience that I have found very difficult to turn down. I have had High Court judges asking me to give work experience to friends of the family and they don't perceive that as being inappropriate or oppressive at all.
>
> (Interviewee 2, non-Inner, F, other prof. assocs.)

Not only were such requests difficult to refuse, interviewees acknowledged that many of those who did agree to such requests did so without realising the negative impact they could have on social mobility.[8] One interviewee recounted having himself offered an informal mini-pupillage to a university friend; it had never occurred to him at the time that to do so advantaged that person over those without such contacts who could not use them to circumnavigate the paper-sifting process. This illustrates the subconscious and wholly unintentional ways in which social closure can be propagated within a profession (Sommerlad, 2007, 2008; Francis and MacDonald, 2006, 2009).

Illustrative of this was that even within a formal, published document setting out chambers' policy on mini-pupillages, one set of chambers expressly stated that 'informal' mini-pupillages could be given by barristers providing that they did not interfere with those given through the direct application process.[9] One chambers' representative interviewed also described chambers as powerless to stop barristers offering informal mini-pupillages, and a consequent resignation to their continuation:

> Obviously, I think with all chambers there's an element of informal mini-pupillages. I can't really stop the barristers from offering private experiences... The only thing that we ask the barristers is that they try not to take on private students when we are running our own scheme, so they are available for the people that have formally applied. And again, there's not much that I can do to stop them if they ignore that. They tend to be quite good about it, to be honest.
>
> (Interviewee 3, non-Inner, F, chambers' rep.)

Such explicit and tacit acceptance of informal mini-pupillages is hard to overcome, partly because such practices are engrained and many barristers do not see their unfairness. Challenging such behaviour is made more difficult by the structure of the field and the lack of coercive power, meaning that individual chambers can, at best, request that barristers do not offer informal work experience, but there are no more forceful, or profession-wide, policies. A 'gentle reminder' of the possible effects is provided by the Bar Council's 'Mini-Pupillage: Good Practice' guide:

> Be aware that making mini-pupillage available, particularly to the children of friends or professional contacts, on an informal basis tends to disadvantage those without existing links to the Bar. Have a policy under which only those who approach you through the formal application system may undertake a recognised mini-pupillage: if informal work experience is offered on a different basis from mini-pupillage, this needs to be clearly understood by all:

---

8 As a mini-pupillage co-ordinator myself I can confirm this from direct experience. Many barristers and clerks have never had cause to consider the wider fairness implications until they are pointed out.
9 Ten Old Square Pupillage and Junior Recruitment Policy (2016: 23, para 101); www.tenoldsquare.com/join-us/pupillage [accessed 31st July 2017].

members of your organisation should appreciate what the differences are and candidates should be quite clear as to whether they are permitted to describe their experience as a 'mini-pupillage' when making pupillage applications.

(Bar Council, 2016: 1)

The emphasis here on recognised mini-pupillages is misleading, however. Whether or not a mini-pupillage is 'recognised' (i.e. acknowledged by the chambers as having been secured through external application) it still provides the recipient with access to important experience: social norms and 'inside knowledge'. Therefore, it is moot whether such an experience is 'offered on a different basis', and how participants can describe their mini-pupillage – it maintains structures propagating disadvantage. It also seems impossible to police how mini-pupillages are later described by a recipient on application forms.

This means that parallel routes to mini-pupillage are operating: the informal route, the direct application route and now the PASS route. In creating a separate route for non-traditional aspirant entrants, it could be argued that PASS is further emphasising their difference (see Chapter 4). It also illustrates that wherever a deviation from the 'standard' (direct application) route occurs, it may indirectly maintain flaws in the standard route. Some of the profession may see PASS as a tacit condoning of the elements of the standard system that disadvantage non-traditional aspirant entrants. Impetus to take stronger action against informal mini-pupillages maybe reduced if PASS is perceived as counteracting the provision of informal mini-pupillages by providing an alternative route to non-traditional aspirant entrants (albeit with a formal application process).

Non-traditional entrants did not have informal links which they could utilise to secure placements: only seven of a sample of thirty-three PASS students had familial contacts in any profession. Only two had contacts in the legal profession (supporting Francis and Sommerlad's findings amongst aspirant solicitors (2009: 71)). This lack of contacts necessitated using external applications to secure mini-pupillages (itself an opportunity to make contacts). They were often unsuccessful:

> Getting mini-pupillages was absolutely impossible. You're applying to all these sets and giving it your all, and they're like gold dust! I remember at my Law Ball, one of the prizes, the top prize, I think, was a mini-pupillage somewhere, and then once you start getting them it's easier and easier to get them.
>
> (PASS FG1 Participant 2, F)

> I'd already applied for mini-pupillages, I think five times, before that, and not got anywhere, and so, being eligible for an access scheme, felt that this was almost something that was set up for people like me who'd tried and not succeeded.
>
> (PASS FG1 Participant 1, F)

One student suggested that these attempts were less likely to be successful than those made by 'traditional' students, as they lacked knowledge both of facts and the profession's unspoken but expected social norms, such as appropriate modes of address and detail (supporting research by Sommerlad, 2007: 200):

> [Non-traditional aspirant entrants] perhaps have not had a realistic introduction to what that career entails. [Traditional aspirant entrants] have also some understanding of that career that is beyond what you can just obtain from Googling 'barrister' or Wikipedia, and I think that once any individual applicant or aspiring barrister has a little bit more of that context in real life, what do barristers have to deal with in real life . . . these kinds of things that you might not get from the very outset, once those are in mind then I think it perhaps gets a bit easier to pass the other hurdles.
> (PASS FG2 Participant 1, M)

Furthermore, non-traditional aspirant entrants' educational achievements are often not contextualised, disadvantaging them in direct application processes for mini-pupillage. The legal profession recognises most easily the 'traditional' route: schooling to A Level, followed by a full-time degree (and the GDL if that degree is not in Law) and the BPTC (Francis, 2011: 38).

Therefore, attempts by chambers' representatives dealing with mini-pupillage applications to contextualise achievement by school type or geographical location, for example, can disadvantage those who have taken a different route. Furthermore attempts, such as this interviewee's, at 'common sense contextualisation' may lead to well-meaning generalisations that actually hinder:

> There is a margin to which I will play with what I think somebody should have, and this may be a little bit of my own illegitimate social engineering, but if somebody has gone to whatever is the really, really good local private grammar school, [a local] grammar or something, and they have got A Levels which are not bad but are not particularly stellar, and I think, 'Well, I went to a state school and got far better than that', they are going to get less credit than someone who went to [a local] comprehensive and did alright, kind of taking a broad view, and then at university they might be doing quite well.
> (Interviewee 5, non-Inner, M, chambers' rep.)

This interviewee was a chambers' mini-pupillage co-ordinator. His quotation demonstrates the challenge of chambers' administration of mini-pupillages, and his deploying strategically adapted institutional structures (de Certeau, 1984). Without knowledge of the challenges facing non-traditional aspirant entrants, barristers may create typologies based on their own views, which may nonetheless propagate disadvantage. This occurred because barristers lack the necessary specialist knowledge of access and education matters, as acknowledged by this practitioner:

> It's very problematic actually because I think the barristers who evaluate the applications can't really be expected to know all the nuances that might be relevant.
>
> (Interviewee 2, non-Inner, F, other prof. assocs.)

However, neither do most chambers have resources to employ someone with that specialist knowledge. This creates a vicious cycle, whereby non-traditional aspirant entrants are unable to gain mini-pupillage through the direct or informal routes, which prevents them from assimilating expected norms and behaviours, further hampering their access.

In the case study, Inner Temple attempted to remove this layer of disadvantage by having an employee with extensive experience of social mobility and higher education matters sifting PASS application forms. By recognising the various ways in which an aspirant entrant may demonstrate commitment to law and gain transferable skills or relevant legal skills, Inner Temple is seeking to open up the opportunity of mini-pupillages to a group who would previously have struggled to access it. This process applies a different conception of merit which contextualises the achievement of non-traditional applicants in their personal and educational circumstances.

This highlights why a professional association may feel that intervening on access to work experience is important. For the profession to benefit from the best applicants, it is necessary that applicants with the necessary intellectual acumen can present themselves as serious contenders, something it is hard to achieve without mini-pupillages, regardless of academic merit. Therefore, providing access to mini-pupillages to students whose academic records, considered against their educational contexts, are impressive could disrupt patterns of social closure. It would achieve this by making the profiles of these students more closely akin to those of aspirant entrants who have followed the 'recognised' path. This, however, does not truly address the profession's failure to recognise skills gained through other experiences, and facilitates continued privileging of mini-pupillages. Consequently, non-traditional aspirant entrants not participating in a programme may continue to be overlooked in favour of those who have followed a traditional route, reinforcing social closure instead of challenging it. Truly transformative change would focus on altering attributes of the profession's 'demand', instead of the candidates' 'supply' (Ashley et al., 2015: 12–13, 54–63; Artess, 2014).

Indeed, for this member of a participating set, there was a realisation during the interview that his chambers' form for direct mini-pupillage applications (i.e. those not through PASS) might actively discourage non-traditional entrants:

> I think this form is not going to do much to encourage people from non-traditional backgrounds because it's long and a bit scary . . . and I said I disagreed with it at the time. Make it shorter, make it more simplistic. There are so many categories and sometimes, inevitably when you see a box on a form you feel that you have to put something down and if it's asking for masses

of details on qualifications and scholarships and membership of professional bodies, awards . . . I think it is going to put people off.

(Interviewee 5, non-Inner, M, chambers' rep.)

Some chambers are operating a more progressive selection policy for direct applications. One chambers participating in PASS already used an education-blind process, requiring 100-word answers to three questions about motivation to join the legal profession, interest in law and whether the applicant had previous mini-pupillages. Such progressive policies, however, seemed little in evidence from interviewees and students, although some remained hopeful that a 'side-effect' of PASS might be encouraging chambers to consider context in their process:

> I would hope that it wasn't just about mini-pupillages. I would hope that in general this scheme . . . It might not be now, it might not be next year, it might take quite a while for that to take place, to see exceptionally talented individuals from disadvantaged backgrounds, and think how their selection processes more generally take into account that disadvantage.
>
> (Interviewee 11, Inner, M, salaried)

Even once non-traditional aspirant entrants have secured work experience, they may find fully participating in it difficult due to personal and financial constraints, and particularly more difficult than for those from traditional backgrounds. These barriers to participation will now be explored.

6.3.2 *Participating in work experience*

Once non-traditional students have secured work experience, whether through direct application or via an access scheme, data suggested that they find undertaking it more difficult than their traditional counterparts for broadly two reasons: financial concerns and social norms.

6.3.2.1 *Financial matters*

Financially, work experience places a burden on students, and disproportionately on those from non-traditional backgrounds (Francis and MacDonald, 2009: 239). The best-regarded mini-pupillages are often London-based, meaning that students from elsewhere will have significant travel costs, and may even need accommodation during their mini-pupillage. Even within London there may be numerous journeys to different courts. Funded mini-pupillages are rare (precise statistics cannot be provided as there is no central database of those chambers providing mini-pupillages and whether they are funded) and tend to exist only in certain privately-funded practice areas.

Of the 185 organisations offering pupillages listed in tabular form in the 2017 Training Contract and Pupillage Handbook, 173 offered mini-pupillages (as evidenced by a tick in the relevant column – pp. 540–549). Of those with more detailed listings (pp. 551–606; thirty-six sets), only two (7 Kings Bench Walk and South Square) explicitly state that they offer funded mini-pupillages which are not a compulsory element of the full pupillage selection process.[10] One Crown Office Row's entry makes no mention of funding but states, 'We also run an equality and diversity mini-pupillage scheme.' A Google search of the phrase 'mini-pupillage expenses' revealed that, considering the first thirty results, all except three chambers had a policy on providing travel expenses. These ranged from paying 'all reasonable expenses'[11] to '£10 per day'[12]. Three explicitly stated that they were unable to provide expenses, and it was notable that all three of these were in predominantly publicly-funded practice areas (criminal and family). This brief exploration suggests some awareness of factors that may prevent aspirant entrants from undertaking mini-pupillage.

A traditional profession may make assumptions about the financial means of mini-pupils; it may be presumed that they have ample financial resources to fund travel or accommodation. This is something which any access intervention concerning non-traditional aspirant entrants needs to address. Of the first cohort of students who participated in PASS and completed Inner Temple's post-placement questionnaire (n=48) twenty-five agreed (eighteen strongly) that 'payment of expenses was essential in allowing me to undertake this placement'. Focus group participants reinforced this; two had cut short other mini-pupillages due to prohibitive travel costs:

> Obviously, you've got to be on peak [travel] as well, so a return, on peak, even with my student railcard, was gonna be £30 for a day, and I can't afford £150 in a week just to get into London. So it's a massive advantage to the scheme. I cut one of my MPs short by two days; I asked for it to be three as opposed to five because I couldn't afford to come in every day.
> (PASS FG1 Participant 2, F)

> I had to ring them up and ask, 'Can I just have cases local to Canterbury so I can actually just walk there?' It's so expensive.
> (PASS FG1 Participant 3, M)

In the case study, it was significant that financial expenses were provided directly by chambers to participating students at the behest of the professional association; no extra cost was incurred by the professional association. Such

---

10 Assessed mini-pupillages, which often form either a pre-requisite to, or part of, the application process for pupillage are discounted in this discussion as they serve a different purpose, though 7KBW does guarantee a pupillage interview for those who successfully apply for a funded pupillage.
11 Atkin Chambers; www.atkinchambers.com/operations/pupillage/mini-pupillages [accessed 31st July 2017].
12 4 Paper Buildings; www.4pb.com/recruitment/mini-pupillage [accessed 31st July 2017].

cost-shifting potentially allows greater provision of access schemes, because the professional association does not itself have to bear financial outlay; its monetary commitment is restricted to employing specialist staff to administer the programme by filtering applicants. However, it will mean that participation is limited to chambers with the resources to pay participants' expenses. In practice areas facing financial difficulties due to cuts in legal aid, chambers which can afford this may be few, as illustrated above by the practice areas of those chambers not providing expenses to direct applicants. Statistics also show that these are the areas that are already comparatively more diverse (Pike and Robinson, 2012: 25, Table 2.11).

In this respect, the mode used by Inner Temple may be replicable by other professional associations in access programmes. The Commercial Bar Association (COMBAR), a specialist professional association, supports PASS by a scholarship through which five students per year who have an interest in Commercial Law are provided with a bursary additional to their expenses provided through PASS; a dedicated mentor, and access to a networking event.[13] Although this is an example of another professional association augmenting an existing programme, it demonstrates potential for greater involvement of professional associations in access to the legal profession. It also demonstrates the possibility of different professional associations complementing one another's programmes, although this will depend on securing agreement to collaboration within both professional associations, which may pose challenges, as discussed in Chapter 4 (and by analogy with the reluctance of legal educators and practitioners to unify; Larson, 1977: 167).

6.3.2.2 'Dear Mr Blah Blah': social norms at the Bar

Every social field has practices and norms that are not articulated or discussed, yet are adhered to by those who inhabit it (Bourdieu, 1984). To 'fit in' within the legal professional field aspirant entrants need to assimilate these behaviours. Such assimilation will be easier for those from traditional backgrounds, as they are more likely to have been exposed to situations requiring those traits at an early age, something which has been highlighted as important. Experiences of PASS participants illustrated that those from non-traditional backgrounds are likely to be hampered unless they assimilate the tastes and outward manifestations perceived as demonstrating a higher social class than their own. It seems clear that when recruiting, the legal profession looks actively (even if not explicitly) for demonstrations of social capital, and is likely to find wanting those who cannot easily demonstrate it, regardless of their intellectual talents (Sommerlad, 2008). Participants in the PASS focus groups cited potential embarrassment from being unsure how to behave in certain situations. This stemmed from a combination of a lack of familial contact and exposure to the legal profession leading to a lack of familiarity with certain rules of legal etiquette, and formal social norms:

---

13 www.pegasus.me/?page_id=162 [accessed 28th July 2017].

> It's like a whole 'nother level, like, when you're writing an email to a judge and it has to be 'Dear Judge' or 'Dear The Right Honourable Lord Justice'. You've never done that before – you don't know. I would've gone with 'Dear Mr Blah Blah' originally! So it makes a real difference to you.
>
> (PASS FG1 Participant 2, F)[14]

This supports empirical work by Francis (2011) and Sommerlad (2007) showing that a key factor relating to success in the legal profession is the aesthetic presentation and other social factors of candidates. Those students who can subtly and appropriately adjust their presentation when they interact with the profession are likely to benefit. For example, Manderson and Turner observed Law students at the 'Coffee House' events run at McGill University. Despite no formal requirement, standards of dress were higher at those 'Coffee House' events sponsored by law firms, suggesting that many students understood the need to demonstrate a professional appearance to firms' representatives (2006: 656). This suggests those students understood that attire, which may carry connotations of socio-economic background, may influence recruiters as it is a demonstration of social and cultural capital (Bourdieu, 1984).

Sometimes capital can be displayed in attributes that identify a student as being different, provided they are also combined with more 'traditional' capital such as education (Sommerlad relates an interview in which a recruiter muses on a hypothetical student wearing a headscarf due to her religion (2007: 206)). One element of a student's personal circumstances or attributes might mediate the lack of cultural capital in other areas, or actively augment it. Many non-traditional aspirant entrants do not possess mediating factors, and therefore feel uncomfortable within the profession unless they are willing and able to conform to or accept these traditions (an even more significant issue for those from other cultural or religious backgrounds, for whom certain traditions may actively conflict with their beliefs).

For non-traditional aspirant entrants, their acute awareness of 'difference' may develop early in the recruitment process:

> The first thing I noticed when I walked into Bar School was that . . . I've never been surrounded by super posh and smart people and then you get there and everyone's just got . . . they even talk in different languages sometimes. They've gone to public schools and boarding schools and they

---

14 I was reminded starkly of this quotation when, as a pupil, I referred to a Silk in chambers whom I had never met as 'Mr [surname]'. My pupil-master warned me that if anyone heard me refer to anyone in chambers as 'title/surname' they'd think I was 'dreadfully pretentious', as barristers always refer to each other by first name, or first name and surname if unfamiliar. Having been brought up with the understanding that 'title/surname' was the politest form of address to someone you did not know, it was a timely reminder of how easy it is to make social errors in spite of, or even because of, good intentions.

talk about the 'boys' maid' and things like this and classes are called different things, and events . . . I don't even understand what they are and that's quite intimidating.

(PASS FG1 Participant 2, F)[15]

One interviewee also raised this, suggesting why it was not widely recognised by many practitioners: once a person had successfully secured entry to the profession, they may forget potential difficulties. This was so even if they themselves had come from a non-traditional background:

> The whole system is quite unclear. I mean, it seems clear to me now but I have been in law for a few years now, but 'Inn of Court' – does that mean anything? An Inn? What is a court? Does that mean anything to people from the relatively disadvantaged backgrounds who haven't spent their school years in courtyards in Berkshire and that sort of stuff? I don't know, probably not. I guess it's easier than it was, with the internet.
> (Interviewee 5, non-Inner, M, chambers' rep.)

For these reasons, non-traditional aspirant entrants often struggle to access work experience opportunities through direct applications. When they do access it, through direct applications or access programmes, they may struggle to fully engage in work experience opportunities. Although PASS addresses the financial aspect, it cannot alter the professions' social norms. This is a particular cause of concern in relation to social mobility matters within the legal profession, due to the importance of identity formation. If non-traditional aspirant entrants become trapped in a cycle whereby they struggle to access work experience, and when they do so are marked out by their presentation as not conforming to the 'desired' profile, their access will be severely hampered. Therefore, a focus on this as part of a professional association's project to increase access suggests that the intervention has the potential to be effective by targeting a source of difficulty experienced by a large proportion of the group of whom it is seeking to increase access.

6.3.2.3 The experience of work experience through an access programme

Some challenges experienced by non-traditional aspirant entrants in direct mini-pupillages remain when mini-pupillages are provided through an access programme; furthermore, additional albeit different challenges may also arise. The efficacy of an intervention will be dependent upon how it is experienced by the 'target group' (here, non-traditional aspirant entrants). As PASS is conducted

---

15 This student subsequently completed pupillage and is now a tenant at a leading London civil set.

mainly within chambers, participating students experience chambers, not the professional association itself. Therefore, the experience will vary between chambers. Such variation may not be material, or it may have a significant effect on non-traditional aspirant entrants' perception of the Bar. It is argued that it has the potential to cause a mini-pupillage to be a less positive experience than it could be if a non-traditional entrant encounters practices or situations that make them feel like an 'outsider'. For example, one PASS participant was placed in chambers that had mini-pupils from its direct application process attending at the same time. These other mini-pupils had different profiles to the PASS participant, and he felt that this made his status notable:

> I undertook the mini alongside three others that had gained a mini at [chambers] through the traditional route, so it was quite interesting to see the dynamic in that respect, 'cause the other three mini-pupils were hugely qualified people . . . and it definitely kind of gave me a somewhat uneasy feeling I suppose.
>
> (PASS FG2, Participant 1, M)

This was not the only set of chambers that had PASS mini-pupils at the same time as those who had applied directly. Furthermore, some others mentioned awareness of their 'outsider' status, with a PASS questionnaire respondent stating that they could not see themselves at their placement chambers as 'I would not meet their very high recruitment criteria', and another stated, 'I am not sure I have the right background to get accepted'. These responses suggest that for some PASS students, their 'outsider' status was reinforced by the programme, and the status quo of social closure supported, instead of tackled, by the programme. Such an experience is not unique to PASS, with Francis finding some non-traditional aspirant entrants felt uncomfortable on vacation schemes because traditional students fitted in without obvious difficulty (2011: 55).

Whilst the candidate quoted above claimed that this did not unduly discomfit him, it raises two concerns. First, even if this participant was unperturbed, other participants might have found this experience unpleasant. If so, it could have contributed to or created a view that the Bar is welcoming only to those with a certain profile. This would operate against an intention of the programme to demonstrate that the profession is open to those of academic ability from all backgrounds. Second, it is possible that the participant did, in fact, feel more than 'uneasy', but did not feel able to say so, knowing that I was evaluating the programme for the providing professional association.

The way in which a participant is presented both by the professional association to the stakeholders (here, chambers) and within the stakeholder is important. To 'label' someone as participating in a programme, especially one which has eligibility criteria clearly published, is to potentially exclude that person further by drawing attention to their 'non-traditional' status. It is difficult for the professional association to control how candidates are presented within chambers, as many practitioners may see it as a simply factual introduction, as some of the students themselves claimed to:

> So when I was introduced to people it was, 'Hi, this is X, he is on the Pegasus Scheme with us, he's a mini-pupil' . . . It wasn't pejorative, it wasn't negative in any way, it was just, sort of, a matter of information as to who I was . . . and it was exactly who I was!
>
> (PASS FG2, Participant 2, M)

Furthermore, some chambers may not see the difficulty in presenting candidates as such. The same PASS participant stated that he felt that being identified as such led to people within chambers taking a greater interest in his background and aspirations:

> They were more interested in me, I think. It was less, 'Oh, you've got another one of these, y'know, quite wealthy public-school people . . . another one.' I felt that they were more interested in how I found university and how's it going . . . They were more engaged and more sort of aware.
>
> (PASS FG2, Participant 2, M)

For some participants this would not be identified as a positive experience, highlighting the inherent subjectivity in 'doing good' (Friedman, 1962: 2); is PASS really making significant changes to the experiences of non-traditional aspirant entrants if it is allowing them access to work experience, but is not truly challenging how the profession perceives them? Such issues are reinforced when participants refer to chambers as being 'nice' to take them, suggesting a power imbalance (see 4.4.1.2). This may be through perceived feelings of pity towards the candidate or indebtedness on the part of the candidate towards chambers, when exposure of chambers to academically-strong, non-traditional applicants is actually a mutually beneficial interaction.

6.3.3 The purpose of work experience

Opinion was divided amongst interviewees, focus groups and questionnaire responses on the reasons why chambers offered mini-pupillages. As already discussed, the main differences of opinion arose between those who felt that the experience was entirely candidate-focussed, and those who felt that there was a mutuality of benefit for both chambers and the student. These two opinions were held equally amongst participants from both student and practitioner groups. Both groups agreed that unassessed mini-pupillages were not themselves an assessment. Unlike on formal vacation schemes, students were not given specific assessed tasks, and neither were they expected to 'put in the hours' and participate in social activities, as students on placements with corporate solicitors' firms were (Francis, 2015: 14).

Some chambers kept rudimentary records of mini-pupils, and there was the obvious possibility that someone who had done a mini-pupillage might be recognised by a member of a pupillage interview panel if they subsequently applied for pupillage at that set. Beyond these basic records and incidental memories, however, mini-pupillages were portrayed as an opportunity for students to experience the profession, and witness the daily life of a barrister. In the pre-PASS questionnaire (n=31), students were asked to rank the reasons why they thought chambers offered mini-pupillages and the answer most commonly ranked as 'most important' was 'to give students a realistic insight into the profession' (n=12). This result was replicated, albeit in a much smaller sample size, in the post-PASS questionnaire, where six students (n=15) ranked it as the most important.

Some participants felt that the information-sharing element of a mini-pupillage was potentially the most important. Both practitioners and students felt this particularly strongly in relation to non-traditional aspirant entrants who may have less opportunity to access information. By undertaking a mini-pupillage they were getting accurate information from people whose professional judgment they would be more likely to respect:

> If an applicant was doing a mini-pupillage you would give them the information, you would give them practical advice, you would say, 'Look, if you want to give yourself the best opportunity to succeed in the profession, you will need to focus on obviously making sure you get the best grades as possible' . . . sometimes it may be that having the experience actually helps them to focus.
>
> (Interviewee 1, non-Inner, M, chambers' rep.)

> I was with [names], these really, really top advocates and they're just giving you . . . they're sitting down and for an hour of their time which they might charge out normally at however many hundreds or thousands of pounds and just giving you, you know, no holds barred, whatever questions you wanna ask, ask away . . . You just couldn't do that unless you're in the chambers with them at the time.
>
> (PASS FG1 Participant 2, F)

This recognition of the possibility of raising aspirations through experience of the profession was another recurrent theme. Although it is not possible to extrapolate from this sample to all chambers, the feeling amongst participants was clear: mini-pupillages are an introduction to the profession for potential applicants. They also allow an element of mutual exposure whereby chambers can 'sell itself' to students.

What many participants emphasised was that reading about the Bar did not give the information necessary for students to make an informed career-path judgment; the experiential element was crucial. One participant who had subsequently secured pupillage went so far as to suggest that it was the immersive element of mini-pupillages that had led to her getting pupillage, as she had not previously experienced the practice area of that set. The sound understanding that she had gained of how the profession worked from her mini-pupillages had, in her opinion, been the decisive factor in her success:

The experience that you'll gain on a mini-pupillage is pretty invaluable. I mean, I am fairly sure that I got my pupillage on the back of the work experience I have and not on the back of anything I've learnt because I've never done family law.

(PASS FG1 Participant 2, F)

Serving no formal assessment purpose, it could be argued that mini-pupillages are simply an institutional logic; something that the Bar has always done and so continues. However, the responses from participants suggested that this was to under-represent the level of knowledge that students gained during them. Nonetheless, it is notable that PASS is not exploring innovative ways of engaging with aspirant entrants to further their understanding of the profession; it is doing so through the attempted alteration of a well-established practice, further supporting the observation that PASS is an example of a professional association 'going with the grain' in a 'safe' innovation.

6.3.4 The privileging of direct work experience

Most non-traditional aspirant entrants will have some work experience. This may include elements relevant to the legal 'arena', albeit that the employment or placement was not in the legal profession, referred to here as 'indirect' work experience. Even those with experience of legal settings through employment (e.g. as a legal secretary) appeared to be disadvantaged (Francis and MacDonald, 2006: 97), and this was mirrored in this research; it is argued that legal work experience is privileged when assessing candidates for entry to the profession, and mini-pupillages particularly so. Non-traditional students who participated in the Pathways focus group identified this as a source of frustration; many had part-time jobs or other work experience that they felt gave them skills relevant to legal practice, but were aware that firms and chambers were unlikely to consider the transferable skills that they had developed as useful for their career prospects:

I think it's good having work experience because there's always something in your work experience that you can bring into law. Like me, I work in an old care home and when I write in my CV I say things like it helped me to work with a wide variety of people that I wouldn't work with outside this . . . but if there's someone that's worked in a top law firm, the people with the top law firm are more likely to be accepted because they've worked like in that kind of aspect, in law . . . You've just worked in an old care home.

(Pathways FG Participant 8, F)

It cannot be stated conclusively from Francis and MacDonald's research (2006) and the data collected in the present research that less value is attributed to work experience gained outside of the legal sphere, or not secured directly through interaction with the profession in the 'pure' form of mini-pupillage. However, it is argued from questionnaires and focus groups in this research, and the focus on mini-pupillages in criteria published online for full pupillages at many sets (e.g. Radcliffe Chambers requires 'applicants who can demonstrate the following: "Evidence of legal experience (such as mini-pupillages, marshalling and other legal work experience)"'),[16] that such under-valuing does occur.

This corresponds with Morley's findings on attitudes to linearity in graduate recruitment (2007: 202, 204). It is likely to discriminate particularly against non-traditional applicants, who are financially more likely to need to work, reducing the opportunity to apply selectively for legal jobs. Furthermore, even the perception of under-valuing may deter non-traditional applicants, if they feel that their skills will automatically be devalued through not being gained within a legal setting, supporting social closure.

It seems likely that the differentiating factor in the value of work experience is partly attributable to the factors identified by Bourdieu: if a student has had legal work experience they have been exposed to the legal profession's doxa and habitus. If they have experience of working in other environments, although they may have developed valuable transferable skills such as communication or teamwork, they have not assimilated social or aesthetic norms of the legal world. Therefore, fragments of an identity conforming to these norms, itself demonstrating prior experience, has not been developed by those without immersive encounters with the legal profession.

The reluctance of the profession to identify as equally worthwhile experience of the legal profession gained 'obliquely' presents a significant problem for non-traditional aspirant entrants. At professional-association level, therefore, initiatives aimed at educating the profession about acquisition of relevant skills through other activities apart from mini-pupillages would benefit those who have followed a non-standard route, and may contribute towards lessening social closure at the Bar.

PASS aims to give non-traditional aspirant entrants the opportunity to undertake direct legal work experience. This may remove one angle of disadvantage experienced by the aspirant entrants who have participated, as the scheme allows them to access direct work experience, and thus fulfil a criterion imposed by the profession for access, as well as providing an opportunity for identity formation. However, it does not challenge the fundamental assumption that the undertaking of mini-pupillage makes an aspirant entrant more suitable for the profession than someone who has not undertaken direct work experience but has nonetheless assimilated knowledge or demonstrated interest by other means. It therefore does not remove this angle of disadvantage from non-traditional aspirant entrants as a group. Privileging of legal work experience may result from the perceived need to assimilate social norms, which is possible to a lesser extent in indirect experience.

In this respect, Inner Temple's challenge through PASS to traditional criteria in mini-pupillage applications that may inhibit access to the profession by

---

16 www.radcliffechambers.com/recruitment/pupillage [accessed 31st July 2017]; fn. 3 above.

non-traditional entrants is not as fundamental as it may first appear. Indeed, it is argued that it actively contributes to the notion that direct work experience in the form of mini-pupillages is a key contributor towards successful access. It does this by creating a programme that gives access to that experience to those who may not otherwise be able to obtain it, instead of raising awareness amongst the profession of the ways in which indirect work experience may nonetheless allow a candidate to assimilate significant legal knowledge, understanding of the profession and transferable skills, which, it is argued, would be a more transformative change. PASS implies that direct work experience is so important that access to it should be available to as many students as possible, instead of acknowledging that other experiences may be as profitable as direct work experience for the generation of transferable, and some legally-based, skills.

PASS therefore contributes to 'maintaining the status quo' (Braithwaite, 2010: 153), albeit allowing more candidates to meet the requirements of that status quo, by continuing to propagate the notion that it is direct work experience which will put a candidate in a better position for entry to the profession. This is an example of a resilient status quo surviving programmes aimed at increasing diversity, notwithstanding initial appearances of breaking down the status quo (Braithwaite, 2010: 153). This may be because the intention was not to break down the status quo at all, but to give an appearance of change, or because the status quo is so resilient that only a programme challenging core underlying assumptions could actually alter it. In this research it is argued that the first, albeit subconsciously, is likely to be the more prominent; it may not have been realised that the programme fails to tackle the deeper issues underlying non-traditional aspirant entrants' reduced access to legal work experience, and why such work experience is perceived as privileged over other forms. However, the latter reason may also be relevant: as argued in Chapter 4, changes to manifestations of the profession's central value system might be occurring; the status quo contributing to social closure may not be as resilient as previously thought. If social mobility eventually becomes subsumed as a core value, then an opportunity to dismantle the status quo from within arises, especially when coupled with embedded agency introducing new institutional logics through staff with different professional experience. This more significant change could potentially cause a dismantling of the underlying assumptions challenging greater social mobility.

Whilst in the long term a programme inadvertently maintaining the status quo is not desirable, if it is a forerunner to an attempt to educate the legal profession about the value of other forms of work experience it may nonetheless provide a sound base for this. By increasing the profession's exposure to non-traditional aspirant entrants, more awareness of the ways in which non-traditional entrants may have gained indirect experience can be built, and percolation to other 'arenas' of the legal profession (Nelson and Trubek, 1992) may occur. In this respect PASS seemed to be successful: some student participants highlighted PASS's mutual exposure (see Chapter 8). It gave non-traditional aspirant entrants the opportunity to discover that the Bar was not entirely white, male and middle-aged, and it gave chambers the opportunity to see the skills and abilities of non-traditional aspirant entrants. As post-PASS questionnaire responses stated:

> Before this mini-pupillage I had the impression that the Bar is 'reserved' for white, upper-class men, it was very traditional and very impenetrable. However, I had the chance to see that things have changed, I had the opportunity to shadow young women barristers, and also one of them had a background similar to mine, which makes me feel more optimistic about pursuing a career at the Bar. As for the environment at the chambers, it was very friendly, modern and forward looking.
> (Inner Temple Feedback Questionnaire, Cohort 1)

> The atmosphere in chambers was friendly, not stuffy, and the barristers I met were approachable and helpful. Before PASS I was uncertain whether I could work in London, but PASS demonstrated to me that the city is actually not as intimidating and unfriendly as I had imagined.
> (Inner Temple Feedback Questionnaire, Cohort 1)

It is argued that PASS's effect on social closure at the Bar will be reduced because it is not challenging the 'game' that disadvantages non-traditional aspirant entrants. Such a challenge might, for example, arise from using PASS as a vehicle to convey how chambers could adapt their own processes to take account of educational disadvantage or non-traditional routes. If this were the case, it might be more likely to cause a demographic shift, as mini-pupillages would become more accessible to a more diverse group of students, increasing access to identity formation and fulfilling a formal criterion. If this can be achieved, then there will be greater potential access to work experience than solely those mini-pupillages provided through PASS.

This case study has examined one form of professional intervention: a programme with a very specific remit of offering mini-pupillages to those who may otherwise struggle to secure them. A lack of work experience has been identified as an additional challenge facing non-traditional aspirant entrants, and therefore this programme has sought to provide assistance in relation to that specific hurdle. However, this is not the only way, and, as this chapter has argued, may not be the most effective way, of ameliorating disadvantage experienced by non-traditional aspirant entrants. In the light and context of the case study, what type of interventions may be most usefully pursued by professional associations looking to improve access is considered in Chapter 8.

6.4 An international comparison

These concerns do not pertain only to entry to the English legal system. A close parallel can be drawn with judicial clerkships in the USA. A clerkship, unlike a mini-pupillage, is a period of paid work assisting a judge. Judges sitting in all the various levels of the state and federal system may hire clerks. The role, and its attractions, are described on the Stanford Law School website:[17]

> Clerkships offer an opportunity to work closely with a judge, learn about the inner workings of the judicial system, and hone your legal research and writing skills. They also provide one or two years of practical training and enable you to make valuable professional contacts in the substantive and/ or geographical areas in which you hope to practice. In short, a clerkship can be an ideal stepping stone into any legal job.

From this description the perceived importance of the possibility of making contacts through a clerkship is clear, and this is echoed throughout the websites of the Law schools of American universities. The University of Wisconsin emphasises similar aspects amongst a list setting out the advantages of a clerkship:[18]

- Engage in a strong, supportive mentoring relationship with a judge;
- Become a member of an active network of former clerks;
- Spend a year or two after law school exploring career options and networking (because of the experience and training, a clerkship is a credential valued highly by law firms, public interest organizations, government agencies, corporations and other employers).

Later in that document, the deeply personal nature of the judge–clerk relationship is noted:[19]

> You should also think about the type of person for whom you would like to work, particularly because the working relationship between judge and clerk tends to be close. For example, do you want to work for a judge who provides a lot of oversight and feedback or one who is more hands-off and allows you to be relatively independent? Does it matter to you if a judge is liberal, conservative, or moderate? There are no comprehensive written resources to help you discover this type of personal information about judges. However, you can find out a great deal about a judge's style and philosophy by asking professors, attorneys whom you know or with whom you work, and/or current and former clerks.

This emphasises the personal nature of the relationship – as observed elsewhere in this book, the role played by background and experiences when one individual is selecting another with whom to work is a key cause of indirect socio-economic discrimination.

These concerns about clerkships and diversity in the legal profession have been recognised by the profession in America, prompting the National Association for

---

17 https://law.stanford.edu/careers/career-possibilities/judicial-clerkships [accessed 24th April 2017].
18 http://law.wisc.edu/career/documents/JudicialClerkshipHandbook_000.pdf [accessed 24th April 2017].
19 Ibid, p.5.

Law Placement (NALP) and the American Bar Association (ABA) to undertake a comprehensive study of judicial clerkships as employment opportunities for Law graduates.[20]

The study, conducted in several phases, sought input from three significant populations: Law school administrations/career service professionals, third-year students, and alumni law clerks. It has captured information on student perceptions about the clerkship application and selection processes; the value students perceive in clerkships; data on the presence of women graduates and graduates of colour in federal, state and local clerkships; the influence of clerkships on attorney careers; and the roles that Law school faculty and administration assume in the student clerkship application processes. The full methodology is available online.[21]

Differential patterns were identified by the NALP and ABA study into judicial clerkships in the USA. Differences were noted in ethnic background and gender, but more pertinently from the point of view of this research, different patterns of clerkship populations emerge based on Law school characteristics. Private Law school graduates were more likely to be federal clerks than other types of clerks. For public Law schools, the skew was towards state clerkships. Both types showed a relatively small, constant proportion of local clerks.

Law schools in all size categories (measured by total J. D. enrolment) reported a higher percentage of state clerks than federal clerks, with the smallest portion being local clerks. However, in the smallest size category (500 or fewer students), prevalence of state clerkships significantly outweighed other levels. The percentage of federal clerks was highest in the intermediate size category (501–750 students).

The Administrative Survey of Law Schools data reflected the differential encouragement and resources supplied to students in England pertaining to mini-pupillages. Although almost all of the Law schools that responded had programmes aimed at encouraging and assisting students in securing clerkships, many lacked specialized informational/support programs for women and students of colour – only about a quarter of the responding schools provided these. Also missing were programs on preparing for a clerkship, which are not offered by 64% of the Law schools. Such programmes might significantly assist a student from a non-traditional socio-economic background in presentational aspects and etiquette.

Law schools themselves viewed the lack of a single and coherent application process for clerkships as a hindrance to fairness. Apart from clearly advantaging those students attending Law schools that put greater resources into assisting students in applying for clerkships, Law schools of all sizes indicated that this issue 'overshadowed all others', with many citing the resource-hungry nature of supporting student applicants and that the clerkship applicant pool for the judges has been negatively impacted. Roughly half of the reporting schools noted that their

---

20 www.nalp.org/courtingclerkships?s=judicial%20clerkship [accessed 24th April 2017].
21 Ibid.

schools are making programmatic changes in response to this issue, by moving up clerkship programming for second-year students to earlier in the fall semester and by including first-year students in their clerkship programming.

Although the structural differences between clerkships and mini-pupillages are clear, what is consistent between them is that the amount of support students receive in being made aware of, and applying for them, is hugely variable. When such importance is attached to these activities by the profession, differential access and support inhibits equality of access. Students from lower socio-economic backgrounds form a higher proportion of those attending public Law schools (Sander, 2011). Therefore, the fact that there are fewer federal clerks coming from those schools suggests greater barriers for non-traditional students in accessing the most highly-regarded clerkship opportunities. At its starkest, the NALP research found that those Law schools that offered more resources to students tended to have a higher proportion of graduates in clerkships, leading to an advantage for those candidates when applying for training and jobs in the future.

6.5 Is the Pegasus Access and Support Scheme fulfilling its aim?

As was set out in Chapter 1, the narrow social demographic seen at the Bar is well-established. A trait of such longevity will not be easy to displace, as a significant number of years of consistent recruitment from across all social classes will be needed before practitioners from non-traditional backgrounds are represented at the Bar proportionally to their representation in society. For this reason, any programme that is targeting only small numbers of non-traditional aspirant entrants is unlikely to have a noticeable effect on the demographics of the profession. Therefore, in the case study, a programme which currently has a throughput of around sixty students per year is not going to cause a perceptible alteration in the demographic. This is not to suggest that it has no utility, but rather that any measures of success need to be predicated on the understanding that the potential effect is limited. Consequently, it is argued that it is important for professional associations initiating such an intervention to be realistic about the programme's goals. As emphasised below, this may also in itself support efficacy of the programme. In interviews, it was suggested that this had not occurred in the case study, with some interviewees maintaining a belief that the programme could cause a profession-wide demographic change.

The aim of PASS as stated publicly on the landing page of Inner Temple's PASS website is modest: 'to support those from diverse backgrounds to consider a career at the Bar'. Some interviewees articulated more ambitious aims, suggesting a lack of agreement across the organisation. This lack of agreement also meant that interviewees' perceptions of what amounted to success differed.

All stakeholders should agree on what a programme is aiming to achieve, and how this will be measured. Without this it will be difficult to make decisions about the programme that are complementary, and aimed at taking it towards a clearly-defined goal. Without such a goal, maintaining cohesion within the running of the programme may also be difficult. When stakeholder interviewees were asked what measures of success were being applied, answers varied widely:

> I think numbers going through is important. I think whether that ... not whether they then end up as barristers but whether that has then been a useful experience for them, either to persuade them to come to the Bar or to show them that the Bar is not what they want to do, but at least then it's on an informed basis rather than a just-guessed basis.
> (Interviewee 4, Inner, M, Bencher)

> We have thought a lot about key performance indicators that we would use and actually it ends up going down to a basket rather than any one ... I don't think success or selection can just be based on one thing ... I would like to see many more successful with Inns of Court scholarships, whether that's at Inner or any of the other Inns.
> (Interviewee 11, Inner, M, salaried)

One interviewee suggested a clear demarcation between the role of Pathways and the role of PASS, perceiving Pathways as an information-disseminating exercise and PASS as having a much more direct link to formal access to the profession:

> I think if somebody or a significant number of people, whatever that is statistically, who go through that scheme then end up in some of the top chambers, that would be the mark of success.
> (Interviewee 7, Inner, M, Bencher, other prof. assocs.)

This illustrates starkly the variation in what even a small number of senior members of Inner Temple perceived as a measure of success. Without agreement on this, it cannot be known whether all efforts are being directed most usefully towards securing a realistic and defined outcome, and this could reduce the efficacy of the programme. Without quantifiable measures of success, and data collection examining whether these are met, it will not be possible for professional associations to know whether their interventions are having any, or the desired, effect (Kuipers et al., 2014: 11). Without this knowledge, it will not be possible for professional associations to build on best practice, and to adapt any programmes that they run to be as effective as possible (see Chapter 8).

Existing literature has identified the potential challenges caused by a lack of clear aims and objectives in the legal profession (Braithwaite, 2010: 143), and more general management change literature (Pettigrew et al., 2001; Ferlie and Pettigrew, 1988; Kuipers et al., 2014) also emphasises the importance of an organisation knowing what it is seeking to achieve before it can take productive steps towards that outcome. Due to the particular idiosyncrasies of the Bar, analysis that emphasises contextual factors provides a more thorough analysis, as it allows consideration of the effect of unusual structures and key historical habits. Pettigrew emphasises that 'causation is neither linear nor singular. There is no attempt to search for the illusory single grand theory of change' (1990: 270).

As Fisher (1997: 455) highlights in relation to development agencies, the 'pursuit of participation ... frequently fails to live up to [its] rhetoric, which seems to promote it and yet can amount to no more than the restructuring of control (Ribot 1996)'. For programmes run by professional associations to truly effect change within a profession, they must pursue genuine change, not only the rhetoric thereof.

6.6 Conclusion

This chapter has argued that the Bar, through its use of social norms and idiosyncratic practices, has continued to indirectly influence entry based on social class by engendering feelings of discomfort amongst non-traditional aspirant and successful entrants, who cannot easily access opportunities to assimilate the social norms of the field (Bourdieu, 1984). This is not confined to the English system, with research from America illustrating similar findings. One way to reduce these feelings of discomfort is by providing non-traditional aspirant entrants with opportunities to assimilate these norms before entry. Mini-pupillages are crucial in providing an opportunity for this to occur, but they are hard to access and participate in for many non-traditional students, meaning they are disproportionately disadvantaged in the application process (Rolfe and Anderson, 2003: 319). Furthermore, well-intentioned interventions may themselves propagate feelings of 'otherness' due to the subjectivity of 'doing good', and this subjectivity further leads to problems of quantification and measurement of an intervention's success. The privileging of legal work experience continues to reinforce the need to conform to the traditional path, as opposed to the treading of a new path which conceives of merit as demonstrable through other activities and experiences more readily available to non-traditional aspirant entrants.

The recommendations of the LETR to gather mini-pupillage opportunities in one place to save students time-consuming research examining the individual websites of each chambers does not address significant problems. It needs to be ensured that the system is widely advertised across all universities, and it still requires chambers to advertise them accurately and for students to choose where to apply. The early life of the Mini-Pupillage Hub demonstrates that centralised advertising does not surmount these hurdles. Furthermore, it does not stop chambers failing to take educational disadvantage into account when paper-sifting candidates, and does not address financial barriers to undertaking work experience disproportionately faced by non-traditional students in the traditional mini-pupillage process.

Alternative methods challenging accepted conceptions of merit may, however, present a challenge to the status quo of the profession which itself compromises acceptance by the profession, and consequently success (Braithwaite, 2010). The extent to which such a genuine challenge can be mounted is likely to be affected by the relative power of the professional association (Halliday, 1987; Chapter 4), and also its perceived motives for acting, which, in practice, are likely to be diverse and encompassing both altruistic and self-serving agendas.

Having established that a central value system's indirect consequences can be challenged, and how this may occur in terms of both structural and human considerations, Chapter 6 moved to a closer examination of the case study. This research suggests that the role of individual experience and stories has been previously underplayed in research into the professions and professional associations. It is impossible to understand how a profession may be best able to respond to societal changes without examining the individual experiences of those who are involved in formulating that response. This research has highlighted the importance of the personal stories of Benchers, salaried staff and practitioners in that respect. Of equal importance, however, are the personal experiences of the students at whom the intervention is aimed. An access programme such as PASS does not stand in isolation. The home, family and friends of young people all contribute to their view of the world, and of themselves.

Furthermore, their educational experiences may already have shaped their prospects for the Bar by university age. Inequality of access to earlier education may compromise a young person's ability to perform well in public examinations, regardless of their raw intellectual ability. The early stage at which the effects of lower-quality education and family poverty begin to affect a child's chance of professional success later in life illustrate that early intervention is likely to be key to social mobility. As the policy documents in Chapter 1 highlight, many of those from lower socio-economic backgrounds are also at an intersection of disadvantage. Even where they are not, the complex interplay of familial and educational factors that exist for many mean that a single access initiative at higher education stage may struggle to effectively address the results of socio-economic disadvantage.

Any significant change to the demographic of a traditional profession will take a protracted period of time. Whilst intervention by a professional association may be effective, and may achieve greater diversity, it will not do so within a few years. Any programme seeking to implement such a change will need to run consistently over some years to noticeably affect the profession's demographics. However, changes which are much harder to quantify, such as more positive attitudes and approaches towards non-traditional aspirant entrants, may occur before any demographic change is seen, but would still be a very positive development. A change in one arena may, especially if that arena is powerful within the profession, affect other arenas, and especially those that are less powerful and influential in their own right (Halliday, 1987; Nelson and Trubek, 1992). Furthermore, other less tangible changes, such as more positive external perceptions, better provision of information and increased aspiration amongst the target group, may happen sooner and from a small-scale programme, but nonetheless be important foundations for greater change.

To be effective in altering the demographic composition of a profession, a professional association needs to either control entry to the profession, or have sufficient influence over those organisations recruiting directly into the profession to alter the recruitment practices identified as propagating social closure. This is a significant challenge, as it will be rare for professional associations to directly control access to the profession (although many will aim to keep as much control as possible; Johnson, 1972). In this respect, the Bar is unusual; the Inns of Court theoretically exercise control over those Called to the Bar, and without having been Called it is impossible to practise. This means that, as professional associations, the Inns of Court are unusually placed to potentially affect the profession's demographic. In practice, this is not the case; the requirements for Call are being 'of good character' and having passed the BPTC. It is the cost of the BPTC that means that many non-traditional aspirant entrants will not even get to the stage of being Called, as they are unable to afford the course fees (see Chapter 7). This illustrates the difference between technical access (being Called) and the reality of access (an environment in which one can qualify to practise without exclusion or discomfort).

The next chapter seeks to build upon the exploration of work experience by addressing those challenges faced by non-traditional aspirant entrants which are outside of the influence of professional associations and interventions which they may initiate. By doing so, it attempts to delineate the limits of professional associations' ability to cause meaningful change within a traditional profession, and considers ways in which a professional association may shape its intervention, such that these limitations are minimised.

7 Wider constraints on interventions by professional associations
Challenges within and challenges without?

The previous chapter examined an attempt to disrupt patterns of social closure by giving opportunities to non-traditional aspirant entrants that they may otherwise be unable to access (using as an example work experience and its role in identity formation; Francis and Sommerlad, 2009: 65). It was argued that this is not the radical move some portrayed it to be, as it fails to challenge fundamental assumptions supporting social closure: the privileging of legal work experience and undervaluing of transferable skills assimilated in other ways. This undervaluation occurs primarily because of the perceived value of social norms. The access programme examined provided an opportunity for non-traditional students to assimilate those norms, instead of valuing their difference.

This chapter therefore explores the wider context affecting the actions of a professional association attempting to change a deeply entrenched characteristic of the profession. No profession is an island, and circumstances beyond the control of a professional association will have a significant impact on the effect of its actions, awareness of which is vital. Specifically, the wider contexts of all stakeholders affect their interaction and may constrain a professional association's intervention.

The two most relevant contexts are that of the professional association and the group at whom the intervention is aimed. For the professional association, constraints may exist within the profession but outside of its control. These barriers may be susceptible to influence by the professional association, but they are likely to be difficult for a professional association to alter as they are profession-wide challenges without a straightforward solution. In the case study, it is argued that there are two significant examples of such barriers. First, increased regulation (such as through the LSA). Second, the BPTC's significant financial cost. Unlike the solicitors' equivalent (the LPC), the BPTC is rarely funded by an entrant's prospective chambers, and has increasingly formal prerequisites. There is the profession's continued desire to retain control over the process of assimilating cultural norms required for a comfortable social existence within it.

In addition to constraints within the profession but outside the professional association's control are those constraints wholly outside of the profession, but which may nonetheless limit the effectiveness of an intervention, such as the educational and social contexts of the intervention's target audience. This is illustrated in the case study through the importance of movement between social fields and a lack of access to information within educational settings.

This research argues that the weakening of professional associations, manifested in these ways, is attributable to a number of causes which can be divided roughly into two groups: first, external factors or events affecting the profession, such as regulatory changes; and second, internal factors such as the structure and structuring properties affecting the perceptions and actions of those within it.

It is therefore argued in this chapter that professions and their professional associations as proxies are no longer as powerful as they once were. Whilst in the past professions controlled entry; the reproduction of their knowledge and culture, and their relations with government, times have changed. Consequently, professional associations now find themselves powerful within a smaller sphere of influence. Entry requirements are under greater scrutiny, as they have been in this research, for fairness and equality amongst applicants. The reproduction of knowledge is no longer necessarily within the control of the profession itself, and nor is a privileged link to government – allowing the influence of policy and practice – a notable feature of professions. Within the legal profession, each of these three factors are readily identifiable. For example, the Legal Education and Training Review (LETR) highlighted weaknesses with the provision of professional education, and the particular barriers faced by non-traditional aspirant entrants.

Professions and professional associations, whilst seemingly weakened, do nevertheless retain the potential for innovative action. More constrained by outside factors than previously, innovation is more reliant on internal actors, and on institutional entrepreneurship carried out both by individuals and the institution within wider constraints.

Finally, a conclusion is drawn together through a discussion of theoretical explanations offered by academics for the relative decline in power enjoyed by professional associations. The main theories considered are post-professionalism (Kritzer, 1999), proletarianisation (McKinlay and Arches, 1985) and deprofessionalisation (Haug, 1973), and restratification (Freidson, 1985). Despite a potential decline in professional associations' power, they are far from powerless, instead adapting their use of power to bolster their position in changing times. This supports the key argument in this research that professional associations have notable capacity for change. However, their evolutionary direction is not under their control as it has previously been, instead being directed by external events (such as legislation or political pressure) and an acceptance that refusing to evolve according to societal concerns would be detrimental to the profession.

7.1 'So limp it's unbelievable': diminishing power of professional associations of the Bar

The general trend depicted in sociological literature of the reduced power of professional associations has been reflected within the legal profession (Abel, 2003), in the solicitors' sector (Francis, 2011) as well as the Bar. A dispute illustrating the lack of power of the professional association is control over entry, and the ongoing discussions between the sites of power at the Bar (see 4.2.3) as to how to best protect the profession's elite status when aspirant entrants are more numerous than ever.

As Abel recognises, the first line of defence against competition is control over entry (2003: 96). In exerting this a professional association issues a clear message to the field that it is securing its place in the market by shoring itself up against competitors. For professional associations, the exercise of control over entry has been key, justified as essential to protect consumers perceived as incapable of judging the quality or integrity of those offering professional services (Abel, 2003: 96). Historically, restricting membership has been a recurring issue at the Bar (Polden, 2010: 1018). Over-supply of non-practising barristers (those who have passed the BPTC but not secured pupillage) has been advanced by some practitioners as a reason not to encourage widening participation (see 7.2).

With pupillages decreasing (437 were available in 2014/15, the most up-to-date figures),[1] but BPTC places remaining largely stable (1,502 in 2014/15),[2] this remains an area of tension between professional associations, members and aspirant entrants. Various working groups have suggested that BPTC places should be reduced (Wood, 2008: 32–4; Neuberger, 2007: 51–7), and how: numerical limits, higher academic requirements, entrance examinations (such as aptitude tests) or English-language requirements (Neuberger, 2007: 51). Whilst control over entry may be necessary to balance supply and demand of practitioners (Abel, 2003: 96) it may nonetheless be exercised in ways that disadvantage certain groups. A consultation paper on the future of training for the Bar (BSB, 2015) raised explicitly for the first time the effect that imposing a 2:1 entry requirement for the BPTC may have on non-traditional aspirant entrants.

There are also formal restrictions. The most recent of these affecting the role of professional associations at the Bar is the (Legal Services Act 2007 'LSA'). This legislation was introduced partly to reduce self-regulation; previously the legal profession and professional associations regulated the profession and oversaw compliance with rules against restrictive practices. The LSA introduced a 'halfway-house' whereby the profession is overseen by an external independent body instead of the Government (Herring, 2014: 77). This external body is the (Legal Services Board 'LSB'), introduced in s.2 as an oversight regulator of all legal services. The independent Office for Legal Complaints (s.114) removes these oversight functions from the profession itself. To increase external oversight, it required existing professional associations such as the Bar Council and the Law Society to separate their representative and disciplinary functions (s.30).

---

1 BSB (2017); www.barstandardsboard.org.uk/media-centre/research-and-statistics/statistics/pupillage-statistics [accessed 27th June 2017].
2 BSB (2017) www.barstandardsboard.org.uk/media-centre/research-and-statistics/statistics/bptc-statistics [accessed 27th June 2017].

This legislation forced changes in professional association functions incongruous with previous perceptions of professional associations, especially in elite professions such as medicine and law (Freidson, 1970).

This, however, was set against a history of increasingly interventionist action against the profession, mainly by the Government but also other sources. One target was entry to the profession, and sustenance of the very junior end. Although funding for pupillages was introduced in 1990, it was not widely implemented as it was not compulsory (Abel, 2003: 99). Furthermore, gaining tenancy remained the main obstacle for those wishing to practise at the Bar. Consequently, in 1990, the Chair of the Young Barristers' Committee urged that BVC places be limited to the number of pupillages (Abel, 2003: 99). This was rejected, and it is interesting to note that the same issue was raised again in the report of the Entry to the Bar Working Party (Neuberger, 2007: 51–8). Once again, it was dismissed as impracticable, and it was suggested that people should be allowed to complete the then-BVC if they had a 2:2 degree and sufficient finances. It was argued that it was not for the profession to prevent people 'taking the risk' of doing the BPTC; potential candidates had to choose for themselves.

In the early 1990s, the young Bar was declared to be 'in crisis' by Peter Goldsmith QC (1993), who had been mandated to assess the environment of, and demand for, legal practice at the turn of the century. He found that the Bar had grown by 23% in four years, but in half that time Magistrates' Court work had declined by 5% and the Crown Prosecution Service had halved the proportion of Magistrates' Court cases for which it briefed counsel. Furthermore, it planned to halve it again, and had already cut Crown Court briefs by 10% (Abel, 2003: 100). It was therefore unsurprising to find that 20% of new tenants had experienced financial difficulties, further underlining the need for those considering the Bar as a career to either have parental financial support or savings of their own on which they could rely when work was scarce.

Attempting to ameliorate the financial crises in which some pupils found themselves, and which were unlikely to be alleviated early in their tenancies (assuming they secured them), in 1997 the minimum wage was held by the High Court to apply to pupils,[3] although most chambers vehemently opposed such minima. The Court of Appeal overturned the High Court ruling,[4] enigmatically concluding their judgement, 'We were not addressed on the potentially far-reaching questions of policy which arise, and which are better considered elsewhere.' The Bar Council agreed to set a minimum pupillage award, initially £10,000, now £12,000 plus some assistance for travel expenses (BSB, 2016: 28). When considering the amount of travelling necessary, and living costs in London, this by no means guarantees an escape from financial hardship. If the pupil earns little in the second six, or the payment of what they earn is delayed (as is often the case with legally-aided work), they may still experience serious financial difficulties.

---

3 *Edmonds v Lawson* [2000] I.R.L.R. 18.
4 *Lawson v Edmonds* [2000] I.R.L.R. 391.

Imposing a minimum award reduced the number of pupillages, a bottleneck tightened further by legal aid reductions. Funding available for the BVC also changed, as the government funding for such vocational courses declined significantly. Simultaneously, the cost of university, a conversion year if necessary, and the BVC were all rising (Abel, 2003: 119).

At the same time, the profession was open to criticism that, although it provided a large amount of money in funding, most of this was distributed through merit scholarships, which did not prioritise financial need:

> The Inns are a bit protective of the data and their scholarships and who gets them, as I am sure you are finding. [We think] they aren't necessarily going to the people who need them the most.
> (Interviewee 6, non-Inner, M, salaried, other prof. assoc.)

This echoed the Neuberger Report (2007: 58–9), and in interviews some practitioners also observed that the challenges faced by non-traditional aspirant entrants in making convincing mini-pupillage and pupillage applications were equally applicable to Inns of Court scholarships (also reported by Neuberger, 2007: 59). Middle Temple, Inner Temple and Lincoln's Inn award on merit, but consider need when deciding the amount of a scholarship.[5,6,7] Gray's Inn retains the fully merit-based system, but candidates in financial need can ask to be considered for further funding.[8]

These funding problems re-opened the debate on quotas to limit the profession's size. The Bar agreed only to fund pupillages on the basis that it could also control their numbers, and thereby replaced the previous implicit entry requirement of ability to pay with a 'modern meritocratic warrant' (Abel, 2003: 119).

The imposition of the minimum award, and the initial success of the Claimant in *Edmonds*, demonstrated that the Bar was no longer untouchable by regulation, as it had been perceived. It would have to adhere to at least some of the requirements made of other professions, even where such seemed incongruous with its elite and self-employed status. The Bar was weakened as a profession, less able to exercise its autonomy to behave in ways perceived by some as being outmoded and unfair.

This challenge to the Bar as an autonomous profession has continued: various subsequent reports conducted by members of the profession have expressly criticised the lack of regulation in certain areas of the profession. For example, the

---

5 The Honourable Society of the Middle Temple (2017); www.middletemple.org.uk/education-and-training/scholarships-and-prizes/bptc-and-gdl-scholarships [accessed 27th June 2017];
6 The Honourable Society of the Inner Temple (2017); www.innertemple.org.uk/prospective-members/scholarships/application-criteria-general-guidelines [accessed 27th June 2017].
7 The Honourable Society of Lincoln's Inn (2017); www.lincolnsinn.org.uk/index.php/education/scholarships [accessed 27th June 2017].
8 The Honourable Society of Gray's Inn (2017); www.graysinn.org.uk/education/scholarships [accessed 27th June 2017].

Wood Report (2008) examined the lack of oversight of BVC providers, whilst the Neuberger Report (2007) highlighted the demographic homogeneity of the Bar.

Furthermore, the legal profession is often ill-thought of by the public, perceived as a profession where all practitioners are earning vast quantities of money for relatively little work.[9] Many participants admitted that they had had such preconceptions themselves prior to participating in PASS, but conversations with barristers during their mini-pupillages had enabled them to gain more accurate information:

> She was making me aware of how little I will be getting paid during a pupillage and she actually said it's not that much different if you're doing family law, but she was saying it's not all about the money and it's just nice to be aware that someone is doing it for the same reasons that you are and not just for a really big pay cheque or anything.
> (PASS FG1 Participant 4, F)

Rogers (2012: 223) noted in her research on Inns of Court recruitment events that barristers speaking at those events conveyed restrictions on the profession's autonomy as a negative circumstance arising from other elements of the legal profession and government action. This suggests an awareness within the profession that it can no longer portray itself as wholly in control of its circumstances; it is now necessarily reactive in situations where previously it would have been the instigator. That these restrictions are perceived in negative terms indicates the profession's distaste for being externally regulated – one interviewee attributed some blame for low social mobility to regulations themselves (see also 5.1):

> I was able to come to the Bar because it wasn't constrained with rules and regulations and that's why social mobility has gone backwards.
> (Interviewee 7, Inner, M, Bencher, other prof. assocs.)

Not only is the Bar experiencing constraints, but it is being forced to acknowledge them and potentially react to them. A point of interest in this research was whether moving away from social closure and the implementation of a programme advocating social mobility could be described as a free and deliberate choice by the professional association, or whether this was a manoeuvre triggered by external factors. PASS participants had very mixed views on this matter when asked 'Why do you think chambers offer mini-pupillages through PASS?', with answers including 'either to address, or, more cynically, appear to address, an issue with lack of diversity', 'to meet a quota' and 'committed to increasing diversity at the Bar and to help those from low-income backgrounds/non-Oxbridge graduates gain access to the Bar' (all from the researcher post-placement questionnaire).

---

9 'Lawyers lament "fat-cat" public perception', *Financial Times*, 7th June 2012.

In advancing a programme of their own making, was the professional association in the case study attempting to disguise forced change as occurring out of choice (Abel, 1985: 12), or had the profession realised that it needed or wanted to encourage entry on merit alone? A combination of both factors seems most likely: this research has certainly discovered within a professional association a core of embedded actors, a number within the elite, who believe strongly that social mobility is important for aspirant entrants as a group, and also the Bar as a profession. It remains contested, however, whether movement towards a more socio-economically representative profession is internally or externally driven. This has been recognised by Maute (2011: 11–12) who suggests that the professions may evolve in these ways, conscious that if they do not, external action may force them to do so. Under such circumstances, evolution in the manner seen in PASS is the preferable option for a profession, as it allows it the recognition of choosing to act, as well as greater control over the way in which such evolution is pursued.

Many of the PASS participants recognised elements of both free choice and external pressure featuring in a decision to initiate a programme such as PASS (for further exploration see Chapter 4), as shown by this response to the question 'What do you think motivated Inner Temple to set up PASS?':

> A genuine commitment to extending access to the Bar to people from socio-economic backgrounds where, historically, the Bar has not recruited from (nor wanted to recruit from). This seems to imply a working towards a long-term change in the make-up of the Bar, not only for the benefit of its future practitioners, but also possibly in order to evolve the Bar in the face of continual existential threats.
> (Researcher pre-placement questionnaire, Cohort 2)

This chapter continues by focussing on four key issues constraining professional associations' actions currently. Externally, there are two main factors: increased regulation and cultural reproduction through professional education. Internally, there are the structuring properties of the field. More generally, there is the challenge posed by the extent to which social fields are permeable, allowing individuals to move between them. First, the two internal factors, legislation and regulation and professional education, will be considered.

7.1.1 Legislation and regulation

As detailed earlier, regulation has increased in many professions. In the legal sector, the LSA was a notable restriction on the self-regulation and autonomy previously enjoyed by the barristers' and solicitors' professions, where disciplinary bodies existed within the representative bodies. The functions of the Solicitors' Regulation Authority (SRA) was performed by the Law Society, and those of the BSB by the Bar Council. Such self-regulation had always been identified as key to the professional project (Larson, 1977: 53). Self-regulation allows a profession to demarcate its own limits, to advance its status, and to negotiate more forcefully with government for situations favourable to it (Abel, 2003).

Constraints occurring through the introduction of the Legal Services Board as a regulator, and the additional duties placed on the frontline regulators in each profession, cannot be ignored. As Francis states 'there is now little doubt that the LSB is a serious actor' (2011: 144). In addition to the broad reasoning behind, and aims of, the legislation, s.1(1)(f) of the LSA sets out as a regulatory objective to be fulfilled by the LSB and frontline regulators (the BSB and the SRA) 'encouraging an independent, strong, diverse and effective legal profession'.

This emphasises the force with which a social mobility agenda is being pursued: diversity has been enshrined in legislation as something which the profession *must* pursue. Similar commitments are observed in the 'Mission and Goals' of the American Bar Association[10] and the Australian Bar Association's 'Priorities'.[11]

The imposition upon the legal profession of such legislation, effectively compromising its right to recruit in a truly autonomous fashion is, it is argued, wholly inconsistent with the powerful portrayals of the legal profession in the past. Whatever theoretical framework was preferred – functional, action, power or other – all situated the professions in powerful and elevated positions not easily constrained by any organisation or exercise of state power. Abel (2003) details various occasions when the legal profession went on a deliberate collision course with the Government over legislation which it felt compromised its ability to recruit in the way it preferred, or to otherwise fetter its discretion in any important matters.

As Boon (2010: 207) notes, the LSB prefers a system of 'principles-based regulation', the less prescriptive counterpart to the 'command-control' system. This middle-ground model emerged after the Clementi Review (2004) highlighted inadequacies in the existing system, but there was fierce opposition to a single legal services regulator. Such regulation, Boon argues, has the possibility to revitalise legal professionalism by increasing order, as the 'hotchpotch' of co-regulating bodies has been reduced (2010: 224). The LETR also articulated concerns about increasing regulatory challenges facing the profession, and suggested that the solution was to encourage greater collaboration between existing regulators (2013: vii). However, the LSB also signalled a move towards entity regulation: the regulation of groups supervising individuals, as opposed to the individuals themselves, introduced in part to address the challenges posed by new professional actors such as global professional services firms (Flood, 2011: 508).

A necessary corollary of introducing a regulatory body such as the LSB, it is argued, is diminished power for the professional associations that previously

---

10 'Goal III: Eliminate Bias and Enhance Diversity'; www.americanbar.org/about_the_aba/aba-mission-goals.html [accessed 3rd September 2017].
11 '2. Improve Our Profession . . . Promote the highest standards of ethics, quality and diversity across the profession'; http://austbar.asn.au/about-the-aba/about-us [accessed 3rd September 2017].

had a much wider scope of unconstrained action. In this jurisdiction, external regulation has been the legislature's path of choice, imposed upon the professions and their professional associations. Semple (2015: 86) characterises the professionalist-independent paradigm of legal services regulation with reference to self-regulation and a focus on the governance of individual practitioners. He notes that in North America, where a system not dissimilar to regulation of the Bar in England occurs, moves by the state towards greater regulation, although appearing to hail significant reduction in self-governance, have in fact not had such notable effects as expected (Fischer, 2006). As Trebilcock writes, the question in North America is currently whether the professionalist-independent paradigm of regulation of legal services can be reformed and revitalised without the threat of more external regulation (foreword to Semple, 2015: vii). We are perhaps already beginning to see some preliminary answers to that question in England and Wales in the decision to introduce the LSB. The LSB's existence has caused at least one regulator to seek to implement further legislation; in 2015 the BSB consulted on further legislation aimed at facilitating it in its role as an approved regulator under the LSA. These included widened disciplinary powers, secured on a statutory footing, and increased information-gathering powers (BSB, 2015a: 1): greater external regulation has also led to the creation of greater internal regulation.

It is not only in regulatory matters that the might of legal professional associations is diminishing. Another area indicative of the power balance in a profession is the method and content of professional education: compulsory training after academic qualifications, before full entry to the profession. This stage is sometimes called 'vocational training'.

7.2 Habituation to the habitus: professional education as cultural reproduction

Tolbert (1988: 104), amongst others, has suggested that ideological processes are key in professional associations as they perceive professional education as providing a common culture and thus shared understanding of problems and solutions. It has long been recognised that professional (i.e. post-higher-education) qualifications play a significant role in shaping students into a profession-desired mould by standardising the knowledge base (Larson, 1977: 46). Professional education also contributes to identity formation and cultural reproduction (assimilation of the field's habitus) for aspirant professionals. If its purpose is fulfilled, they will complete the education as a member of the profession possessing the general ideology and practices required by the profession, referred to by Larson as 'cognitive standardisation' (1977: 40). Such cognitive standardisation will include not just knowledge but certain values and beliefs.

This standardisation gives the monopolistic professional project the appearance of neutrality, and consequently legitimacy (1977: 41), partially disguising the internal stratification within professions which is often outwardly invisible (Abbott, 1988: 121). Furthermore, appearances of commonality within the profession stemming from educating aspirant entrants into an appearance of homogeneity lead the elite section of the profession (Shils, 1975) to perceive commonality amongst the rest of the profession. They therefore present what they perceive to be the interests of the profession as shared by the whole profession, further serving the force with which the profession's desires can be pursued: a facade of united action arising from a 'facade of homogeneity' (Abbott, 1988: 106).

Professional education leads to the formation of a body of knowledge required for entry to the profession. For these reasons, it is in a profession's interest to have a high degree of control over the content and teaching of a professional qualification. However, that body of knowledge will be applied differently by each individual due to their personal differences. Larson suggests that three things arise from this: social characteristics prevalent within the profession will influence the standardisation at any one time; leading producers will define those requirements that cannot be taught, and third, that the role of individual talent will vary (1977: 41). This is at variance with PASS's stated aim: that the role of talent should not vary (see 4.4 and Chapter 5). Many interviewees and students perceived PASS as an attempt by Inner Temple to frame individual talent, measured flexibly, as an aspect that does not vary but is considered paramount in all recruitment for the Bar.

In the legal profession the second of those elements identified by Larson, that the leading producers will define those requirements that cannot be taught, has been key. Many outward manifestations of crucial qualities that the profession is looking for in aspirant entrants are difficult to teach; many of them are learnt from parents and carers very early in life (Bourdieu, 1984). A move towards increasing access is reflective of the third element, with initiatives favouring ability over traditional background giving a greater role than previously to individual ability. This is something PASS is seeking to further.

The translation of these values into the legal profession through a standardised knowledge base therefore begins at the legal education stage (Francis, 2011: 17). This stage is influenced by the profession, which often has strong links to the providers of professional training, and may even part-run or fund such training, although it may not retain as much control as it would like. In the legal profession, professional education in the form of the BPTC (and the solicitors' equivalent, the LPC) is run by commercial providers who are not connected to or funded by the Inns of Court in any way. This is contentious, with many commentators and members of the profession arguing that private providers do not have the interests of the profession or students at heart, simply pursuing profit. During this research, the LETR was published. Although it made recommendations regarding the provision of the BPTC, it did nonetheless declare that the system overall was 'fit for purpose', despite recurring concerns about the quality and provision of the course in some parts (2013: Chapters 4 and 5).

Less control over legal education is one way in which the profession's power is reduced. Before European competition laws forbade monopolies, there was only one provider of the BVC (the forerunner to the BPTC): the Inns of Court School of Law (ICSL). One of the interviewees recalled this as generally providing appropriate education:

> [Professional associations] have no control over that. When I did it you had to go to the Inns of Court School of Law to do your Bar Finals, it was the only place . . . I thought the teaching was good, the support was okay . . . but once they stopped that because of competition rules and everything else, all of these places started springing up all over the county where you could do your Bar Finals, which was great, because in theory you could live at home or close to home or at least be in a part of the county which was cheaper than London, but then they just hiked up the course fees.
>
> (Interviewee 10, Inner, F, Bencher, other prof. assocs.)

Provision of the BPTC is a source of continued debate within the profession. Despite the introduction of competition supposedly aimed at increasing the standard and choice for students, interviewees felt that this had not occurred. Although the Wood Report stated negativity evinced by some students was not consistent with the teaching seen by members of the team (2008: 56, para 131), deep concerns remain about the course, with little faith in providers. One participant undertaking the BPTC when she participated in a PASS focus group had particularly strong views:

> I have a massive thing with the Bar Course because I don't think there is even half enough regulation . . . of the course; on the fees that are being charged, on the amount of places that are being offered, on the providers and how they are regulated. I just think . . . it's really, actually, quite appalling.
>
> (PASS FG1 Participant 2, F)

Various reports have examined the course's content and efficacy, and potential effects on access to the profession (Neuberger, 2007; Wood, 2008). The course is a compulsory pre-requisite for obtaining pupillage; it cannot be circumvented. It is offered by providers, some private commercial, some university-based.[12] The course is usually undertaken in one year on a full-time basis, although most providers also offer it part-time over two years (BSB, 2014: 24).

More recently, an alternative model for the BPTC has been suggested by the Council of the Inns of Court ('COIC') (COIC, 2016), after research funded by the Legal Education Foundation. In 2015 the BSB launched a consultation entitled 'The Future of Training for the Bar: Academic, Vocational and Professional Stages of Training',[13] described as 'a programme of review and reform that will bring our training regulation up to date and assure high standards in barristers' services for the future' (BSB, 2015: 1). Arising from the LETR's observations on barriers to training for the Bar, it focussed particularly on affordability and cost (2015: 6). Having used the 2015 report to finalise the options on which there would be open consultation (2015: 11), in October 2016 the BSB opened

---

12 BPTC Provider Information 2014–15; www.barstandardsboard.org.uk/media/1664258/bptc_info_table_2014-15.pdf [accessed 30th July 2017].
13 www.barstandardsboard.org.uk/media/1676754/fbt_triple_consultation_9_july_2015.pdf [accessed 30th July 2017].

a full consultation, 'Consultation on the Future of Training for the Bar: Future Routes to Authorisation'.[14]

Using as guiding principles 'flexibility; accessibility; affordability, and sustaining high standards' (2016: 5), the BSB proposed three possible future approaches: 'Evolutionary' (Option A), 'Managed Pathways' (Option B) and 'Bar Specialist' (Option C) (2016: 6–7). Option B, which provided for several routes which the BSB might authorise, was the BSB's preferred option.

The profession, however, was underwhelmed. A letter to the Chair of the BSB, signed by over 500 members of the profession, lambasted the BSB for, amongst other things,

> fail[ing] to identify the underlying cause of the current problems, namely the fact that BPTC provision has become a self-serving industry that has vastly outgrown its raison d'être of training people in preparation for their becoming one of the people who commence providing legal services every year as members of the Bar of England and Wales.[15]

COIC, supported by the Bar Council, created a fourth possibility, and in December 2016 the BSB added this fourth option to the consultation and extended the deadline for responses to the end of January 2017. COIC's proposal (2016: 32–6) was for a two-part BPTC: 'knowledge' and 'skills'. The first part – 'knowledge' – could be studied in myriad ways. Self-taught, online, distance; it is up to the student how they assimilate the knowledge they need to pass the centralised assessments. This would enable this stage of the course to be studied alongside employment or family responsibilities. As passing the 'knowledge' element is a pre-requisite for enrolling for the structured, classroom-taught, 'skills' element, this filters candidates who are unlikely to meet the required standard before they have expended large sums of money, something COIC, as many participants in this research, highlighted as a current problem.

The COIC proposal was greeted with more enthusiasm, especially for its recognition of social mobility issues (e.g. Young Legal Aid Lawyers' response[16]). In March 2017 the BSB indicated that it would approve the COIC model,[17] and by June 2017 there were already rumours of exactly what a number of participants in this research had favoured: a BPTC delivered by the Inns of Court.[18]

---

14 www.barstandardsboard.org.uk/media/1794621/future_bar_training_routes_consultation__final.pdf [accessed 16th July 2017].
15 www.graysinn.org.uk/sites/default/files/documents/news/BPTC%20BSB%20consultation%20open%20letter.pdf (this link contains the body of the letter but does not contain the full list of signatories) [accessed 16th July 2017].
16 www.younglegalaidlawyers.org/sites/default/files/YLAL%20response%20to%20BSB%20Consultation%20-%20January%202017.pdf [accessed 16th July 2017].
17 www.barstandardsboard.org.uk/media-centre/press-releases-and-news/bsb-announces-decision-on-the-future-of-bar-training [accessed 16th July 2017].
18 www.legalcheek.com/2017/06/exclusive-inns-of-court-prepare-to-launch-new-bptc [accessed 16th July 2017].

Concerns about the current course's quality were rife amongst case study interviewees, both students and practitioners. A recurrent theme was the low entry requirement: a 2:2 at undergraduate level. Statistics show that 26.3% of BPTC students commencing the course full-time in 2014 (the most recent year for which data is available) had a 2:2 degree classification.[19] Of the BPTC graduates from that cohort, 202 had secured a first six pupillage by the time of data collection (2017a: 130). The data released by the BSB is regrettably imprecise, but states that of those '<5' had a 2:2 and an 'Outstanding' grading on the BPTC, '<5' had a 'Very Competent' grading on the BPTC, and <5 in both the Outstanding and Very Competent categories had not declared their degree classification (2017a: 130). In summary, very few students with a 2:2 secured pupillage, and those that did had achieved either an Outstanding or a Very Competent on the BPTC. It is a clear cause for concern that so many are being Called to the Bar with little chance of practising. Much emphasis was placed on this in COIC's response to the BSB's consultation. This was also a cause of concern to many interviewees, and recurred as a conflict within the profession. The vast over-supply of the BPTC led to accusations that access schemes were 'giving false hope' to non-traditional aspirant entrants, as statistically the likelihood of success is so low:

> [Lady Hale] also said the Bar shouldn't be doing so much outreach work because it was giving people false hope about being able to enter the Criminal and Family Bar when there simply wasn't going to be the pupillages available ... I mean I have always seen outreach as providing good careers advice and hopefully aspiration-raising more generally to those who otherwise wouldn't have it.
> (Interviewee 11, Inner, M, salaried)

This level of competition seemed to be something of which students were aware, especially after participating in PASS, and they understood that undertaking the BPTC without first securing pupillage was a significant risk:

> I think it made me value the competitiveness of getting a pupillage, because I never really understood it before I did my [PASS] mini-pupillage.
> (PASS FG1 Participant 4, F)

> And it's not even certainty. It's not even a half chance; it's like a 1 in 10 chance after that that you're gonna get the job that you need to secure. There's no way round it ... so if you don't get a pupillage you can't get to the Bar, and you've got five years to use these qualifications which you've really worked hard for.
> (PASS FG1 Participant 2, F)

---

19 This figure comes from a calculation as follows: in 2014, 1,502 students enrolled on the BPTC (BSB, 2017a: 99), and 304 of those had a 2:2 degree (2017a: 304). There were no separate statistics for those who had any other degree classification.

Entry requirements cannot be dictated by professional associations, despite their open acknowledgement that many students embarking on the BPTC will, predictably, be unsuccessful; although they may secure a BPTC place with a 2:2, they are unlikely to obtain scholarships or pupillage without extenuating circumstances. This is one way in which professional associations are appearing in this research as weakened entities. This reduced level of control was also emphasised in the case study by the unrest regarding introducing an aptitude test for entry to the BPTC – further controlling who receives standardised knowledge in a setting aiming to facilitate the cultural reproduction of the profession's norms. The Future of Training for the Bar consultation explicitly raised the question of whether a 2:1 should be the academic minimum required for entry to the vocational stage of training (2015: 14). Accompanying discussion within the consultation paper is consideration of potential negative effects on certain groups, particularly ethnic minority candidates or those with disabilities; no specific mention is made of those who have experienced socio-economic disadvantage (2015: 15).

The official academic standard of a 2:2 was, for the 2013/14 academic year, supplemented for the first time by the Bar Course Aptitude Test (BCAT). The BCAT was introduced in response to recommendations made by the BVC Review Group, chaired by Derek Wood QC (2008: 3), which suggested various possible forms that the test may take, and at what stage it should be administered (2008: 39, para 78). A pilot took place in 2009–10 with about 200 student volunteers, and a second pilot (in which the writer participated whilst a BPTC student) took place between November 2010 and November 2011 (BSB, 2013: 10). The BCAT was then approved by the LSB in July 2012.[20] The *BCAT Handbook* describes the test as assessing critical thinking, which it does by measuring three core areas of critical thinking: recognising assumptions, evaluating arguments, and drawing conclusions (2013: 3). In other words, it is aimed at identifying those raw and innate skills that participants in this research routinely identified by the over-arching term 'talent' (see 4.4 and Chapter 5). A practice test is available free of charge online from the website of the body that administers it, Pearson Vue.[21]

The idea behind measuring these skills is that they are innate, and therefore not subject to teaching or coaching effects (Ogg, Zimdars and Heath, 2009: 784). Large quantities of research suggest that this is not the practical effect of such tests, and that bias is found in many. Race (Jencks and Phillips, 1998), gender (Connor and Vargyas, 2013: 17) and cultural biases have all been discovered, with the latter including bias against those from lower socio-economic backgrounds (Stringer, 2008). Research commissioned by the LSB into legal aptitude tests drew a balanced conclusion highlighting both strengths and weaknesses of aptitude tests (Dewberry, 2011). It concluded that caution should be employed when considering the use of aptitude tests, as their results were

---

20 http://l2b.thelawyer.com/lsb-approves-introduction-of-bar-course-aptitude-test/1013628.article [accessed 30th July 2017].
21 www.talentlens.co.uk/BCAT [accessed 30th July 2017].

affected by candidates' prior experiences, and those from privileged backgrounds tended to perform better than their counterparts from less privileged backgrounds (2011: 72).

Those who had sat the test, including a chambers' representative in an administrative position undertaking the BPTC part-time, were unconvinced of its usefulness:

> Before you have even started the course you've now got to pay £150 for an aptitude test which if you fail, it's ridiculously easy, it doesn't test anything, it's the biggest waste of £150.
> (Interviewee 3, non-Inner, F, chambers' rep.)

Practitioners involved in conceiving it felt that the test in its final format was not true to what had been intended, and what had thus been supported by the profession. In its final format, it was felt to serve very little purpose:

> I thought, everybody thought, the aptitude test might be a way forward but the test was watered down by the LSB and so it hasn't . . . all it's done in my view is just to take another £150 off the students . . . The actual nature of the test is not what was intended by the BSB or the profession.
> (Interviewee 10, Inner, F, Bencher, other prof. assocs.)

Furthermore, PASS focus group participants perceived aptitude tests negatively, as an exercise in identifying privilege as opposed to talent:

> So, given that this aptitude test probably doesn't shed as much light on how clever you are [or] how hard you've worked in your academic degree and your academic grades I think it's just another way of trying to sort the wheat from the chaff, and I don't think that it's very accommodating towards people who will be put off by that.
> (PASS FG1 Participant 1, F)

'Sort the wheat from the chaff' is a powerful metaphor. It carries connotations of desirable and undesirable; some are fit for the task and some not. Akin to the 'sifting' phase described in appraising mini-pupillage applications (see 6.3.1), aptitude tests provided another way in which the profession could apply standardised measures to reduce the workload of scrutinising individuals and their circumstances (although in this case it was in relation to entry to the BPTC instead of obtaining mini-pupillages). This participant further suggested that success in the aptitude test could potentially come to be regarded as another marker of a traditional background, as she had earlier mentioned that she was aware that research suggested that traditional candidates would score more highly.

Access to the standardised knowledge has therefore become more closely guarded; not at the behest of the profession, but commercial providers who run the courses purely for profit. To gain control over the stage of professional education, a professional association would be faced with a stark choice: to run the courses itself. Furthermore, it would face the challenge of European laws on monopoly, as it had when the ICSL was the sole provider. When competition law prevented this continuing, the ICSL became one of many providers, before being absorbed into City Law School in 2008.[22]

Whilst some interviewees felt strongly that a return to monopoly was undesirable, they did feel that standards needed raising, and that a professional-association-run course could potentially achieve this. This assertion partly seemed to rest on the professional associations' status as not-for-profit, and the possibility that such an ethos and set-up could be used in any training provision:

> Education should really be education, it shouldn't be a profit-making exercise, and whether that means in future the Inns coming together, because they have got a lot of financial resources, [and] maybe produce their own, maybe a not-for-profit charity or some sort of arm to deliver what training needs to be done.
> (Interviewee 1, non-Inner, M, chambers' rep.)

Using professional association resources to run the BPTC not-for-profit would significantly reduce fees. With lower fees, scholarships could be less, releasing some funds currently given in BPTC scholarships. Such funds could, for example, be used for bursaries for living costs. For non-traditional aspirant entrants, such funding would help those who had successfully secured a place to undertake the course without threat of financial hardship.

When considering further barriers caused by the BPTC disproportionately affecting non-traditional entrants, its year-long duration is criticised as unnecessary (contrary to prevailing opinions communicated to the Neuberger Working Group; 2007: 47). Particularly for non-traditional aspirant entrants, the duration – time during which they cannot work full-time – is likely to be important, especially if they have caring responsibilities or have to be financially independent. Thus, a less radical and more common suggestion than professional-association provision of the BPTC was shortening it.

This has already occurred on the LPC, where an accelerated course of around seven months is now available to all students at certain providers,[23,24] and is compulsory for some firms' trainees.[25] On a 'streamlined' BPTC, it was suggested by case study participants that professional associations could play an important role:

---

22 City Law School, 'Our History'; www.city.ac.uk/law/about/our-history [accessed 30th July 2017].
23 www.law.ac.uk/about/press-releases/2011/col-to-offer-accelerated-lpc [accessed 7th August 2017].
24 www.thelawyer.com/bpp-caves-in-to-pressure-with-fast-track-lpc-for-all/1006555.article [accessed 30th July 2017].
25 https://l2b.thelawyer.com/issues/l2b-online/ao-unveils-fast-track-lpc-despite-fears-over-two-tier-system [accessed 7th August 2017].

> For example, perhaps the Inns could have a role in that, having resources available. We obviously subsidise our members hugely with qualifying sessions which we do, perhaps that's something we could do for the Bar Course.
> (Interviewee 8, Inner, F, salaried)

When interviewees were asked to comment on the challenges they perceived to social mobility at the Bar, the BPTC featured heavily:

> I think it's a disgrace actually because it seems to be ripping people off. But every attempt that the profession has made to look at how we deal with that was ground into the dust on competition grounds.
> (Interviewee 9, Inner, M, Bencher, other prof. assocs.)

When asked about solutions to challenges posed by the BPTC, all suggested a greater role for the Inns as professional associations, supporting assertions in earlier chapters about the high regard in which practitioners held them. More generally, it demonstrates the power held by professional associations in an attempt to restrict the provision of specialist knowledge as a commodity produced by that profession (Larson, 1977: 14). It is argued that such increased participation, whilst potentially a way to make the BPTC more accessible, may be viewed as bringing a professional association into a commercialised arena in an undesirable way (Faulconbridge (2012) considers the challenges of close integration between education providers and City law firms).

Alternatively, however, such involvement by a professional association could be perceived as hope for a return to the levels of power previously enjoyed by the profession. Whilst the current picture of professional education for the Bar paints a somewhat dreary picture of private providers with purely commercial desires, a number of those interviewed clearly felt that greater professional association involvement in the standardisation and teaching of professional knowledge would benefit both the profession and aspirant entrants.

A resultant tension could be observed between the 'old school' model and the newer, commercial model. In such a traditional profession, lamenting for the 'old times' might be expected. For those interviewees that could remember it, there seemed to be a genuine belief that the ICSL's monopoly had had advantages: keeping costs relatively low, combined with acceptable standards of provision. These practitioners portrayed commercial providers as financially greedy and without care for the students whom they admitted knowing that their hopes of obtaining pupillage were slim at best. Younger participants had no memory of the ICSL, and consequently had few suggestions for improving the situation. Nonetheless their distaste at what they perceived to be unethical behaviour of commercial providers was clear.

It is not only those things outside of the profession which may hinder the effectiveness of interventionist behaviour by a professional association within it, however. The structure of the profession itself may pose particular challenges to such action, and these will now be explored, focussing particularly on the unusual structure of the Bar, and how this has affected the ability of Inner Temple to take interventionist action.

7.3 Structuring properties of the field

Any profession has its own structuring properties. It has both its 'hard' structuring properties, such as the hierarchy of its organisations (see Chapter 2), and its 'soft' structuring properties. Soft structuring properties are the accepted ways things are done within the profession, and how people within the profession think about things: their frames of reference and pre-conditioned choices and perceptions. When altering established practices, the field's structuring properties may exert as much force in determining whether change occurs as those external matters detailed above such as regulation and education.

The structuring properties of the field for the purposes of this research draw on many things already discussed, particularly the attachment to traditional practices, incorporating Bourdieusian ideas of habitus and doxa, and matters of institutional logics and how organisational change may be secured. Within a profession, established links between different organisations and specific roles for individuals may constrain the action that a professional association wishes to take. The significant constraint of multiple sites of power at the Bar was addressed in Chapter 4.

7.3.1 Soft structuring properties

If a profession is seeking to bring about a change, it may need to alter elements of its internal 'soft' structure to achieve this. Specifically, the recruitment of new, specialist staff (Braithwaite, 2010) with experience of different institutional logics (Friedland and Alford, 1991) may be necessary if a professional association is struggling to depart from time-honoured practices that have assumed a fallacious position of necessity, when in fact they are merely habitual (see 5.3).

A key 'soft' structural element at the Bar was recognised by Abbott as internal stratification (1988: 120). Even where access to a profession is open, once within the profession individuals stratify according to their specialist practice areas. Those dealing directly with lay clients (such as solicitors, and barristers in some practice areas) are regarded as lower in the hierarchy than those dealing only with professional clients, who are 'unsullied' by contact with non-professionals. Abbott argues that this is because the more a professional's work employs their specialist knowledge alone, and not other skills such as general communication or fact-gathering, the greater their claim to being a professional (1988: 118, 120). In certain practice areas at the Bar, Direct Access and realities of criminal and family practice mean that barristers compromise their knowledge with practical reality, lowering them in the perceived status hierarchy within the profession. In the case study, this soft structuring was recognised as having a significant effect. For many chambers specialising in criminal and family practice, there was seen to be less need to participate in access programmes, as they were already more diverse than most commercial and chancery chambers (Bar Council, 2014: 27, 105).

With greater emphasis on fact-management and people skills, any programme aimed at increasing diversity at the Bar is likely to hinge around the altruistic ideological commitment to the potential of every individual in the short term, whilst also marketing itself to the profession as a longer-term gain through creating a more diverse pool of talented candidates. There is also likely to be reliance on the transformative nature of a group being diverse to gather greater lived experience within its members (Sommerlad, 2008: 193). It may be for this reason that those whose main area of practice is criminal or family are more diverse and show greater social mobility than those whose main areas of practice are chancery and commercial, with the Working Lives Report in 2011 showing 65% and 60% of those whose main practice areas were crime and family respectively had been state-educated (Bar Council, 2011: 25). By the time of the 2013 Working Lives Report, this had decreased to 61% for criminal practitioners, but stayed the same for family (Bar Council, 2014: 105). Meanwhile, 71% of those mainly practising in 'Admiralty or shipping' and 66% in 'patent or IP' had been educated at fee-paying schools. Recent figures show that even within the traditionally privately-funded practice areas, students who are state-educated (and thus arguably more likely to be from a non-traditional background) are more likely to carry out publicly funded (and consequently less well-paid) work:

> State-school education is associated with an increased likelihood of doing publicly-funded work in the professional negligence/personal injury practice area (where 53% of state-school-educated barristers have received fees from publicly funded work compared with 33% of those who attended fee-paying schools), and commercial and chancery practice areas (where 32% of state-educated barristers and 16% of those educated at fee-paying schools received fees from publicly funded work.)
>
> (Bar Council 2014: 105)

Arguably a greater array of lived experience is more important in publicly funded work, focussing as it often does on matters of human interaction and difficult circumstances, in opposition to privately-funded work, much of which is conducted for businesses and hinges on interpretation of legal documents. The Bar itself shows some hints of recognising this difference of diversity between practice areas, with most PASS partner chambers carrying out most of their practice in commercial, chancery or related areas (such as media or intellectual property), as compared to proportionally much smaller numbers of participating chambers which concentrate on criminal or family work.[26]

7.3.2 Hard structuring properties

Hard structuring properties were observed to play two main roles in this research. First, the self-employed nature of the profession meant that fragmentation

---

26 According to the classifications on www.pegasus.me/?page_id=71 [accessed 30th July 2017].

between chambers was almost inherent, so any concerted effort needed to be headed by an organisation with the capacity to unite members from across sets of chambers. Second, many sets did not have the resources to employ staff who were experienced in access matters to run a programme themselves. Inner Temple could surmount these: it employed specialist staff, and facilitated links and idea-sharing between members who wanted to promote access.

When practical hurdles were removed, the willingness to support access programmes, which many interviewees said was prevalent at the Bar, could come to the fore. A recurring theme in interviews was that challenges to elements of the central value system were hampered by structural matters. For an ideology of social mobility to develop, there needed to be sufficient administrative help, which Inner Temple supplied for PASS. For many interviewees, it seemed that administration remained the biggest barrier to a professional project without social closure:

> Particularly at chambers' level we don't have administrative support that a big firm has; if you want to run your own programme it's often a barrister who's got to do that. He doesn't have time or skills necessarily to set it up and administrate it whereas bigger firms have HR departments ... I think the Pegasus scheme is very good at playing to the strengths of the different organisations involved.
> (Interviewee 2, non-Inner, F, other prof. assocs.)

The elite and removed position of Inner Temple allows the programme to have a much wider reach than it would if it was run by chambers, and it has a respect that seemed less present for other professional associations of the Bar, possibly because practitioners feel a greater attachment to their Inns. Such differential attachment was found by Francis amongst STEP practitioners, with many feeling more attached to their originating profession, regardless of the area they were currently working within (Francis, 2011: 130).

Crucially, Inner Temple also had the funding to run a programme. Some interviewees stated that specialist Bar associations benefitted from many of the same attributes as the Inns (a strong field position, community and wide reach across chambers). They were unable to run such programmes due to funding constraints, with an even greater reliance on voluntary support from practising barristers for co-ordination of activities:

> I suppose just thinking about how we do things with the FLBA [Family Law Bar Association] and what not, what the FLBA do when they need to get a message out or they need to get a job done, they contact every set of chambers and they identify a member within that set, an FLBA member who will be responsible for collating all the information, and they get fantastic responses as a result of doing that.
> (Interviewee 10, Inner, F, Bencher, other prof. assocs.)

The number of sites of power within the Bar differentiates the profession from most others. In both its general actions and setting up PASS, Inner Temple acted with relative autonomy. However, where there are other professional associations operating within the arena, the relationship between bodies exercising power will affect the interplay of actions (see 5.4).

Inner Temple's ability to act is increased by the structural properties of the field, bringing together members with a shared interest, usually through a committee led by a Bencher of the Inn. It is then possible to take directed action that would be difficult to achieve with the whole membership due to the plurality of views (Halliday, 1987: 136). In Inner Temple this group was the Outreach Committee as the decision-making body, supported with relevant practical knowledge by individuals within the Education and Training Department. One interviewee suggested that it was Inner Temple's decision to have a committee focussing on these matters that allowed it to take decisive action, meaning some perceived it as having 'moved ahead' of the other Inns:

> I suspect it is just because there is a committee dedicated to it and people care about it but I don't think people care more at Inner than they do at any other Inn. It's just that once you have a committee dedicated to it and people willing to work, then you can actually get things done.
> (Interviewee 4, Inner, M, Bencher)

This interviewee's focus on the ability to harness a willingness to act was echoed by others who also highlighted the interplay between willingness and the challenge caused by the structural properties of the profession in bringing that enthusiasm into a useful and co-ordinated form:

> I don't think there is a difference in terms of enthusiasm – I think the one really striking thing is there is a huge amount of goodwill in my experience right across the Bar for social mobility programmes. The problem is harnessing that effectively, and that's the really difficult thing.
> (Interviewee 2, non-Inner, F, other prof. assocs.)

The idea for PASS started life within a committee with the specific remit of outreach and access issues. When formulating an intervention aimed at encouraging social mobility, the Outreach Committee had started with an entirely blank slate to consider how best to pursue its aim:

> The first two sessions were just entirely 'blue sky' thinking of how can we ensure that we get the best possible candidates to Inner. It wasn't just getting numbers, we wanted the best possible candidates and to ensure that there are no barriers to anyone applying and no barriers on the basis of any protected characteristic, including, and it's not a protected characteristic under the Equality Act yet, socio-economic barriers.
> (Interviewee 4, Inner, M, Bencher)

This apparent willingness to consider any options for supplying the best candidates suggests that, theoretically, the committee was recognising that a programme to improve social mobility and thus supply the best candidates regardless of background might require a departure from established patterns of practice stemming from the central value system. The quotation also illustrates the close links between an altruistic act and one which is designed to supply the best candidates to the profession for its own gain (see 4.4).

However, when considering potential forms of intervention, entrenched practices were a challenge. The Inns have, for many years, been giving scholarships for the BPTC, a key function of the modern-day Inns. This focus could be detracting from meaningful consideration of other possibilities. One practitioner interviewee suggested that the Inns of Court formed part of the challenge, as their practices were entrenched – they focussed on particular matters and were reluctant to examine afresh how their efforts could be focussed in innovative ways to address challenges:

> Personally, I see the Inns as quite a big barrier because they each have their own way of going about things and historically have. For example, they put a lot of resources into their sponsorship programmes for BPTC students. My own view is that it comes too late in the process actually to assist the people that need it and if we could redirect those really very significant resources that are put in at that stage to an earlier stage we could make a much bigger difference. I don't think any of the Inns have got their head around it at all, because for so many years they have been supporting the BPTC, they see that as very much part of their role.
> (Interviewee 2, non-Inner, F, other prof. assocs.)

This suggestion of re-directing money to programmes engaging with non-traditional aspirant entrants earlier in their education fits with research on the importance of early intervention (see 1.1.2). This could heighten aspirations, prior to GCSEs and A Levels which have significant effects on future options. Despite the possibility of radical new programmes through the open-thinking exercise undertaken by the Outreach Committee, the programme created avoided a radical approach (see Chapter 6).

7.3.2.1 The role of committees

Within the professional association, and more narrowly within the Outreach Committee, opportunities for communication are created; the professional association is recognised as an arena for collective interaction, a role contributing to professional associations retaining influence over their professions (Greenwood, Suddaby and Hinings, 2002: 61). Undoubtedly the Inns form communities which allow communication both amongst members and between members and the professional association which would not otherwise occur. It also allows collaboration between organisations on projects such as PASS. In a committee setting, a common interest in the subject matter of the committee may also bring members together in a more than merely formalistic way, giving a forum for the sharing of ideas and reinforcing the community nature of such associations (Larson, 1977: xiii).

This internal collaboration facilitated within an Inn also extends to external collaboration, or at least the potential there for, between the Inns of Court. The four Inns liaise, allowing agreement and collaboration on a much greater scale than could be facilitated between individual barristers or sets of chambers. However, the level of co-operation between Inns was not agreed upon by interviewees, and a source of different opinions seemed to be their mode of connection to the Inn, illustrating the different opinions apparent even within one association (see 4.2.2)

It may further be said that a key structural matter is where the 'edge' of the profession is found (Francis (2011) explored cause lawyers and paralegals as occupants of this area). Arguably, with significant legal aid cuts under the Legal Aid, Sentencing and Punishment of Offenders Act 2012, the Bar, and particularly those practice areas in which non-traditional aspirant entrants are better-represented, is moving increasingly towards the 'edge of law'. Butler, Chillas and Muhr point out that every profession will sometimes be operating 'at the margins', an area described as contested, unstable, liminal and perilous (2012: 259). It may not seem immediately obvious what relevance the margins have to well-established professional associations, but it is argued that a desire to stay away from the margins contributes to professions behaving in novel ways. For example, a professional association may move away from occupational closure in an attempt to further secure its central status in a profession. In a modern world concerned with social mobility and success based on merit, it is embracing notions of social mobility that is likely to assist a professional group in staying away from those margins, whilst a deliberate continued focus on methods of admission which indirectly discriminate in favour of those who have followed traditional educational paths or have familial or social links to the profession propagates a view of the profession as 'outdated' and 'old-fashioned'. Increasingly, a policy of inclusivity will nowadays be more advantageous to a profession (Rogers, 2012).

The implementation of such a policy may be laborious. Not only might a professional association be constrained by its own structural properties and limits on its power, but it may also be constrained by events outside of its control. In this research a key challenge to the success of Inner Temple's intervention was external influences operating on PASS participants, who often had experience of a relatively limited range of social fields. These social fields were usually quite different to those encountered at the Bar.

7.4 'It's not the well-trodden path, really': peers, family and education of non-traditional aspirant entrants

As non-traditional aspirant entrants were likely to have experienced very different social fields to those existing at the Bar, part of the challenge is their ability to accept or minimise the cognitive dissonance that comes from entering a profession in which they are currently a minority group (Costello, 2005: 3–4).

Most young people's worlds are framed by their peers, family and school, all of which influence attitudes to education and career choices. A number of the focus group students displayed uncertainty about their 'future selves' (Markus and Nurius, 1986: 954); specifically, whether they would succeed in entering the profession, and their personal and professional lives if they did. Research has shown that students who are positive about their future selves are more likely to achieve their goals, as the 'future self' concept provides motivation (Markus and Ruvolo, 1989). Those who do not receive encouragement and support in their schooling from family, peers and schools are much less likely to have positive occupational future selves (Leondari, 2007). This was reinforced by focus group participants' comments that educational and occupational choices made by their peers influenced their hopes about a career at the Bar:

> Obviously some are influenced easier than others, but generally it's your peers, because if your peers are saying, 'Personally, I don't wanna do this anymore, school's not for me, I'm just gonna drop out and probably just live off Job Seekers' Allowance' or something then, and they're doing pretty good at it, you'll think, 'I don't see why I can't do the same thing.'
>
> (Pathways FG Participant 7, F)

Academic research explored earlier sets out the theory of institutional logics (5.3), and the abilities of staff to 'glide' between different fields (e.g. Meyer and Hammerschmid, 2006). Similarly, students need to 'glide' between Bourdieusian social fields to maintain friendships and community links whilst also behaving appropriately in professional settings (Francis, 2015: 192). For non-traditional students there may be a clash between practices and habits of schools and peer groups, and the Bar, and their relative marginalisation may make it harder to recognise and adapt to the differences needed in behaviour (Bauman, 2005: 135). Academic literature on these matters has highlighted the difficulties faced by those moving from one setting to another, especially if these settings are very different (e.g. Hinchliffe and Jolly, 2011), and this was perceived by participants in their own lives:

> And then my friends, it was again this slightly more obscure, slightly more niche choice, it's not the well-trodden path, really.
>
> (PASS FG2 Participant 2, M)

> We're not used to, I mean, I'm not used to the p's and q's that go with [the legal profession].
>
> (PASS FG1 Participant 2, F)

At their educational establishments, the PASS students had come across very differing approaches to their hopes of becoming a barrister from tutors and lecturers:

> I told my tutors, or at least one of them, and got sort of approval, as that's basically what he had done for a bit before he became a tutor, and you know, it ticks the academic box.
>
> (PASS FG2 Participant 2, M)

> I got told that by my uni; I got told several times to not bother with the Bar because you were like . . . [a non-traditional entrant] . . . In the nicest possible terms they couldn't've made it more clear that I should have a back-up plan.
>
> (PASS FG1 Participant 2, F)

Such (potentially well-intentioned) concern for a non-traditional student who is academically-able – the latter-quoted student had a first-class Law degree from the University of Surrey – suggests that some higher educational professionals are propagating stereotypical views of the Bar, and these may discourage non-traditional aspirant entrants who place trust in this information. Although not a focus of this research, there may be advantages to educating higher education institutions about the profession to support the efforts of other organisations in helping students make informed career decisions, a suggestion also made by the Neuberger Report (2007: 40).

To maximise the positive effects of interventions, partly by considering social fields, it is crucial that any group at whom an intervention is aimed are consulted about their perceptions and realities (Shah, Pascall and Walker, 2006: 9), as opposed to having assumed perceptions projected onto them by others (in Shah et al.'s research, young people with disabilities, or in this research, young people from non-traditional backgrounds). Such consultation is more likely to be possible where someone with relevant experience is employed by the professional association running the intervention, and in the case study feedback was sought from every participant. This research contributed towards an evaluation of that feedback for improving the programme.

Despite a knowledgeable employee and consultation with programme participants, it is not possible for a professional association's intervention to alter the personal and social contexts of aspirant entrants. However, formulating interventions with an awareness of these contexts means that the impact of a programme is less likely to be attenuated by them. This will require someone with expertise in education or access, as opposed to the profession's expertise, as experience with PASS has demonstrated. A key strength of professional associations in undertaking work to improve access to the profession is that where stakeholders within a profession (such as chambers at the Bar) are small entities it is likely that funding for such a specialist post will only be available at professional-association level. It would be both expensive and inefficient to have people doing a similar job in many chambers. Such a model where specialists are employed by the professional association, however, is only likely to be appropriate where professional associations are large and perceived as representative, but each operating unit of the profession is much smaller (e.g chambers), and many are therefore willing to hand over the formulating of such interventions to a central, trusted body.

The remaining question then is: how much power does that body continue to hold when it is a professional association? For some years academics have postulated that professions are declining. Either that they no longer exist as an entity, as jobs formerly done by professionals are broken down and compartmentalised in smaller, more specialised jobs done by employees (proletarianisation), or that they remain, but in a much less powerful form (post-professionalism). Muzio and Ackroyd (2008: 49) suggest that professionalism adapts through professionals taking defensive manoeuvres to maintain their privileges. The next section addresses whether, in modern society, a professional association is likely to have sufficient power to intervene effectively.

7.5 Effects of a post-professional world on the Bar

This research has depicted a profession and professional association reduced in power but by no means completely powerless. A key explanation for the loss of professional power has been advanced by Kritzer (1999), who suggests that a state of post-professionalism has now occurred due to societal changes affecting how the public interact with the legal profession, and how the legal profession carries out its business.

Kritzer's assertions certainly find support in the English legal system, and were recognised in the LETR (2013) (see 3.1.3). Some occurrences flowing from such changes have aroused suspicion, however, with Atlas Chambers' merger with 4–5 Gray's Inn Square having to be defended against rumours of a 'rescue deal', instead being portrayed as a controlled and strategic manoeuvre.[27] The increase in tasks done by those not fully legally-qualified has reduced barriers to occupational involvement with the law, but other research, as documented above, has suggested that professionalism, and the barriers that it creates, is still a live issue which the Bar needs to tackle to secure the best candidates.

Other legal scholars have suggested that rather than a changing conception of professionalism which nonetheless preserves its main tenets albeit in an altered form that may be construed as being less powerful, professions are, in fact, dwindling in their very existence. Neo-Marxist theorists have proffered theories of proletarianisation (McKinlay and Arches, 1985) and deprofessionalisation (Haug, 1973). Neo-Weberian scholars, meanwhile, focus on the ability of professional associations to change under the label of 'restratification' (Freidson, 1985). 'Restratification' developed from the academic counteraction of the 'deprofessionalisation' school of thought with the 're-professionalisation' thesis, which argued that where professional practices are redefined, negotiated and amended due to external actors such as markets and consumers, there remained a foundation of defining features of professions such as autonomy, collegiality and monopoly, with organisational and professional boundaries blurred (Muzio et al., 2008).

27 www.thelawyer.com/news/practice-areas/bar-news/merger-for-4-5-grays-inn-square-is-not-a-rescuesays-chambers-head/3001026.article [accessed 30th July 2017].

This research has illustrated that the elite within an organisation may still play a significant role in shaping the actions of a professional association, and that their role should not be overlooked. Therefore, any theory advanced as contributing towards an explanation of the actions of Inner Temple needs to recognise the potentially transformative role of the elite on a professional association, as well as its own capacity for evolution. The theory of restratification (Freidson, 1985) allows for this. Most research examining this theory focussed on the medical profession, and further academic investigation into the presence of restratification in the legal profession in England and Wales could be usefully undertaken. Existing research depicts a 'halfway-house' approach in which the professions retain their elite status and collective interests, but in a modern legal workplace with increased bureaucracy, managerialism and service-provision (Rogers, 2012: 208).

In the legal profession the elite remain instantly recognisable, especially within the professional associations, where Benchers continue to hold a lot of power in the Inns of Court. Therefore, a model which recognises the structural nuances of the field but still provides a method of explanation for the significant changes that it is undergoing offers an appealing alternative to those theories which sound the death knell for the professions as previously portrayed. However, restratification theory relies heavily on the presence of managerialism within the elite, something not apparent at the Bar, as the managerialist activity is not carried out by the Benchers themselves, but by support staff. Furthermore, the extent to which managerialism can develop at the Bar remains limited due to the autonomous nature of chambers.

The change within the elite's demographic itself as observed in this research also requires explanation, as such evolution is not catered for in original articulations of restratification, which assume that on joining the 'elite' (in this research, becoming a Bencher), a newcomer will largely conform to the existing norms. More recent scholars, however, have acknowledged that the elite can change (Waring, 2014: 696). In the case study, there was evidence to suggest that some Benchers were deliberately not altering their professional identities, instead continuing to manifest their previous behaviours and identities (as 'outsiders'), giving the elite a more 'accessible' feeling. These Benchers were credited with helping push PASS forward, as they themselves either came from non-traditional backgrounds, or had for other reasons felt like they were 'outsiders' when they arrived in the profession:

> I went to a state school and didn't tick any of the boxes really that I should have ticked if I had wanted to become a barrister.
> (Interviewee 10, Inner, F, Bencher, other prof. assocs.)

> I can't say I don't fit the natural stereotype barrister myself, I was at public school and so on – not one of the top few, but I remembered distinctly feeling a bit of an outsider when I first came to the Bar. I don't know if that is just a personal thing but if I felt like that I dread to think what someone from a more economically- or socially-challenged background would feel like.
> (Interviewee 9, Inner, M, Bencher, other prof. assocs.)

This was suggested by a member of salaried staff as important not just in garnering 'official' support for the programmes from the elite (necessary for internal support and funding), but also having programmes overseen and encouraged by Benchers with genuine ideological commitment to the programmes' aims. Where traditional structures nonetheless hold progressive groups, it is argued that it will not necessarily constrain action as might be expected:

> We have quite a young group of Benchers for the Inns, so [at] some of the other Inns the Benchers are just that much older, so I don't know what that might do to their perception of the Bar . . . I think just being a bit closer to the prospective students and seeing what that meant . . . And for whatever reason, from what I have seen, the Inn has quite a number of Benchers who come from less traditional backgrounds or at least they have felt comfortable enough speaking out to ensure that the Inn rides along with that course.
>
> (Interviewee 11, Inner, M, salaried)

This supports arguments made in Chapter 5 on the ability of individuals and small groups within organisations to effect change (Battilana, 2006; Braithwaite, 2010), and embedded agency. It also supports arguments that not only can demographic change occur within even a traditional profession, but it may do so openly, without a requirement that difference is disguised or denied. These Benchers had not felt the need to assimilate entirely the identities formerly associated with being Benchers; rather they held onto their identifying non-traditional features, despite the potential cognitive dissonance and discomfort (Costello, 2005: 3–4).

The elite appears to be evolving. New Benchers are not simply turning themselves into the existing elite, but are retaining their identities and, in doing so, are moving forward the wider commitment to social mobility. This may also be key to the maintenance of an elite, as it is not 'stuck in the past' but is progressive whilst maintaining elevated status, and it is argued that this allows the conception of professionalism to advance as well. In this way, the profession may evolve with less strife than expected, whilst still retaining what appears to be a traditional professional model.

7.6 Conclusion

Earlier chapters considered why a professional association might act to challenge a consequence of its central value system, and examined how this might occur. The case study, it was argued, was not as radical as it may first appear, due to its failure to challenge certain underlying assumptions which continue to privilege those from higher socio-economic backgrounds in entering the profession. It is not, however, only the formulation of the specific programme examined which may obstruct a professional association's attempts to improve access for those from lower socio-economic backgrounds.

Matters internal and external to the profession may influence the effectiveness of such a programme. Increased regulation of the profession may either arrest or assist innovation. Other matters outside of the control of the profession, such as professional education not governed by the professional association, may have a serious effect on social mobility within the profession, but be outside of the control of the professional association. Similarly, even matters internal to the profession may cause barriers. At the Bar, particularly notable are the structuring properties and the impermeability of social fields. The experiences of students may have a defining role in their perception of the profession, but also in their self-perception. The lack of control which a professional association has over many of these factors means that interventions must consider them, and be formulated with the intention of having a meaningful effect despite these constraints.

This chapter has portrayed a somewhat conflicted field. Whilst professional associations undoubtedly retain power, and particularly within their own spheres of operation, their general position appears much weakened. This has resulted from increased regulation, and a loss of control over key elements of the identity formation undertaken by aspirant entrants. Meanwhile, professions fight a battle in balancing their recruitment practices, seeking to balance exclusivity in talent with inclusivity in demographics. This is hampered by the relative lack of permeability of social fields, with aspirant entrants struggling to fit into a profession with very different social norms. Events external to the profession affect its operation in such contentious matters, with happenings in the political sphere and the educational sphere being particularly notable (see Chapter 1). To succeed in forming an effective intervention, a professional association must actively consider these constraints on its ability to act, not ignore them.

Politically, a commitment to social mobility generally, and reduced self-regulation for professions, has caused the profession's recruitment practices to be under greater external scrutiny than ever before. Huge gulfs in the educational attainment of children from different geographical areas and socio-economic backgrounds pose a challenge to establishing parity of achievement without parity of provision or qualifications.

Theoretical explanations for the reduced power of professions have been offered through post-professionalism (Kritzer, 1999), proletarianisation (McKinlay and Arches, 1985), deprofessionalisation (Haug, 1973), and restratification (Freidson, 1985). It is argued, however, that despite diminished power, professional associations, and especially those within the legal profession, do retain some potency. The appearance of retention of power has been reinforced by the framing of actions as voluntary choices rather than imposed necessities. In the case study, therefore, one perception of what has happened could be that, aware of the requirements set out in the LSA and enforced by the LSB, Inner

Temple felt that it needed to take steps to promote diversity, and did this by introducing a programme with this aim. By introducing their own programme, they retain control over it, and portray it as wholly their own choice, introduced free from external pressures and regulations, in line with Abel's observation that professions have generally sought to exert control over progressive initiatives instead of blocking them (1985: 12). This area is, it is argued, ripe for further academic investigation.

8 Putting theory into practice
General themes for access schemes

The preceding chapters have focussed on the 'behind the scenes' elements of an access scheme within a profession: how it might move from idea to reality through numerous stages and with various actors' involvement. They have looked at the theoretical underpinnings of how such a scheme is created, why, and by whom. Evaluation of PASS as a case study indicates which aspects of that programme are viewed as successful by stakeholders and participants.

Findings from that evaluation have much wider applicability. From the PASS data it is possible to identify attributes contributing to a successful programme. Some of these attributes are relevant to any access programme, whilst others are most relevant where the access programme is devised by a professional association but provided by individual collectives within the profession (e.g. firms or chambers). All have wider applicability than programmes within the legal profession.

This chapter does not claim to set out a blueprint for a successful access programme. The factors that influence whether any specific programme succeeds in meeting its aims and objectives (however they are devised) are many and varied, and depend on the context and structure of the profession within which the access scheme is set.

8.1 General principles

Some practical and theoretical aspects were raised consistently by participants, and these will need consideration by those developing any access programme. These are access to information; mutual exposure and benefit; aims and objectives; and challenging perceptions.

8.1.1 Access to information

A significant barrier for many non-traditional students to any profession is the provision of information. Even with swathes of information available publicly for free on the internet, this research illustrated differentiation between '2D' advice, such as that available on the internet, and '3D' advice, where the giver and students meet in an environment that permits and encourages interaction. When considering access to information, three matters need to be examined:

(a) Where are aspirant entrants currently getting information?
(b) What is the quality, accuracy, and quantity of that information, and where are the gaps?
(c) How might an access programme be placed to remedy flaws in the accuracy of that information?

Finally, this section highlights through the experience of participants in this research how information played a leading role in their attempts to access the profession.

A. SOURCES OF INFORMATION OUTSIDE OF ACCESS PROGRAMMES

There are many ways in which aspirant entrants might access information. This section's discussion is structured around a consideration of the main ways – formalised information through school, and publicly-available material.

Many students' careers information comes through school, often delivered as part of Personal, Social and Health Education lessons, and later more specialist advice through a university careers service if the student chooses to use that service. Existing research has demonstrated that such careers advice often offers 'solutions' to young people's 'deficiencies'. An employer-centred paradigm, focussing on increasing students' 'employability', serves the needs of students through meeting the needs of employers (Artess, 2014). Artess, however, suggested a more student-centred approach based on 'career-adaptabilities', focussing on the student as an individual, shaping a sense of identity and career-construction. By building upon prior learning (of any type) this is a more inclusive approach with students at the centre of career-related interventions (2014: 23). Programmes providing information through practitioners can reinforce this approach by empowering young people to make career decisions.

Such an approach might also ameliorate the suspicion young people feel about school-based careers' advice; a comprehensive literature review by Hughes and Gration illustrated that students perceived school guidance as subject to 'spin' (2009: 19–20). This may in part arise because it is impossible for careers advisors in schools and universities to be experts on every career path, particularly smaller professions with specific and somewhat specialised entry routes, and they may shy away from advising on 'difficult' or ambitious career paths.

Where entry to a career is heavily influenced by matters such as work experience undertaken at or by certain educational stages to be of maximum benefit, specialist advice will be desirable in addition to the general guidance and support given by careers advisors, the general value of which this research does not seek to impugn. One note of caution, however, is that some careers advisors may subscribe to particular stereotypes about the professions, which they share with the students, with potentially negative consequences (see 7.4).

This illustrates the importance of a rounded approach to access work. Outreach activities need to include careers advisors in further education settings. Much might be gained by access programmes running sessions with careers advisors, tackling myths about entry to professions, so their propagation, whether well-intentioned or otherwise, is discouraged.

As school careers advisors are advising students at an early stage, and thus fairly broadly, it is unlikely that targeting them with large quantities of in-depth specialist information will be helpful. Establishing a communication channel provides access to more information if needed. At higher education level, it is necessary that those who are advising have access to specialist information to reduce the risk of inaccurate or misleading information being given to students.

Events run by a professional association can offer effective outreach to university careers advisors through sessions providing targeted information about the profession. Proportionate approaches are likely to be materials put together by the profession for use in schools, and a more pro-active approach towards careers advisors at the university stage, including more direct contact with the opportunity to ask questions and engage with the profession in a relatively informal setting. Such information needs to highlight the importance of work experience, at what stage students should be undertaking this, and how students can be supported in making competitive applications, especially if prior to university they experienced educational disadvantage.

Students need information at a level of detail that they can understand, but which also addresses the complexities of the career, and is realistic about required skills and prospects of success. As emphasised throughout this book, access should not be about giving false hope to aspirant entrants, but supporting informed decision-making. For some participants in this research, it was access to information that was the attraction of contacts within the profession, not necessarily 'greater' advantages such as informal work experience:

> If I hadn't been on this course I wouldn't've met the people I've met and I wouldn't've got the contacts I've got. Then I wouldn't be able to ask questions that I wanted to. So I still think that you still need contacts in this area of work.
>
> (Pathways FG Participant 7, F)

The accuracy of the information provided is more important than the quantity of it. As demonstrated through Pathways and PASS, however, students also value subjective personal experiences, alongside the necessary objective factual information on qualifications, work experience and applying for scholarships. For this, direct interaction with members of the profession was necessary and appreciated, and may offer a stronger counterpoint to the information students receive through peers and family, which may be incorrect, and which higher education research has shown exerts a strong effect on career choices (Foskett, Dyke, and Maringe, 2004: 10).

Students in the focus groups had had very different experiences at university of the levels of support that they were offered when they told staff members that they were considering the Bar as a career. Some academic staff communicated strong views to students that they were 'not the sort of people' who would succeed at the Bar, even where they had achieved highly academically, compounding doubts students already had about whether they would fit in (see 6.3.2.2):

> The first thing I noticed when I walked into Bar School was that . . . I mean, I went to a state comp in Essex, I went to Surrey University. Always worked hard, got As and Firsts and stuff across the board, but I've never been surrounded by super posh and smart people, and then you get there and everyone's just got, they've got, they even talk in different languages sometimes.
> (PASS FG1 Participant 2, F)

Such advice may be well-intentioned; it is impossible to deny that the Bar is a highly competitive profession, and that many capable young people do not succeed as so few pupillages are available. Advice to 'have a back-up plan' may be perceived by higher education staff as prudence. What is crucial is that such warnings about the competitive nature of the Bar are not conflated with a perception that a student will not succeed at the Bar because of their socio-economic background. Better information provision for those in higher education about the Bar, how it recruits, and what it is looking for in candidates would be one way of addressing misunderstandings about the nature of the Bar leading to advisors discouraging non-traditional aspirant entrants on non-academic grounds. This was also recommended by the Neuberger Report (2007: 36–7).

At some universities, academic staff had experience of the Bar (often through those who had practised themselves) and in these institutions there seemed to be more awareness, and a stronger dialogue between the profession and the institution, allowing access to better information for the students:

> Inner's quite prominent in my university though, so most members of the Bar who are now academics are all Inner . . . How our dinners work, the barristers come from London are usually the people they network with quite often and so it's through them that they then get on to the scholarship interviews and what not and pretty much all of them are Inner.
> (PASS FG1 Participant 3, M)

Some practitioner interviewees also felt that more general careers information was not always accurate or helpful, with one saying that they felt that networking's importance was a myth perpetuated by universities:

> Students now are fed the idea that it's a lot about networking and it's not open to them if they are not networking, and I don't think there is any truth in that at all.
> (Interviewee 2, non-Inner, F, other prof. assocs.)

This is an example of a difference in perception of the profession internally versus externally. Whilst practitioners tended to attribute little weight to connections, students (both from Pathways and PASS) felt that they were important. Students and practitioners attaching weight to different issues highlights that an understanding not just of the challenges, but also of perceived challenges, is important. This again illustrates the importance of information dissemination; even if a profession does not agree that a particular matter is contentious, if aspirant entrants and educational institutions believe that it is, the profession will need to address it to maximise the effectiveness of the programme.

One PASS team member suggested that every university would have at least one young person who is a competitive applicant for the Bar academically, and that chambers need to recognise that talent can be found in every university:

> I think we're of the view there is at least one exceptional student at every single university and that is often very difficult for chambers necessarily to take account of. Especially when there is this level of competition and this many applications, some of the easiest things for them to do are to go back to those, 'Oh, the student from here must be good because they must have had really high A Levels to be able to get into this university', and so on.
>
> (Interviewee 11, Inner, M, salaried)

A lack of understanding within the higher education sector may be symptomatic of a wider lack of understanding of a profession that has historically 'kept its counsel'. This was perceived by participants as a further challenge to access that needed to be surmounted; first, the public needed an improved general understanding of the profession from which to advance the message of access based on ability. As some interviewees noted, the messages that the public receive through the media about the Bar are improving from previous times:[1]

> *Judge John Deed* is great TV but I am afraid it's not the reality. The recent programme with David Tennant [*The Escape Artist*] ... That at least had a character who wouldn't have been perceived to be traditional establishment ... and *Silk* shows a diverse range of characters and, very importantly, successful female practitioners.
>
> (Interviewee 4, Inner, M, Bencher)

Whilst the media is relied on by many for their understanding of the profession, that can lead to inaccurate perceptions. Participation in PASS had significantly improved many students' perception of the profession:

---

1 *The Trial*, a 2017 Channel 4 series featuring practising barristers, a recently-retired judge, actors as the defendant and witnesses, and 12 members of the public as a jury in a simulated case, was lauded by the profession for its realism. It attracted some criticism for editing decisions such as omitting the entire summing-up, and thus the burden and standard of proof. This led to some characterising it as a missed opportunity to educate the public about the process (www.kingsleynapley.co.uk/insights/blogs/criminal-law-blog/the-trial-a-murder-in-the-family-the-verdict [accessed 4th August 2017]).

> It still is Oxbridge dominated and it can't change that, so I don't think it changed my perception in that respect, but it certainly made me realise that they don't sit there in their wigs, or in suits, and even though they might be frightfully upper class and somebody who I will never have come across in my life before, it doesn't mean that it's not accessible or welcoming and they don't want you to be there or they're going to judge you because you're not like them, and I think that is what had changed for me in my perception of the Bar.
>
> (PASS FG1 Participant 1, F)

Effecting such a change in public perception remains a challenge which a professional association instigating an access programme needs to consider addressing through its wider outreach activities (see below). Educating the public about a profession is likely to need the effort and resources of more than one organisation.

B. QUALITY AND QUANTITY: HOW CAN ACCESS PROGRAMMES CONTRIBUTE TO THIS?

This research demonstrates that access programmes, when properly constructed, can contribute to fulfilling needs for both subjective personal information and objective facts. Members of the profession provided more detailed information in direct interaction with students, and explored more personal issues unlikely to be addressed in general careers material. This was praised by students in both the Pathways and PASS focus groups, suggesting that it should be integral to access programmes regardless of the target age group. Indeed, where there was variation between the topics covered by the separate small groups run by different barristers on the Pathways day, it was noted by the students that one thing that had been missing from some of the groups was a discussion of the more personal aspects of the career path:

> I was thinking our group session with barristers when we split up could have been more personal. We just concentrated on the cases the whole time . . . It could've been even more personal with a barrister, which I would've thought would've been much better.
>
> (Pathways FG Participant 5, M)

> Obviously, she can't tell us about it in too much depth cos that's her personal information, but, she was good I think. She gave enough information [that] personally I understood.
>
> (Pathways FG Participant 7, F)

As illustrated by the difference in the experience of these two students from different groups on the same Pathways day, small-group work also increased variation (as in chambers; see 6.3.2.3). This sometimes strayed to incorrect or out-of-date information. Such difficulties are almost inevitable when trying to reconcile students' desires to hear barristers' personal experiences with the need for up-to-date information. Where participating barristers have been Called some years previously different procedures applied. These journeys were, however, particularly valued:

> Listening to the barristers talking about how they got to where they are now; the path to the career from where you are now to where they are now.
>
> (Pathways FG Participant 8, M)

One way to address this is for members of the profession participating in access events to receive a regularly-updated briefing document for reference, whilst also being encouraged to discuss subjective experiences where these remain relevant.

Exposure to professionals can occur through access events where the aspirant entrants visit a location linked to the profession (i.e. a large firm or professional association) where members of the profession can be brought together to meet students, such as the Pathways model. Alternatively, such engagement can occur through students going into workplaces individually or in smaller groups in programmes such as PASS. The fewer students involved in each engagement, the greater the interaction. When asked about their favourite element, Pathways students mentioned the focussed attention of barristers in small groups, and hearing their personal experiences:

> I enjoyed everything, but thought that the group one was the best bit, as it allowed [an] opportunity to speak to the barristers in smaller groups, more privately.
>
> (Pathways FG Participant 6, M)

This value is not only from practical provision of information, but also the symbolism of time given by members of the profession engaging in such activities. This made students feel that the profession viewed them as worthy of its time and effort as potential future entrants (see 4.3.1).

C. MEDIUM OF INFORMATION

The value students placed on interaction with practising barristers, as an opportunity to access honest and realistic information about the profession, demonstrates that direct contact in less formalised and more routine settings facilitates both the provision of accurate information and exposure to the profession's human side. They could build a rapport with someone and consequently discover their experiences in a more personal way. This is supported by existing research showing that the value of work experience in later securing employment in that field seems largely related to the experiential element of having been within a workplace. Part of the experience is being able to meet and speak to existing members of the profession, and in this way assimilate linguistic and behavioural norms.

Having done this, an aspirant entrant is better able to present themselves in the way that chambers expect of aspirant entrants (Francis and Sommerlad, 2009: 65). This makes them a more convincing candidate when applying for pupillage, and may mediate socio-economic background (Sommerlad, 2007: 206). Direct experience also allows aspirant entrants to talk more convincingly about their desire to be involved in a particular area of practice. For those practice areas where very little experience can be gained apart from within chambers, due to the nuances and practicalities of the subject not being taught at degree level, mini-pupillages are especially important for this reason:

> You can't come to the chancery Bar without having done at least one mini-pupillage in chancery work, you just can't get there. I just don't think you can talk meaningfully about the work of the chancery Bar in a way that's likely to get you through interview unless you have actually experienced some of it, so I think it's absolutely vital.
> (Interviewee 2, non-Inner, F, other prof. assocs.)

This was reinforced by a PASS student who had selected 'chancery' because he was not sure what it entailed, and that this opportunity to explore a wholly new area of law had been very valuable to him:

> It does still give people a chance to say that this is something they're not very familiar with, or something they want to investigate as . . . I didn't really know what the word 'chancery' meant when I applied for it. I think it still gives people that opportunity, and so yeah, it was very valuable.
> (PASS FG2 Participant 2, M)

In professions with sub-specialisms this will be particularly important. At the Bar it is uncontested that different practice areas provide very different professional experiences. There are, for example, very few similarities between the typical days of criminal and chancery practitioners. The differences are stark: many people with the skills and temperament for one practice area would not be as happy or successful within another.

For these reasons, it is important to chambers that an aspirant entrant truly understands the area of law in which they are asserting a desire to practise. It is also important that they have experienced the realities of life at the Bar through the shadowing of a practising barrister:

> I didn't really, until gaining that experience, realise that a barrister's schedule on any normal day is that hectic, requiring them to lope across London; various courts, various hearings, juggling a multitude of cases in just one single day, going from one case to have something totally different, perhaps a preliminary hearing to something completely different, and then returning back to chambers in order to write an opinion, for example.
> (PASS FG2 Participant 1, M)

Whilst it is possible for it to be written down in an account of a barrister's day that all these things occur, it is only when experiencing them that it is possible to really appreciate the various dimensions – trains that run late, overcrowded Tubes, nowhere to get lunch and needing to wear comfortable shoes. Such practical aspects of life at the Bar, and its importance to understanding the profession, were not underestimated by practitioners, and students acknowledged that the only way to gain this accurate, mundane information was from practitioners:

> The ability to walk fast enough. It's very important in this profession; I didn't understand the importance of having good shoes and things like that. You have to walk around a lot and we move at quite a pace, so you know they have got to be able to keep up, so sensible shoes always.
> (Interviewee 1, non-Inner, M, chambers' rep.)

> Talking to actual barristers because there is no one better than them to tell [aspirant entrants] what it's really about.
> (PASS FG2 Participant 2, M)

When answering the pre-PASS questionnaire circulated to the 2014 PASS cohort (the second full cohort), many answers to the question 'Why do you think it might be important for you to gain work experience?' not only focussed on this value of experiential engagement with the profession, but many students explicitly linked their lack of familiarity with the professions with the need to undertake work experience:

> I believe it will allow me to experience the set of skills required to be a successful barrister. Also, it will give me an insight into a professional career that none of my family members currently hold.
> (PASS participant, 2014, pre-placement questionnaire)

Many responses to the questionnaires explicitly referred to a lack of familial or social links within the profession as a barrier to entry, regardless of the thoroughness of their own individual research:

> I've always wanted to be a barrister and I've done so much research; I've watched like every video there is on YouTube about being a barrister, and I've looked at every website possible. And then I came today and I found out stuff that I didn't actually know.
> (Pathways FG Participant 7, F)

Not only was there an opportunity to ask questions, but the PASS participants often emphasised how generous the barristers whom they had shadowed during their PASS mini-pupillage had been with their time:

> My supervisor was really, really lovely and he explained it all to me, and took me . . . spent a lot of time, a real surprising amount of time; I wouldn't really expect anyone to spend so much . . . so many hours just explaining about how the particular trust arrangement worked and this kind of thing.
> (PASS FG2 Participant 2, M)

This emphasises that any attempt to make participation in an access programme compulsory should be treated with extreme care. Barristers were the programme's direct contacts with students, and were repeatedly commended for their generosity of time and knowledge (see 6.3.3).

The students realised that this generosity could not be commanded by an organisation. It had to come from practitioners wanting to be involved. Had it been otherwise, the students would not only have had potentially negative views of the profession instilled or developed, but would also not have gained as much from the experience as they did in terms of assessing whether the profession was a career route they wanted to pursue.

For some non-traditional students, there was also the realisation that, even for those who were already practising within the profession from very traditional backgrounds, there was a desire for fair access:

> Even though they might be frightfully upper class and somebody who I will never have come across in my life before, it doesn't mean that it's not accessible or welcoming and they don't want you to be there or they're going to judge you because you're not like them, and I think that is what had changed for me in my perception of the Bar.
>
> (PASS FG1 Participant 1, F)

This individual openness to difference is key to building a perception of the profession as open to anyone able. Many PASS participants expressly stated how helpful and friendly barristers who were from very traditional backgrounds had been towards them, although one stated that 'background and schooling is still a focal point in conversation, especially with other barristers'; a challenge to access efforts.

A key transferable finding of this study is that access schemes will be most beneficial if members of the profession engaging in them do so with the intention of positively contributing to access. Many student participants remarked on the genuine enthusiasm which many of the barristers showed for the programme and its participants.

They also found that spending time with barristers exposed them to practices and social nuances that they could not have picked up elsewhere, but which might have inhibited them in gaining further opportunities (see 6.3.2.2).

As Beck and Beck-Gernsheim (2001: 23) note, every person has myriad identities, each of which is engaged when they undertake a different activity. Students will deploy different identities at school/university, with their friends and with family. Non-traditional students may not have had chance to develop a 'professional' identity that gives them the social tools that they need to present themselves well in a professional environment. These tools include ways of addressing others and self-presentation. Through mini-pupillage, students have an opportunity to witness the ways those already in the profession present themselves, and to develop an identity suitable for interviews and other interactions with the profession. Students identified this as an important opportunity. Equally valued, however, was openness and honesty about the realities of life at the Bar, and the situations and challenges that the students were likely to encounter as they moved from their university education through the BPTC and then pupillage applications.

Although many students perceived access initiatives as having one-way benefit through them accessing information, this was not necessarily shared by the profession. In programmes based on work experience it is particularly likely that there will be some mutual benefit; chambers can market themselves to, and assess, those undertaking mini-pupillages. The next section of this chapter addresses this mutuality of benefit, and how its benefit to both parties can be maximised to encourage participation in the programme.

8.1.2 Mutual exposure and benefit to participants and profession

All chambers took notice of the presence of mini-pupils. To what extent, and whether it was officially recorded, varied hugely between practice areas and individual chambers. Generally, in chambers that undertook principally commercial or chancery work, mini-pupillages were a compulsory requirement before an individual could even be considered for pupillage. For this reason, these sets tended to formally monitor the performance of mini-pupils. Many of these sets also required assessed written work, which was retained for reference should that individual then apply for pupillage. Meanwhile, at most criminal sets no record was made of mini-pupils beyond their name being written in the diary; a rudimentary record of their having had a mini-pupillage with the set.[2]

Even at sets where performance on mini-pupillage was important, it was emphasised that mini-pupillage was a two-way process. It allowed potential applicants to identify whether the set was one that they wanted to apply to, and chambers to 'sell themselves' to good students:

> We like to see mini-pupillages as a shop window for the good candidates to apply here for pupillage and so we like therefore to select people on merit.
>
> (Interviewee 9, Inner, M, Bencher, other prof. assocs.)

Some interviewees were upfront that participating in PASS gave chambers a chance to 'sell themselves' to promising aspirant entrants with whom they might not otherwise have had contact.

Alongside directed aims (such as the provision of work experience), most access schemes have at their core an implicit idea of mutual exposure where two parties who might not otherwise come into contact are brought together. Although this is often not a stated aim, it cannot be underestimated. Exposure both to the physical workplace and working norms allows students to assess whether the job's reality corresponds with their perception of it, facilitating an informed choice by someone who may not otherwise have sufficient information.

---

2 But nonetheless a long-living record: I was a mini-pupil at my set in July 2013, and in July 2017 received an amused email from the chambers' business manager with a screenshot of the 2013 diary for that week with my name in it.

For organisations this is also an advantage. Many employees and professionals would openly subscribe to ideals of equal access and opportunities for all talented young people. Nonetheless, they may permit practices implicitly disadvantaging such students without realising (see 6.3.4). An access programme allows members of a profession to meet young people who have been identified by a third party (either an unconnected individual within that workplace or by a linked but external organisation) as having potential. Through this interaction, existing members may realise that the absence of qualifications they would usually expect does not automatically mean that a young person is not a competitive candidate as a result of skills assimilated through other experiences (see 4.4).

8.1.3 Aims and objectives

To know whether a programme is 'succeeding', it is necessary to have defined that success, and how to quantify and measure it. Access programmes will be subject to constraints and tensions generated by a wide range of views as to the aims and objectives of the programme. Particularly at the level of a professional association or other organisation large enough to run an access scheme, there is likely to be at least a small committee which is taking decisions about the format, scope and administration of the scheme.

There are two ways in which a lack of clear aims and objectives may inhibit an access scheme. If there is explicit disagreement about the aims of a scheme it will be hard for it to be established at all, as such disagreements are likely to stem from, or contribute to, disagreements about the programme's structure and focus. Second, even an initial failure to consider and set out expectations for discussion and consensus causes difficulties. This may lead to internal tensions amongst those running the programme if there is no consensus on what the scheme aims to do, or how it relates to other initiatives, as seen in the case study:

> Interviewer: Do you think they form a cohesive path, the Pathways and then the Pegasus Scheme?
>
> Interviewee: No, because I very much hope that by the time someone has been through the Pathways programme they wouldn't need the Pegasus programme.
>
> (Interviewee 4, Inner, M, Bencher)

Although there was a broad agreement on the aim of PASS being 'to increase social mobility' and 'get the best candidates', there was no overarching consensus on how or why this should be achieved. A number of participants tracked the source of impetus for social mobility back to the Entry to the Bar Report (Neuberger, 2007), but there was also a feeling that the Bar had been making gradual, organic progress in this area for some time, even if that progress had gone unnoticed:

> I do think quite a lot of outsiders to the Bar would be surprised by the extent to which barristers are concerned about social elitism and social exclusivity at the Bar. I think outsiders all think we are quite happy in our bubble, as it were.
>
> (Interviewee 2, non-Inner, F, other prof. assocs.)

Indeed, one practitioner participant stated that she felt that the Bar had been in error in not drawing more attention to the progress it had made:

> I don't think the Bar is actually very good at saying actually we do do these things and we have been doing it for a long time . . . I think attitudes changed a long time ago and they are continuing to change. I am not saying it's perfect because it's not but, yeah, I think they are changing.
>
> (Interviewee 10, Inner, F, Bencher, other prof. assocs.)

Salaried staff who had come in from other organisations, however, disagreed with this. This illustrates that the internal perception of a profession may be very different to the external perception, and that incrementalism is a real risk when progress is being evaluated internally (Abel, 2003: 25–6). It also suggested that external staff felt that the Bar had been overly self-congratulatory when it had made belated progress. One member of staff who had been working for the Inn for five years observed a significant change within that time to the Bar's attitude as a whole towards access matters:

> I would say, though, when I started the line would be that the Bar doesn't have a problem. Perhaps it was denial, but I think it was more fundamental than that, that they truly believed that the Bar was meritocratic and that was their own self-perception. It was this own view of themselves: 'I got here and therefore anyone can if they work hard enough.' Almost [a] 'pick yourself up with your boot-straps' mentality and I think that has changed.
>
> (Interviewee 11, Inner, M, salaried)

Such differences of opinion even as to the starting position of the intervention may challenge its efficacy; Lewin (1952: 228–9) suggests that organisational change happens in three stages: unfreezing of the current practice, a move to the new practice, and then the refreezing of the new practice. Without each of these steps, a new practice cannot supplant an existing one. It is argued that such 'freezing' cannot successfully happen if it is not agreed exactly what it is that is being frozen. In the case study, it would be possible for Inner Temple to, within its own practices, 'unfreeze' (as termed by Lewin, 1952) social closure, implement PASS as a manoeuvre towards a commitment to social mobility, and then 'refreeze' its practices, including PASS.

Similarly, other literature discusses the need to 'anchor' or 'institutionalize' change (Jepperson, 1991: 148). Where institutionalisation of a new institutional logic occurs, it is likely to be secure as a new part of the framework by which those within the institutional logic relate to one another. If, however, it is simply 'action', Jepperson argues that it is susceptible to rebuttal by collective action. Where a professional association wishes to introduce a new facet into its institutional logics, it will see long-term effects only if it successfully institutionalises the new 'rule' within the central value system. This, however, remains subject to the inherent limitations caused by a lack of agreement and clarity on that which is being accepted as a new practice, or a new element incorporated into existing practice.

Rather like setting out on a journey as a group, if the end destination is not agreed it is likely that some of the travellers will end up frustrated, confused and disappointed. A lack of stated aims and objectives also makes evaluating success a very difficult task. Similarly, the inter-relation with other programmes needs to be clear within the mind of the organising body. If they are to form a cohesive structure offering specific support at different stages, then the inter-relation between them needs to be clear. In the case study, the only clear relationship between the programmes was that participating in the earlier programme (Pathways) was an eligibility criterion for the later programme (PASS). If no measures of success have been agreed, then against what will the outcomes of the programme be measured? Is participating in both programmes seen as a failure of the first? Furthermore, there are implications not just for those running the scheme, but also for the participants. If they do not know the aims and objectives of the programme before participating, unmanaged expectations may develop.

If programmes with the same target group and similar aims are not co-ordinated, duplication of effort to no greater benefit for the aspirant entrants or the profession is likely. Collaboration both within and between professional groups can extend the reach of such programmes by generating opportunities to engage in different ways or with different groups.

A strong influence on the comparison (non-PASS) chambers' decision to initiate their own programmes was that they felt that they were 'stretching themselves too thinly' by committing to various external programmes, and that creating their own would both increase cohesiveness within chambers, and also, through focussing resources, have one effective programme that they controlled, instead of different members committing to other programmes and efforts potentially being diluted:

> We were very keen to help out where we could but a lot of our clients, law firms, would have projects . . . and we would help out on all of these, we were always keen to help out, but it was usually very last minute, it was quite reactive rather than being pro-active. You couldn't measure how successful you had been. You do one one year, you might not do it the next year, and we weren't big enough to be able to take an active part in all the schemes, so we decided to stop all of those schemes and let other chambers take those on and just do our own scheme.
> (Interviewee 12, non-Inner, F, chambers' rep.)

When establishing a new programme, what it is seeking to achieve, and how this is to be measured and monitored, should be set out in clear language. Aims and objectives should be considered by all involved in setting up the programme, whatever their specific stakeholder position. Disagreements at this stage can be solved, allowing the programme to proceed with all parties understanding what the desirable end-point of the programme is, and how progress towards that point will be measured. This also assists with managing expectations, which is key for all stakeholders. In this research, the possibility that this had not been fully achieved was highlighted both by differences in opinions conveyed in interviews and also the implied perceptions of some student participants.

8.1.4 Funding

As noted at 6.3.2.1, financial assistance was greatly valued by participants: 51% of PASS respondents 'agreed' or 'strongly agreed' that payment of expenses had been crucial to them undertaking the placement. Whilst this does not mean that it was not helpful for the remaining 49%, it does raise the question of whether students should be able to opt out of receiving expenses if they feel that they do not need them.

This is not offered as a recommendation for an access programme due to concerns about the operation of a 'two-tier system'. It is, however, something to be considered when an access programme is being established. Only providing travel expenses to those who state that they need them is a way of maximising the number of students who can benefit from a programme in the aspects in which they need its assistance: there may be some students who can afford to pay travel expenses, but need the assistance of an access programme for other reasons, i.e. difficulty demonstrating traditional educational attainment.

Where a scheme is run at 'firm-level', if unfunded places are offered by some firms this may allow more firms to participate, for example those in areas where funding is problematic and thus cannot pay expenses for a student but may be wholly committed to the ideology of an access programme and wish to participate to show that support.

Another possibility is for the co-ordinating organisation to provide a set amount of expenses to participants for them to undertake work experience where and when they choose. This, however, would require them to apply through that organisation's usual application route, meaning that the student would not get the benefit of the specialist consideration given to application forms processed through a central system such as Inner Temple provided for PASS.

Requiring individual firms or chambers to pay expenses may have a limiting effect on which organisations can participate. For example, in the legal context, chambers doing mainly legal-aid-funded work are less likely to be able to fund mini-pupils. This will also be the case for many smaller organisations. At the Bar, data shows that it is the publicly-funded areas of practice which are already the most diverse (Working Lives Report, 2013: 27, 105), so an argument may be made that PASS's requirement for the payment of travel expenses does not exclude chambers in those areas of practice where both students and chambers are likely to benefit most from the mutual exposure of PASS. It is not safe to assume, however, that less well-funded and/or smaller organisations within a profession will be more diverse.

8.1.5 Changing the rules of the game, or teaching more people to play by them?

Information from some focus group participants suggested that participating in PASS simply allowed non-traditional aspirant entrants to 'play the game', instead of challenging the rules of that game which disadvantaged them. For example, they met people who then offered them informal work experience opportunities in the way that traditional aspirant entrants may be able to access them through family or friends:

> The lady I was sitting next to was a circuit judge at Southwark Crown Court, so I . . . got talking to her and she offered me a marshalling experience for the week, which was really good.
>
> (PASS FG1 Participant 4, F)

> I came to the Dinner to the Universities in March, and through the person I was sat next to got another mini-pupillage, so, in that sense, as well as the experience of coming to that event and meeting loads of people – lots of law students, lots of barristers – and being in this environment it was also making new contacts.
>
> (PASS FG1 Participant 1, F)

This highlights the risk that access programmes can limit their own reach by addressing deep issues in a superficial way. If aspirant entrants' gain from an access programme is an ability to conform with norms which are themselves fundamentally inhibitory to equal access, the programme has limited its own success. The highest measure of success for such a scheme is its ability to challenge underlying norms hindering equal access.

As discussed in Chapter 4 this may include norms such as how merit is conceived, or the weight attached to activities traditionally viewed as necessary, such as specific work experience. When designing a programme, it is necessary to consider whether there might be deeper underlying issues preventing a more diverse group of aspirant entrants entering the profession. If so, a programme will need to make attempts to tackle these if it wishes to secure longer-term change. Programmes which 'paper over the cracks' may seem appealing in the short term, but they will, ultimately, achieve little if there is a deeply engrained practice underlying them which is working against wider access.

The challenges of deconstructing underlying matters which made wider access difficult were illustrated in PASS – the ultimate conclusion as expressed earlier in this book is that it was well-intentioned, but failed to dismantle the importance of mini-pupillages. Perhaps the biggest hope for such a programme going forward is that gradually the challenges to underlying practices in the programme will permeate through the general practices observed in the profession. If chambers reformed their own mini-pupillage recruitment processes to be education-blind, this would obviate the need for an access programme aimed at mini-pupillage provision, as the changes it had sought would now be 'built in' to the general processes employed by the profession.

For a programme to truly challenge the 'rules of the game', it will need to target the inequalities of which unrepresentativeness is the outward manifestation. If it can do this its potential reach is much wider than those students participating in the programme. As it would be almost impossible for a programme to be of such a scale that it could reach every person who would be eligible under the selection criteria, it is only if the programme is mounting a challenge to the underlying practices that there will be change across the profession as a whole.

8.2 Context is everything: practical challenges

However an access programme approaches its endeavour, it will be affected by factors outside of its control. To ignore these factors is to ignore significant influences that will contribute to whether an access programme is successful or not. 'Context is everything', wrote Margaret Atwood in *The Handmaid's Tale*, and this is an area in which that is particularly apposite. Whilst Chapter 7 illustrated the general challenges faced by a profession-based access programme, there were also practical challenges relating to the delivery and organisation of a programme.

8.2.1 Challenges where a scheme is delivered at firm-level

In this section the phrase 'firm-level' refers to an access scheme delivered by autonomous organisations, such as individual firms or chambers. 'Professional association-level' refers to a scheme delivered at a higher level within a profession, such as an overarching organisation. PASS was a combination of these; it was administered at 'professional-association level' but delivered at 'firm-level'.

Administration at firm-level will only be possible where there are sufficient funds and administrative support within the firm to support a scheme. This is undoubtedly the case in some professions, and it is not suggested that schemes should not be run at firm-level where that is financially and practically possible. What is potentially lost, however, is the possibility of greater parity across a profession. If schemes are run at firm-level then there is no higher-level oversight.

As chambers are autonomous, variation between PASS chambers was inevitable. This is not in itself negative as it illustrates that chambers have different 'feels' to them. Variations that materially affect the experience of a PASS student may be a more significant issue, as highlighted below in the specific example of the integration of PASS students with direct applicants.

PASS students are explicitly required by Inner Temple to be placed within existing mini-pupillage availability and frameworks in chambers. For chambers, this was often an attraction of the scheme:

> The administration is done by Inner, which has its own resources and expertise, and then chambers just need to provide the same as they do to their other mini-pupils. I just think it's really clever to have set it up like that.
>
> (Interviewee 2, non-Inner, F, other prof. assocs.)

This, however, led to significant variance of experience. Some chambers had well-established and comprehensive mini-pupillage programmes which included additional activities such as advice on applications and mock interviews. Other chambers, often those that were smaller, had very little structure for mini-pupils, and their experience depended entirely on which barrister they were with, and their type and amount of work. Similarly, different chambers offer mini-pupillages of differing lengths; those participating in PASS varied from two days to a working week. Students who undertook mini-pupillages lasting two days expressed a wish to stay longer, or to have another mini-pupillage at another chambers so that their overall experience lasted five days. This was especially so where they undertook their mini-pupillage during a quiet time of year; one student on a two-day mini-pupillage was sent home early on one day as there was nothing for them. Many benefits of the programme are experiential from spending time with, and conversing with, barristers. Therefore, it is possible to see why students on short placements may feel that they have not benefitted as much.

The autonomous nature of chambers means that they cannot be made to change their own mini-pupillage set-up to give standardisation across PASS chambers. Whilst chambers could be asked to comply with certain requests about the experience PASS students have, the variety of sizes and types of chambers, as well as their practice models, make this difficult. However, a 'best practice' document may reduce avoidable variations impacting a student's experience. A number of the matters that impacted on students' experience concerned how they were presented within chambers and integrated into the chambers' mini-pupillage framework (see 4.4.1.2). Any professional association considering a firm-level access programme needs to consider how it will be affected by inevitable variations between the providing firms, what effect this will have, and what, if any, steps can be taken to ameliorate it.

8.2.2 Timing of the programme

Some students felt that they would have benefitted from participating in PASS earlier in their academic careers. The general advice is that students apply for PASS in their second year of undergraduate study, although some focus group participants had applied later (during the GDL) and one had applied earlier (first year of university). The latter student felt strongly that he could capitalise on its benefits by applying for further mini-pupillages whilst still at university. Some who had participated at a later stage felt they would have gained greater benefit earlier in their university careers.

Many firm-level organisations, however, will only take students over a particular age or level of education. For example, many chambers will not take mini-pupils until they have completed two years of a Law degree, or three years of a non-Law degree:

> The problem is that about a quarter of the chambers on PASS will take first-year students. And those are in specific practice areas as well, so it can be quite difficult for us to do that [take students earlier], while all of them will take final-year law students.
>
> (Interviewee 11, Inner, M, salaried)

Logistical issues make work experience-based programmes difficult to introduce for younger students; interviewees noted particular issues in family practice due to courts sitting 'in camera' and thus students having to be 18 to attend. Others talked about the difficulty of the subject matter and inter-personal skills needed in other areas making having a young person accompanying the barrister a potential problem. Other professions are likely to encounter similar considerations.

An Inner Temple employee justified the stage at which PASS has been placed:

> I think we were also mindful that we wanted something to sustain the relationship with our Schools Project students entering university stage and then hopefully thereafter. So it was a bit two-pronged insofar as we are missing those students that might not have been on the Schools Project but that would have fit in that category, and I don't mean 'we' as an Inn, but 'we' as a profession, and secondly that a lot of the students from our Schools Project would then have this issue going forward and we want to support them.
> (Interviewee 11, Inner, M, salaried)

Nevertheless, some participants, both students and practitioners, suggested earlier intervention:

> Just talking to barristers, so barristers visiting schools and that kind of thing, perhaps at the earlier stage; year 9 or 10, maybe, while their GCSE and A Levels are still in the future, or people who are about to start university.
> (PASS FG2 Participant 2, M)

Earlier intervention before public examinations such as GCSEs is also supported by general research on social mobility. Jerrim, Vignoles and Finnie (2012: 22) highlight the need for early intervention and encouragement for children from lower socio-economic backgrounds so that their attainment at a very young age does not bar their path to higher education. For the Bar, where academic achievement is important, there is an argument to be made for intervention before such examinations, due to their ongoing impact:

> Academics are important. If somebody had got A Levels that are C's, B's, D's and they have got 2:2's in [areas of chambers' practice] that probably is almost certainly going to be a 'no'.
> (Interviewee 5, non-Inner, M, chambers' rep.)

Profession-specific intervention at such an early age is likely to be contentious, however, and for many professions placement-focussed interventions would be practically impossible. There are other ways of the profession engaging with younger students, as demonstrated by the Pathways programme. What is not possible in such engagement, however, is the experiential element so valued in PASS.

The non-PASS chambers involved is known for its progressive approach within the profession. In this spirit, it had decided against the offering of mini-pupillages from its beginning:

We decided not to do it because they traditionally were [. . .] whilst you were at university and you would know somebody and you would go along or there might be a more open system, but it was mostly through people that you knew and then you would go along and you would shadow a barrister and go to court and see what it was like . . . It seemed to us to be very unfair to people who didn't have anyone that they knew, and also that they were unpaid [which] we thought was awful.

(Interviewee 12, non-Inner, F, chambers' rep.)

Instead, it offered work experience which was the same as mini-pupillage in many material ways, but at an earlier age and with expenses paid:

It's for people through from GCSEs to A Levels. Now that isn't to say, we have had sometimes had people who are at university, but that is who it is meant to be for . . . So there is an application form that you have to fill in, your teachers have to fill in a bit or somebody has to fill in a bit . . . It's not a CV, it's an actual application form about you, and we read those quite carefully and then we allocate places against that. We pay travel expenses and we pay expenses whilst you are here, so [we] make sure you get your lunch and pay for you to go to court.

(Interviewee 12, non-Inner, F, chambers' rep.)

This chambers had rejected the entire premise of unpaid work experience, instead offering two different alternative options. The first being that described above, and the second a broader programme of access activities targeted at a school local to the chambers (in central London), through which it fostered a longitudinal relationship with students which began in the school, and then extended to work experience:

We do that with a local school and one of the reasons why it's so empty downstairs is because some of the staff have gone this morning. They have got . . . it's like a skills morning, it's some kind of careers morning for the kids in school . . . They are all having to fill in application forms. They have had to do that in advance, send them to us in advance. We sifted them as we would sift the usual, and then we are interviewing them, so they are getting interview practice.

(Interviewee 12, non-Inner, F, chambers' rep.)

This chambers felt that its work experience programme addressed the need for earlier intervention to give students information about the academic qualifications needed:

We thought we needed to start at a much earlier point . . . You have (a) to know that it is available and then (b) you have to know what kind of grades you need . . . I think it's important that people know it is a role that they could do but that you do have to work hard for it.

(Interviewee 12, non-Inner, F, chambers' rep.)

This chambers did a lot of criminal work, and found that taking younger students into the criminal courts had not posed a problem. Criminal trials are ordinarily open to the public, so provided a younger student is suitably-behaved, this is unlikely to be problematic. Section 73(1) Access to Justice Act 1999 amended s.36 Children and Young Persons Act 1933 to allow a child (defined as under 14 years old) to be in court if the Judge permits. As stated above, however, this may not be so in all areas of practice. This provided an interesting model for comparison with PASS. It addresses concerns over intervening too late to make a substantial difference, and also removes the focus from traditional mini-pupillages. Instead it focusses on engaging young people with the profession before they have taken important educational choices and public examinations, prioritising the provision of information which many participants felt strongly was lacking for many non-traditional aspirant entrants. It also uses a model of work experience which does not favour pre-existing links to the profession, coupled with information provision and skills-building.

8.3 Going forward: incorporating an access programme into usual practice

A way to make a programme's contribution lasting is to engage 'firm-level' organisations in examining their own practices surrounding the target matter. It was clear from interviews that shorthand measures for success were often used when reviewing direct applications to chambers. This was usually not out of malice or discrimination, but lack of understanding around social mobility and educational disadvantage, and time constraints on those reviewing applications and selecting mini-pupils. Barristers, not administrative staff, were administering applications alongside heavy workloads of their own. Therefore, although some tried to make rudimentary adjustments aimed at increasing the fairness of the system, they accepted that it was not ideal (see 6.3.1).

For many participating chambers, therefore, the administrative support that Inner Temple gave by receiving applications and selecting successful applicants was very important. However, if a programme is to have a long-term wider impact, individual firms need to be encouraged to adopt relevant practices, e.g. from PASS, similar education-blind application forms and sifting practices. These aim to identify interest, motivation and skills, not simply traditional academic achievement.

One chambers from which a representative was interviewed was already doing this, but this was a large chambers with more dedicated administrative staff than most. This allowed it to run a comprehensive mini-pupillage programme, including networking events, application workshops and mock interviews. Although this scale of undertaking could not be provided by many chambers, it would be a one-off process for many to re-structure their mini-pupillage application forms, procedures and selection criteria to focus more on motivation and potential for a career at the Bar through skills gained, and less on traditional measures of academic achievement. This is a more effective way to open mini-pupillages to a more diverse range of applicants in the long term. By incorporating best practice from PASS into the usual practice of more chambers, non-traditional aspirant entrants would be more likely to succeed through direct application processes.

An access programme can be the seed for change. Unless it is big enough to incorporate the whole profession, however, it needs to germinate ideas and good practice which can be tested and, if effective, spread through the profession. Also relevant to a programme's reach are its duration and extent of intervention.

8.3.1 Extension of support

All research participants were asked how they would construct an access initiative with limitless funding, or how they would develop PASS further on those terms, to explore what elements they would prioritise. Many stated that Pathways and PASS worked well, but had narrow reach, particularly geographically. This quotation is representative of many interviewees' views:

> I am very conscious of the fact that Pathways is London-centric and limited in the number of people it can help, but that's no excuse for doing nothing, and I am also conscious of the fact that the Pegasus Access Scheme is very important for some, but I would like to have more people applying through it. But I think as people become aware of that, the academics we talk to become aware of that and recommend it to their students, then it will do that.
> (Interviewee 4, Inner, M, Bencher)

8.3.1.1 Longitudinal

Many interviewees and students wanted the programme to continue after the mini-pupillage. Commonly, suggestions for such a continuation were networking events, individual mentoring or workshops on completing application forms, for example. The value of such ongoing programmes is supported by longitudinal research over two years showing that careers information, advice and guidance for adults was generally more effective when experienced as part of an ongoing process, rather than as an isolated event, and in-depth support was positively associated with a range of observable learning and career outcomes (Pollard et al., 2007).

The main hurdle to this is finite financial and human resources:

> I think a lot more can be done with PASS. We are looking at how we can make it a more [indistinguishable] scheme as well, so CV workshops, or networking or quite practical apart from just the mini-pupillage, but capacity-wise we are incredibly stretched and while you don't think those things might take too much effort, actually they do. So it's less what we want to do but more whether we will be able to do it at this stage and it always means if we do change things, which almost invariably requires resources in terms of time, that we have to let something else go.
> (Interviewee 11, Inner, M, salaried)

This quotation, however, demonstrates that both Inner Temple and the student participants envisaged similar activities in extension of PASS. Students were aware that, even after they had secured mini-pupillages through PASS they still had to clear further hurdles: additional mini-pupillages, scholarships, the BPTC and ultimately securing pupillage. These were all perceived as difficult things to achieve, and especially so without specialist support from those who understood how the system worked.

Therefore, a further recommendation from this research was that consideration is given to the extension of PASS by, for example, mentoring, workshops on applications or informal events where students can mix with barristers. As discussed below this may raise a difficult question as to whether more support is given over a longer period for fewer students, or whether the current support level is maintained but with the numbers currently involved.[3] Discussion on extending the programme also focussed on geographical reach, and the possibility and desirability of involving more chambers that were out on circuit through England and Wales.

8.3.1.2 Geographical

PASS currently focusses on London chambers, though eight regional sets participate.[4] Such a narrow geographical spread will limit the number of students who can participate. Although travel expenses are paid there remain large areas of the country from which travelling to London every day is not feasible. In response to this research, PASS students who are not London-based now get self-catering accommodation (and an allowance for food) for the duration of their mini-pupillage.

The clear issue is cost. Using funds for accommodation in an access programme may mean that fewer students can participate as less money is available for travel expenses. The question therefore arises whether more financial support should be given to fewer students, so that it is possible for students from anywhere in the country to participate, or whether less support should be given to more students, with a focus on travel expenses, restricting the geographical reach of the programme.

Expanding the reach of a programme is also reliant on ensuring that students hear about it. With advertising costs potentially taking money away from the programme, careful thought needs to be given to whether to purchase professional advertising, or rely on word of mouth.

---

3 PASS now includes a two-day skills session including interview practice, resilience training, advocacy training delivered by practitioners, and a mock trial.
4 Atlantic Chambers – Liverpool, Enterprise Chambers' Leeds' annexe, 37 Park Square – Leeds, Chartlands Chambers – Northampton, Guildhall Chambers – Bristol, Linenhall Chambers – Chester, No5 – Birmingham, St John's Chambers – Bristol; www.innertemple.org.uk/becoming-a-barrister/how-to-get-involved/pass/our-partners [accessed 19th November 2017]

8.3.2 An ethical conundrum?

Careers-based interventions on access raise additional tensions in a competitive profession. Are access programmes in such professions aimed solely at 'recruiting' those from socio-economically disadvantaged backgrounds, or are they aimed at a more widespread audience to generally improve access by disseminating information about the professions? This issue has caused tensions more widely than simply amongst participants in the case study of this book, with current President of the Supreme Court Baroness Hale speaking on the matter at least twice in the few months prior to the fieldwork. She stated in an interview that legal aid cuts would cause the Bar to return to being 'white, male and Oxbridge'.[5] This had been preceded by her keynote speech in October 2013 at the launch of the Young Legal Aid Lawyers' report into social mobility, 'One Step Forwards, Two Steps Back', in which she stated:[6]

> What is the point of all our outreach work with schools, of the Sutton Trust's splendid Pathways to Law programme, and similar initiatives by the professions, if we tempt more and more young people to aspire to a legal career that most of them can never have?

This logic was hotly disputed by a key figure in PASS at Inner Temple:

> I have always seen outreach as providing good careers advice and hopefully aspiration-raising more generally to students who might not otherwise have it, and careers advice includes realistic expectations of what the profession's gonna be like. You don't get that by closing the doors. By lifting the bridge you will not get a more informed prospective group of students.
>
> (Interviewee 11, Inner, M, salaried)

Much of the data collected for this research suggests, with all due respect, that Baroness Hale has misconstrued the effects of programmes on participants. Most of the responses, both in focus group settings and on the online questionnaires filled in by Pathways students and PASS participants, suggested that students were under no illusion as to the challenges that they faced in pursuing a career at the Bar. Akin to Sommerlad's cohort of LPC students (2007: 200), many student participants acknowledged scant understanding before participating in the programme, with one describing his knowledge of the Bar as 'quite insubstantial up until [PASS]', and a Pathways student not understanding how self-employment worked, thinking that it meant not getting paid at all (some of

---

5 'Legal aid cuts will help public school boys get to the top, says top female judge', Louisa Peacock, *The Telegraph*, 18th April, 2014.
6 Keynote speech, Young Legal Aid Lawyers Conference, London Southbank University, 30th October 2013.

my colleagues at the Criminal Bar may share that understanding at the moment). Lack of knowledge and misunderstandings seemed to be ameliorated by the programmes, to the extent that this could be judged in responses. It is argued that this is an element of access schemes in the professions that is vital, and the dissemination of information should never be discouraged on the basis that entry to a profession is already very competitive.

Furthermore, even for those students who concluded that the profession concerned is not their desired career, participating may nonetheless raise their aspirations by illustrating that a professional career is an achievable goal. This was also recognised by practitioners whose chambers participated in PASS, identifying that non-traditional students gained something more fundamental from mini-pupillages than simply a knowledge of the law or an understanding of the daily realities of being a barrister:

> You see these kids on the Monday morning and they look terrified. By the time you see them on the Friday afternoon and they have completed their week, they are walking two foot taller, they say they have confidence and you can see it in them and they say things like, 'Even if I don't come to the Bar there are things that I have learnt this week that I will always carry with me' . . . We are not trying to turn them all into barristers, we are trying to give them a look into a world that maybe they think is not for them.
> (Interviewee 10, Inner, F, Bencher, other prof. assocs.)

The most important factor in the content of interventions such as this is not the information given that is specific to the profession (although for some participants that will be of the most interest) but the more general information about occupational success, and raising aspirations to professions by showing them as open to anyone with strong academic achievement, and guidance on how to achieve this:

> The most important things I took away were not at all connected to the Bar, it was just about useful life skills: how to do well at university, this kind of thing. They were the most important things that I actually learnt on the way back from this thing in Kent at Chatham County Court, on the train talking to my supervisor. That was the most useful conversation, and that's really the gold.
> (PASS FG2 Participant 2, M)

Whilst the legal knowledge content of access interventions is useful and interesting for many students, if the programme is viewed as fundamentally an aspiration-raising exercise, as well as a method of gaining work experience, the general encouragement which comes through close contact with professionals is as crucial. For the specific information relevant to the Bar to be conveyed in this way it is necessary that practitioners are engaged in these programmes, and that it is the profession itself telling its story. This gives accuracy and shows willingness to engage with aspirant entrants. This is particularly important due to the sometimes misleading (albeit well-intentioned) information given by peers, the media and sometimes staff in educational settings.

8.4. Conclusion

Disproportionately higher attainment by students from a higher socio-economic group relative to their peers in lower socio-economic groups from a very young age (Feinstein, 2003) illustrates that early intervention is likely to be key in ensuring that young people from disadvantaged backgrounds attain the school-level qualifications needed to make them realistic and competitive entrants for the legal profession. Nonetheless, in the case study Inner Temple chose to focus its intervention on providing work experience (other events, such as Dinners to the Universities and careers presentations often attract more traditional entrants).

For any change made to be sustainable, it is necessary that the profession as a whole embraces different recruitment practices. Established professions tend to take on a 'caste-like appearance' (Larson, 1977: xv). This is unsurprising when it is well-established sociologically that people tend to choose others similar to themselves when, for example, administering recruitment processes (Mossman (2006) details this phenomenon's effect on women seeking to enter the profession for the first time). The situation then becomes cyclical: the profession is comprised of demographically-similar people, because when recruiting, the people already within the profession choose those most similar to themselves, perpetuating homogeneity within the profession. It therefore becomes increasingly difficult for people from other demographic backgrounds to enter. Although there is often no malintent, or even conscious intention, borne by those who select others similar to themselves, it clearly represents a significant hurdle to entering the profession to those who are under-represented within it that cultural reproduction within the workplace leads to certain candidates being more likely to be successful.

Broadly speaking, there are two strands to the problems facing the legal profession that mean that non-traditional practitioners are under-represented. First, proportionally fewer non-traditional aspirant entrants consider seeking entry to the profession, and second, a large proportion of those that do are inhibited from fulfilling the requirements to enter the profession as the course fees for the LPC and BPTC are prohibitive. The interventions explored here are aimed at the first of those problems. They are, unfortunately, not able to solve the second problem, which, due to provision by private providers of the training courses, is somewhat stand-alone.

However, non-traditional aspirant entrants being discouraged from a profession by feeling that it is for 'different people to them', or is unwelcoming, is more susceptible to influence through a change in the way the profession portrays itself. In the case study, much focus fell on the potential of PASS to change perceptions of the profession held by non-traditional aspirant entrants, with themes of diversity, inclusiveness and meritocracy prevalent, especially in response to the open-ended question on Inner Temple's feedback form, 'Has PASS changed your perception of the Bar and barristers? If so, how?' This quotation is representative of responses:

> The Pegasus Access Scheme has changed my perception of the Bar and of the barristers. Before the scheme, I felt that becoming a barrister would be very difficult due to my background. However, I was impressed at how diverse the Bar was becoming and the PASS is a good example of this. Having undertaken work at a top chancery set, I now have a renewed confidence to pursue my goal as a barrister.
>
> (Inner Temple Feedback Questionnaire, Cohort 1)

For many stakeholders, in fact, this possibility seemed uppermost in their minds, above the potential for a change in the demographic composition of the Bar, which many raised but then discounted as being unrealistic for a programme of this limited reach; a legitimate concern.

Programmes will be restricted structurally by the nature of the originating profession. At the Bar, the prevalence of self-employment in autonomous chambers and the consequent lack of consistency in the provision of work experience meant that PASS had to accommodate these variations to include as many chambers as possible. As the professional association in a self-employed profession it also lacks coercive powers (and it is not suggested that, even if coercive powers were held, their exercise would be appropriate in these circumstances).

Action could be taken, however, to surmount variations in the expectations of participating students by communicating clearly to them what participation will involve, and by providing 'best practice' documents for programmes delivered at firm-level. This could reduce variations whilst recognising that, in the case study, all chambers had established mini-pupillage programmes, as this is a requirement of them joining PASS. Geographical reach, advertising, and longitudinal support are all factors that need consideration prior to a programme beginning to maximise benefit to participants.

9 Conclusions

Multiple factors affect whether a professional association is capable of instigating change within a traditional profession. It is the interplay between these factors, as well as their presence and strength, that influence the professional association's ability to act. Exploring these factors sheds light on professions and professional associations more generally, although no generalisability is claimed due to the methodology used. In focussing on one profession through a case study, and specifically on the actions of one professional association, this research has sought to explore an area previously neglected: the Bar of England and Wales. In examining this particular profession, it has also examined why social mobility appears to be less-demonstrated at the Bar than in other professions.

The role of the profession's elite has been identified as key. Despite some scholars' suggestions that the elite's influence is diminishing, implied by theoretical frameworks confining it to a peripheral role (e.g. McKinlay and Arches, 1985; Haug, 1973), this research suggests that, at least at the Bar, this decline is not evident. Within a professional association the elite may retain control over the direction in which the professional association is moving, and in the case study its influence was clear. Its support brought access to funds and internal influence that were necessary where a professional association with a longstanding central value system was seeking to create an intervention challenging practices that had developed through that value system, which were themselves longstanding.

Not only does the elite retain more power than some scholars have suggested, it may evolve. In the case study members of the elite did not conform as strongly to the traditional demographic of the Bar as may be expected. This was acknowledged by participants as crucial to the willingness of the professional association to undertake activities aimed at encouraging non-traditional aspirant entrants, and of increasing awareness within the profession of the additional challenges faced by such entrants in trying to enter the profession. On joining the elite, these individuals retained large parts of their non-traditional or otherwise 'outsider' identities, and seemed to use these as both motivation for encouraging increased participation, and to demonstrate to non-traditional aspirant entrants that success was a possibility for them. They also used their awareness of these challenges to encourage the profession to consider the importance of access and how to support it. Evolution of the elite has previously been overlooked by research, and further exploration could yield more information about the elite's relative power within more modern and differently-structured professions, as well as factors influencing evolution within the elite.

The importance of individuals at all levels, recognised in existing research, was supported in the context of the Bar. Particularly key was the collaboration between individuals who personally possessed various resources, or had access to them through their position within the organisational hierarchy. No one group could access everything it needed to establish an intervention targeted at a longstanding manifestation of the central value system. Instead, each group had a niche: salaried staff brought specialist knowledge about the target matter, and different institutional logics assisted them in utilising their knowledge effectively. They questioned accepted practices and innovated, influenced by their experiences of other institutional logics assimilated from previous workplaces. Collaboration with similar-level staff in other professional associations within the field maintained cordial relations. Meanwhile, as discussed above, the elite had access to funding, hierarchical leadership and internal influence, which they used to gain both practical and theoretical support for the project.

Hierarchical leadership alone was not enough, however, and this research supports management theories (e.g. Kotter, 1995; 2013) expounding the distinction between management and leadership. This distinction was notable; a member of salaried staff who occupied a fairly low hierarchical position was regarded by members of the professional association as showing influential leadership crucial to driving the project.

Whilst this research illustrates the continuing relevance of factors such as size and field position to the ability of a professional association to act, it makes two notable observations on the attributes of an effective professional association. The first is the role of individual loyalty. A recurrent theme is the role of individuals at all levels in creating capacity for change in a professional association. Key to this was individuals' loyalty to the professional association, a factor not previously explored. Whilst some academics have considered the affective domain of professionalism (Francis, 2011: 137), within which such loyalty falls, further research could be valuable in understanding this way in which professional associations can potentially increase their ability to cause change.

The second observation is that the effect of field position on the professional association's ability to act may not be as clear-cut as previously suggested. The potentially paradoxical nature of a professional association needing to be both central and peripheral to effect change has been addressed by academics; resolutions have included movement from central to peripheral, and simultaneously occupying both positions (Francis, 2011: 30). This research, however, suggests that field position may not be as important as the driving force exerted by individuals. A field position which may be expected to inhibit innovative behaviour can be counteracted by other attributes of the professional association, such as elite actors or individuals showing particularly strong leadership. Similarly, strong attachment to the central value system arising from field position may actually facilitate, instead of inhibiting, innovative action.

For the Bar, this research aimed to contribute to an improved understanding of a profession often invisible in research in England and Wales. Such neglect is regrettable; the profession's idiosyncrasies and nuances make it a fascinating research area, and one ripe for exploration. Whilst many questions remain unanswered, this research has built upon the foundation of Rogers' research (2010, 2012, 2014), examining aspirant entrants' perceptions of their chances of success (2014), and the portrayal of the profession to aspirant entrants by the Inns of Court at recruitment events (2012). This book builds upon that knowledge of aspirant entrants by focussing on the particular challenges that non-traditional aspirant entrants may experience in entering the profession; something not confined to England, but also noted by research in the USA.

Although PASS improves access to mini-pupillages by having applications assessed by someone with specialist knowledge, it only aids students who apply for, and secure, mini-pupillages through the scheme. It does not change chambers' practices in selecting mini-pupils, often giving preference to those who have followed a traditional educational route and supplemented this with 'standard' extra-curricular activities and work experience. This traditional conception of merit disadvantages many non-traditional aspirant entrants. In time PASS may encourage chambers to use alternative conceptions of merit if PASS students undertake mini-pupillages successfully. Participating chambers may realise that a traditional conception of merit applied when selecting mini-pupils excludes some very able applicants who have followed a non-traditional route. Such a change may, however, be hampered by a lack of availability of specialist access knowledge within chambers, and a lack of resources to recruit such.

Evidence of PASS's amelioration of challenges to participation was more mixed. Its provision of financial assistance was reported by many student participants as crucial, and the opportunities that it gave to meet and talk with practising barristers gave students access to information about the profession, and a snapshot of daily life in practice. However, as a programme run by a professional association but delivered by chambers, there were variations between students' experiences which had potentially negative effects on the programme's ability to encourage non-traditional aspirant entrants. One example was the incorporation of PASS students with direct-applicant mini-pupils with traditional profiles, highlighting the non-traditional status of the PASS student.

Overall, it is argued that PASS is unlikely to have a significant effect on the demographic of new entrants to the Bar. This results both from its small scale, and its avoidance of challenging traditional conceptions of merit and the status quo of the value attached to mini-pupillages. It also does not challenge the privileging of direct work experience; the view of many aspirant entrants and chambers that mini-pupillages are key to success in the pursuit of a career at the Bar. This maintenance of the status quo in the privileging of mini-pupillages is key to the argument made that PASS is unlikely to be truly transformative on a profession-wide scale. PASS gives non-traditional aspirant entrants an 'opportunity' for conformity, a route to more closely resemble their traditional counterparts through the provision of mini-pupillages and contingent experiences such as exposure to social norms. Instead of seeking to change the rules of the game, it simply allows a small group of non-traditional entrants to play.

Notwithstanding these observations, however, this research argues that programmes such as PASS can be truly transformative for student participants, whose comments illustrated that they valued and gained from their mini-pupillages. There is also the possibility that, more broadly, a programme such as PASS may increase the understanding of non-traditional aspirant entrants by the mutual exposure of students with such profiles going into chambers. Students who had a good experience (the majority who participated in this research) often cited an improved perception of the Bar and a better understanding of the profession. This may contribute, in a small way, to engendering a better appreciation amongst non-traditional entrants of how the profession operates; many participants had discussed their experiences with friends, family and university staff.

More general lessons about the content of access programmes can also be gained. Existing research suggests that intervention at a much earlier stage would ensure that young people have the information that they need to make informed decisions that will be relevant to their career choices. For example, participants in this research cited matters such as not knowing how important state examinations were at the time that they were taken, meaning that some students had poor grades hampering their access to the Bar. In some cases, these grades were not the result of lack of ability, but lack of application, which many suggested could be improved by knowledge of the competitive nature of the profession at an earlier stage, giving aspirant entrants information so that they knew what would be expected of them academically by the profession. However, it seems unlikely that profession-specific intervention before Sixth Form stage would be successful. Opportunities to experience professions are rare for those under 18. An initiative aimed at promoting one specific profession to younger students, instead of generally raising aspirations, could be controversial. Furthermore, attempts by programmes to 'bleach out' non-traditional characteristics of aspirant entrants makes for a deeply uncomfortable situation; care must be taken to ensure that programmes do not progress from supporting young people to learn as much as possible about the profession to deliberately setting out to morph non-traditional aspirant entrants into traditional entrants.

The interplay between tradition and social mobility has illustrated that professional associations, despite not being as powerful as they once were, nonetheless retain a key role at the Bar. This is especially marked in relation to the Inns of Court, which benefited from a combination of favourable attributes allowing powerful engagement with, and support from members. As the preceding chapters have demonstrated, the likelihood of success of an interventionist professional association will come down to a combination of internal and external matters. Some of those will be within the control of the profession, and some outside that control. The interplay of all these factors, along with intrinsic attributes of the professional association, and some of its target audience, will determine whether an intervention will succeed or not. Furthermore, the current research has highlighted that it may often be impossible to tell whether an intervention has 'worked' as there may be a lack of stated aims and objectives against which success can be assessed, stymying evaluation and development.

What is clear, however, is that certain actions and attributes of a professional association may indicate the likelihood of success. Whilst previous research has been criticised in turns for ignoring, and then overplaying, the roles of individuals, the importance of them is confirmed in this research. Whilst not every individual who acts in a way contra-indicated by the prevailing institutional logics of the organisation is necessarily a brave institutional entrepreneur charging into battle against their elitist and evil institutions, the capacity of a single, or small group of, individual(s) within a larger institution should not be doubted under certain conditions. This research illustrated that a whole may be more powerful than the sum of its parts.

The success of individuals' efforts is often affected by other matters, particularly the specialist knowledge from their own professional backgrounds, and whether they can bridge gaps between different levels and groups within the organisation, thus gaining both financial and human support for their project. Forging links with those in other, related organisations, which may otherwise perceive competition or hostility in an institution's actions, is also important. If individuals can do this then they may, with enough support, be able to move incrementally to challenge elements of the central value system even in an elite and traditional profession. It was unclear how genuinely PASS challenged the central values, although it was clearly perceived to by many practitioner and student stakeholders. The level to which such views of genuine challenge can ever be supported, however, is also likely to be compromised by the lack of clear aims and objectives against which longitudinal outcomes can be measured.

This book paints a picture of professions and professional associations weakened, but by no means without power to influence and direct the development of the profession at the English Bar. The professional association, already well-used to the structural challenges and idiosyncrasies of the Bar, has willingly brought in outside expertise, whilst determination on the part of internal actors seeking a way to demonstrate their personal ideological commitments to social mobility and access on merit have provided important human resources for the project.

In developing PASS, Inner Temple has certainly established itself as an innovative thinker within the profession, and made a statement to other professional associations about what it values within the profession and what, amongst the myriad of issues currently facing the profession in times of turbulence for the publicly-funded Bar, it feels is worthy of attention. There is much about it that is praise-worthy and to be admired. This does not mean, however, that it is safe to admire PASS as the epitome of an access programme run by a professional association. Rogers' research characterised the English Bar as portraying a meritocracy as a defensive strategy in a wider climate of general suspicion of the fairness of entry to the professions (2012: 218). This is lent some support by the reality that access programmes may, whether intentionally or otherwise, contribute to maintenance of the status quo.

Postscript

Whilst this book has addressed the challenges facing young people from socio-economically disadvantaged backgrounds accessing the profession, for those who do succeed the hurdles do not fall before them. Considering Lady Hale's comments, it would feel disingenuous to conclude this book without addressing in brief the continued challenges within the profession. As I expressed in Chapter 8, I do not agree that due to the competitive nature of the Bar non-traditional aspirant entrants should be discouraged. There is nothing to be lost by encouraging those with a realistic prospect of securing pupillage from entering the race – that is not, to paraphrase, 'tempting young people to aspire to a legal career that most of them can never have'. However, Lady Hale's other concern, that legal aid cuts will inhibit the socio-economic diversity of the Bar, cannot be denied.

Those who secure tenancy in sets doing legally-aided work will face some time of low and unpredictable earnings, due to the fixed fees of legal aid. Solicitors claim their costs under a Representation Order from the Legal Aid Agency, from which counsel are paid, often by cheque. All the while, new tenants will be charged chambers' rent (up to 20% of income), and will need to keep back at least a further 20% of what they earn for tax at the year-end. For many, the dreadful uncertainty of cashflow is as much a source of stress as the paucity of the amounts paid. Rent, bills, and travel expenses to court (which are often significant, especially with rising rail fares, and are not eligible for reimbursement in many Crown Court cases) cannot be paid as and when the money is received.

These problems are most pronounced at the junior end of the legally-aided Bar (criminal, immigration and some family work predominantly) because in areas where most work is privately-paying it is generally better-paying, and with a shorter time lapse between work and payment. With the introduction of the minimum pupillage award of £12,000 many pupils find that although their life during pupillage is far from luxurious, they at least have a reliable (usually monthly) income. As soon as a pupil is taken on as a tenant that security abruptly ends.

In reality, there will be cases done for which there will be no payment. Errands to far-flung courts to appease solicitors who instruct more senior members of chambers, on spurious and improper legal aid transfer applications for which there is no payment to which either the solicitors or counsel are entitled. Such trips are imposed upon counsel too junior to say no (although the Handbook permits refusal if there is no proper fee – BSB, 2017: 45, rC30.8) by clerks who see the benefit to chambers of keeping such solicitors sweet for further instructions. This cost–benefit analysis does not favour the welfare of junior tenants, even in chambers with excellent clerking. There will be Magistrates' Court trials for which the preparation takes all night and the trial lasts all day, miles outside of London, for £70, which is never paid.[1] There will be Prosecution lists before District Judges who berate counsel because the Crown Prosecution Service is too understaffed to review cases properly or answer the phone when counsel require instructions on how to respond to that failure, as they are not permitted to exercise any discretion.

For many counsel, once they pass these difficult times, they forget them. They establish comfortable earnings, and their refrain is that 'it will get better'. After all, it did for them. And that is what many who utter those words really mean: 'It got better for me'. But the question at the junior end is, 'Will it for us? When?' Increasingly it is an assurance that it is hard to believe in at all. How much of our careers will be dictated by the bureaucracy of the Legal Aid Agency and a government that is unwilling to recognise that legal aid is a crucial tool if there is to be any access to justice for all but the wealthiest, and repeatedly cuts it as a result? Three years on from the 'One Bar, One Voice' event,[2] little has changed. The most junior speaker at that event was Hannah Evans. Then a third-six pupil, she became a tenant at 23 Essex Street, and her much-applauded speech resonates in 2017 as it did in 2014. It can be accessed in full online,[3] and I would urge anyone who is concerned about social mobility at the Bar to read it. I can say from my own experience that nothing Hannah said has changed for the better.

Efforts to improve access are all but meaningless if there is not more done to support the junior Bar, including by more senior barristers and the judiciary. We cannot expect young people from any background to train for this profession only to find that having succeeded in getting pupillage, and then tenancy (neither of which happen without remarkable graft) they cannot be financially independent. Many go on secondment to government departments or regulatory organisations such as the Financial Conduct Authority or the Serious Fraud Office: these provide regular pay, regular working hours, a fixed place of work and in some cases paid holiday and sick leave. It is not hard to see their attraction for the 'baby Bar'. There needs to be attention paid to the effect of decisions on the junior end of the profession, ensuring that decision-making bodies are not comprised only of those who are successful and have forgotten how life was before they were.

For meaningful efforts not just to increase access but to address problems of attrition having secured access, senior figures must engage with the reality of life at the junior end of the Bar. As soon as my pupillage award came to an end, I

---

1 The extent of this problem is endemic, as highlighted by the Bar Council's Young Barristers' Committee in September2017-https://www.criminalbar.com/files/download.php?m=documents&f=170918090745-170916Annex5YBCreporttoBarCouncilSeptember2017.pdf [accessed 7th Jan 2018]..

2 www.barcouncil.org.uk/media-centre/news-and-press-releases/2014/february/speech-to-'one-bar,-one-voice'-event-by-hannah-evans,-third-six-pupil,-23-essex-street [accessed 17th April 2017].

3 www.barcouncil.org.uk/media-centre/news-and-press-releases/2014/february/speech-to-'one-bar,-one-voice'-event-by-hannah-evans,-third-six-pupil,-23-essex-street [accessed 17th April 2017].

took a part-time academic job in addition to my work at the Bar so that I had a reliable income. I was incredibly lucky to secure a job sympathetic to my self-employed commitments, and extremely flexible (and for that I am lucky to teach at a university where Saturday teaching is permitted, and I thank all my students who endure it). At the junior end of sets doing predominantly legally-aided work we are struggling. We stay because we dreamed of this, worked hard for this and most of all, still believe that it is important. We are buoyed by the occasional private brief, or the kindness of a chambers colleague who lets us keep their brief fee when we cover a hearing at the Crown Court when the Crown offers no evidence or the Defendant pleads guilty. If this reality is not recognised soon by the Government and the profession, it will be harder than ever for the Bar to encourage disadvantaged, talented young people to come to the Bar without then being accused of being disingenuous when it transpires that having succeeded, many cannot afford to continue in this career.

References

Abbott, A. (1988) *The System of Professions: An Essay on the Division of Expert Labor*, Chicago, IL: University of Chicago Press.
Abel, R. L. (1985) 'Lawyers and the Power of Change', *Law and Policy*, 7(1), 5–18.
Abel, R. L. (1988) *The Legal Profession in England and Wales*, Oxford: Basil Blackwell.
Abel, R. L. (2003) *English Lawyers Between Market and State: The Politics of Professionalism*, Oxford: Oxford University Press.
Artess, J. (2014) 'Changing Conceptions of Students' Career Development Needs', in M. Lazic (ed), *Serbia within European Paradigm of Career Guidance – Recommendations and Perspectives*, paper presented at the International Careers Conference, University of Niš, Serbia, 24th October 2013 (pp. 18–24).
Ashley, L., Duberley, J., Sommerlad, H., and Scholarios, D. (2015) *A Qualitative Study of Non-Educational Barriers to the Elite Professions*, London: Social Mobility and Child Poverty Commission.
Ashton, A. J. (1924) *As I Went on My Way*, London: Nisbet & Co.
Auerbach, J. S. (1976) *Unequal Justice: Lawyers and Social Change in Modern America*, New York, NY: Oxford University Press.
Bachman, R., and Schutt, R. K. (2011) *The Practice of Research in Criminology and Criminal Justice*, 4th ed, Thousand Oaks, CA: Sage.
Bar Council (2011) *Bar Barometer: Trends in the Profile of the Bar*, London: Research Department of the General Council of the Bar of England and Wales.
Bar Council (2014) *Barristers' Working Lives: A Second Biennial Survey of the Bar 2013*, London: General Council of the Bar.
Bar Council (2014a) *Bar Barometer: Trends in the Profile of the Bar*, London: Research Department of the General Council of the Bar of England and Wales.
Bar Council (2016) 'Mini-pupillage – Good Practice Guide', London: General Council of the Bar.
Bar Council Joint Working Party of the Young Barristers' Committee and Legal Services Committee (Peter Goldsmith QC, Chair) (1993) *The Work of the Young Bar*, London: Bar Council.
Bar Standards Board (2013) *BCAT Handbook*, London: Bar Standards Board.
Bar Standards Board (2014) *Bar Professional Training Course Handbook 2014–15*, London: Bar Standards Board.
Bar Standards Board (2015) *Consultation: The Future of Training for the Bar: Academic, Vocational and Professional Stages of Training*, London: Bar Standards Board.
Bar Standards Board (2015a) *Consultation: Amendment to Bar Standards Board Powers*, London: Bar Standards Board.

Bar Standards Board (2016) *Pupillage Handbook*, London: Bar Standards Board.
Bar Standards Board (2017) *The Handbook*, 3rd ed, London: Bar Standards Board.
Bar Standards Board (2017a) *BPTC Key Statistics Report*, London: Bar Standards Board.
Bar Standards Board Education and Training Committee (2012) *Response to LETR Discussion Paper on the Review of Legal Education & Training*, London: Bar Standards Board.
Battilana, J. (2006) 'Agency and Institutions: The Enabling Role of Individuals' Social Position', *Organization*, 13(5), 653–676.
Battilana, J., and D'Aunno, T. (2009) 'Institutional Work and the Paradox of Embedded Agency', in T. B. Lawrence, R. Suddaby and B. Leca (eds), *Institutional Work Actors and Agency in Institutional Studies of Organizations*, Cambridge, Cambridge University Press.
Bauman, Z. (2005) 'Chasing Elusive Society', *International Journal of Politics, Culture and Society*, 18, 123.
Beck, U., and Beck-Gernsheim, E. (2001) *Individualization: Institutionalized Individualism and its Social and Political Consequences*, London: Sage.
Becker-Bruser, W. (2010) 'Research in the Pharmaceutical Industry Cannot be Objective', *Evid Fortbild Qual Gesundhwes*, 104(3), 183–189.
Bero, L. A. (2013) 'Why the Cochrane Risk of Bias Tool Should Include Funding Source as a Standard Item [Editorial]', *Cochrane Database of Systematic Reviews*, 12.
Bindman, G., and Monaghan, K. (2014) '*Judicial Diversity: Accelerating Change*', London: Judicial Appointments Commission.
Blanden, J., and Machin, S. (2007) *Recent Changes in Intergenerational Mobility in Britain*, London: Sutton Trust.
Bloom, B. S., Engelhart, M. D., Furst, E. J., Hill, W. H., and Krathwohl, D. R. (1956) *Taxonomy of Educational Objectives: The Classification of Educational Goals, Handbook I: Cognitive Domain*, New York, NY: David McKay.
Boon, A. (2010) 'Professionalism under the Legal Services Act 2007', *International Journal of the Legal Profession*, 17(3), 195–232.
Bourdieu, P. (1984) *Distinction: A Social Critique of the Judgement of Taste*, Cambridge, MA: Harvard University Press.
Bourdieu, P., and Wacquant, L. (1992) *An Invitation to Reflexive Sociology*, Cambridge: Polity Press.
Brady Leigh, P. (1827) *The Law Student's Guide*, London: Henry Butterworth.
Braithwaite, J. P. (2010) 'Diversity Staff and the Dynamics of Diversity Policy-Making in Large Law Firms', *Legal Ethics*, 13(2), 141–163.
Bridge Group (2011) *Call for Evidence by Alan Milburn on Child Poverty and Social Mobility: Response from the Bridge Group, 12 October 2011*. Retrieved from www.thebridgegroup.org.uk/evidence/MilburnResponse.pdf
Bruce Baker, C., Johnsrud, M. T., Crismon, M. L., Rosenheck, R. A., and Woods, S. W. (2003) 'Quantitative Analysis of Sponsorship Bias in Economic Studies of Antidepressants', *British Journal of Psychiatry*, 183(6), 498–506.
Bucher, R., and Strauss, A. (1961) 'Professions in Process', *American Journal of Sociology*, 66(4), 325–334.
Butler, N., Chillas, S., and Muhr, S. L. (2012) 'Professions at the Margins', *Ephemera*, 12(3), 259–272.
Carbado, G. W., and Gulati, M. (2000) 'Working Identity', *Cornell Law Review*, 85, 1259–1308.
Carr-Saunders, A. M., and Wilson, P. A. (1933) *The Professions*, Oxford: Clarendon.

Causa, O., and Johansson, A. (2009) 'Intergenerational Social Mobility', *Economics Department Working Papers No. 707*, Paris: Organisation for Economic Co-operation and Development.

de Certeau, Michel (1984) *The Practice of Everyday Life*, Berkeley, CA: University of California Press.

Charmaz, K. (1990) 'Discovering Chronic Illness: Using Grounded Theory', *Social Science and Medicine*, 30(11), 1161–1172.

Charmaz, K. (1995) 'Grounded Theory', in J. A. Smith, R. Harré and L. van Langenhove (eds), *Rethinking Methods in Psychology*, London: Sage.

Charmaz, K. (2000) 'Grounded Theory: Objectivist and Constructivist Methods', in N. K. Denzin and Y. S. Lincoln (eds), *Handbook of Qualitative Research*, 2nd ed, Thousand Oaks, CA: Sage, pp. 509–535.

Charmaz, K. (2002) 'Qualitative Interviewing and Grounded Theory Analysis', in J. F. Gubrium and J. A. Holstein (eds), *Handbook of Interview Research: Context and Method*, Thousand Oaks, CA: Sage, pp. 675–693.

Clark, G. (2015) 'Social Mobility Barely Exists But Let's Not Give up on Equality', *The Guardian*, 4th February.

Clementi, D. (2004) *Report of the Review of the Regulatory Framework for Legal Services in England and Wales*, London: Ministry of Justice.

Cocks, R. (1983) *Foundations of the Modern Bar*, London: Sweet and Maxwell.

Collier, R. (2002) 'The Changing University and the (Legal) Academic Career: Rethinking the Relationship between Women, Men and the "Private Life" of the Law School', *Legal Studies*, 22, 1–32.

Comte, A. (1851/1973) *System of Positive Polity, Volume 1: Containing the General View of Positivism and Introductory Principles*, translated by John Henry Bridges, New York, NY: Burt Franklin.

Connor, K., and Vargyas, E. J. (2013) 'The Legal Implications of Gender Bias in Standardized Testing', *Berkeley Women's Law Journal*, 7(1), 13.

Costello, C. Y. (2005) *Professional Identity Crisis: Race, Class, Gender, and Success at Professional Schools*, Nashville, TN: Vanderbilt University Press.

Costley, C., Elliott, G., and Gibbs, P. (2010) *Doing Work-based Research: Approaches to Enquiry for Insider-Researchers*, London: Sage.

Council of the Inns of Court (2016) *Response of The Council of the Inns of Court to the Bar Standards Board's Consultation (October 2016) on the Future of Training for the Bar: Future Routes to Authorisation – And – Addendum Dated 1 December 2016*, London: Council of the Inns of Court.

Cox, E. W. (1852) *The Advocate*, London: John Crockford.

Crawford, C., Johnson, P., Machin, S., and Vignoles, A. (2011) *Social Mobility: A Literature Review*, London: Department for Business, Innovation and Skills.

Creswell, J. W., and Plano Clark, V. L. (2011) *Designing and Conducting Mixed Methods Research*, London: Sage.

Crooks, D. L. (2001) 'The Importance of Symbolic Interaction in Grounded Theory Research on Women's Health', *Healthcare for Women International*, 22, 11–27.

Crowne, D. P., and Marlowe, D. (1960) 'A New Scale of Social Desirability Independent of Psychopathology', *Journal of Consulting Psychology*, 24(4), 349–354.

Dent, M., and Whitehead, S. (2002) *Managing Professional Identities: Knowledge, Performativities and the 'New' Professional*, London: Routledge.

Dewberry, C. (2011) *Aptitude Testing and the Legal Profession*, London: Legal Services Board.

Durkheim, E. (1957) *Professional Ethics and Civic Morals*, London: Routledge and Kegan Paul.

DiMaggio, P. J. (1988) 'Interest and Agency in Institutional Theory', in L. Zucker (ed), *Institutional Patterns and Culture*, Cambridge, MA: Ballinger, pp. 3–22.

DiMaggio, P. J., and Powell, W. W. (1983) 'The Iron Cage Revisited: Institutional Isomorphism and Collective Rationality in Organizational Fields', *American Sociological Review*, 48(2), 147–160.

DiMaggio, P. J., and Powell, W. W. (1991) 'Introduction', in W. W. Powell and P. J. DiMaggio (eds), *The New Institutionalism in Organizational Analysis*, London: University of Chicago Press, pp. 1–38.

Duman, D. (1982) *The Judicial Bench in England 1727–1875: The Reshaping of a Professional Elite*, London: Royal Historical Society.

Faulconbridge, J. (2012) 'Alliance "Capitalism" and Legal Education: An English Perspective', *Fordham Law Review*, 80(6), 2651–2659.

Feinstein, L. (2003) 'Inequality in the Early Cognitive Development of British Children in the 1970 Cohort', *Economica*, 70, 277.

Ferlie, E., and Pettigrew, A. M. (1988) 'AIDS: Responding to Rapid Change', *Health Service Journal*, 1st December, 1422–1424.

Fischer, J. M. (2006) 'External Control over the American Bar', *Georgetown Journal of Legal Ethics*, 19, 59, 97.

Fisher, W. F. (1997) 'Doing Good? The Politics and Anti-Politics of NGO Practices', *Annual Review of Anthropology*, 26, 439–64.

Flood, J. (1981) 'Middlemen of the Law: An Ethnographic Inquiry into the English Legal Profession', *American Bar Association*, 2, 377–405.

Flood, J. (2011) 'The Re-landscaping of the Legal Profession: Large Law Firms and Professional Re-regulation', *Current Sociology*, 59(4), 507–529.

Flood, J., and Whyte, A. (2009) 'Straight There, No Detours: Direct Access to Barristers', *International Journal of the Legal Profession*, 16(2), 131–152.

Foskett, N., Dyke, M., and Maringe, F. (2004) *The Influence of the School in the Decision to Participate in Learning Post-16, DfES Research Report*, London: Department for Education and Skills.

Francis, A., and MacDonald, I. (2009) 'After Dark and Out in the Cold: Part-time Law Students and the Myth of "Equivalency"', *Journal of Law and Society*, 36(2), 220–247.

Francis, A. M. (2004) 'Out of Touch and Out of Time: Lawyers, Their Leaders and Collective Mobility within the Legal Profession', *Legal Studies*, 24(3), 322–348.

Francis, A. M. (2011) *At the Edge of Law: Divergent and Emergent Models of Legal Professionalism*, Surrey: Ashgate.

Francis, A. M. (2015) 'Legal Education, Social Mobility and Employability: Possible Selves, Curriculum Intervention and the Role of Legal Work Experience', *Journal of Law and Society*, 42(2), 173–201.

Francis, A. M., and MacDonald, I. W. (2006) 'Preferential Treatment, Social Justice, and the Part-time Law Student – The Case for the Value-added Part-time Law Degree', *Journal of Law and Society*, 33(1), 92–108.

Francis, A. M., and Sommerlad, H. (2009) 'Access to Legal Work Experience and its Role in the (Re)production of Legal Professional Identity', *International Journal of the Legal Profession*, 16(1), 63–86.

Freidson, E. (1970) *The Profession of Medicine*, New York, NY: Harper Row.

Freidson, E. (1985) 'The Reorganization of the Medical Profession', *Medical Care Review*, 42, 11–35.

Freidson, E. (1994) *Professionalism Reborn: Theory, Prophecy and Policy*, Cambridge: Polity Press.
Friedland, R., and Alford, R. R. (1991) 'Bringing Society Back in: Symbols, Practices, and Institutional Contradictions', in Walter W. Powell and Paul J. DiMaggio (eds), *The New Institutionalism in Organizational Analysis*, Chicago, IL: University of Chicago Press.
Friedman, M. (1962) *Capitalism and Freedom*, Chicago, IL: University of Chicago Press.
Garud, R., Hardy, C., and Maguire, S. (2002) 'Institutional Entrepreneurship as Embedded Agency: An Introduction to the Special Issue', *Organization Studies*, 28(7), 957–969.
Gasson, S. (2004) 'Rigor in Grounded Theory Research: An Interpretive Perspective on Generating Theory from Qualitative Field Studies', in Michael E. Whitman and Amy B. Wosczynski (eds), *The Handbook of Information Systems Research*, London and Hershey, PA: Idea Group Publishing.
Glaser, B. G. (1978) *Theoretical Sensitivity*, Mill Valley, CA: Sociology Press.
Glaser, B. G. (1992) *Basics of Grounded Theory Analysis: Emergence vs. Forcing*, Mill Valley, CA: Sociology Press.
Glaser, B. G., and Strauss, A. L. (1967) *The Discovery of Grounded Theory: Strategies for Qualitative Research*, Chicago, IL: Aldine.
Globe Business Media Group (2015) *The Training Contract and Pupillage Handbook*, London: Globe.
Goode, W. J. (1957) 'Community within a Community: The Professions', *American Sociological Review*, 22(2), 194–200.
Greene, J. C., Caracelli, V. J., and Graham, W. F. (1989) 'Toward a Conceptual Framework for Mixed-method Evaluation Designs', *Educational Evaluation and Policy Analysis*, 11, 255–274.
Greenwood, R., and Hinings, C. R. (1993) 'Understanding Strategic Change: The Contribution of Archetypes', *Academy of Management Journal*, 36(5), 1052–1081.
Greenwood, R., and Hinings, C. R. (1996) 'Understanding Radical Organizational Change: Bringing together the Old and the New Institutionalism', *Academy of Management Review*, 21(4), 1022–1054.
Greenwood, R., and Suddaby, R. (2006) 'Institutional Entrepreneurship in Mature Fields: The Big Five Accounting Firms', *Academy of Management Journal*, 49(1), 27–48.
Greenwood, R., Suddaby, R., and Hinings, C. R. (2002) 'Theorizing Change: The Role of Professional Associations in the Transformation of Institutionalized Fields', *Academy of Management Journal*, 45(1), 58–80.
Halliday, T. C. (1987) *Beyond Monopoly: Lawyers, State Crises and Professional Empowerment*, Chicago, IL: University of Chicago Press.
Hanlon, G. (1997) 'A Profession in Transition? Lawyers, the Market and Significant Others', *Modern Law Review*, 60(6), 798–822.
Harris, L. C. (2002) 'The Emotional Labour of Barristers: An Exploration of Emotional Labour by Status Professionals', *Journal of Management Studies*, 39(4), 553–584.
Haug, M. R. (1973) 'Deprofessionalization: An Alternative Hypothesis for the Future', *Soc. Rev. Monograph*, 20, 195–212.
Haywood, C. P., and Mac an Ghaill, M. (1997) 'Materialism and Deconstructivism: Education and the Epistemology of Identity', *Cambridge Journal of Education*, 27(2), 261–272.
Herring, J. (2014) *Legal Ethics*, Oxford: Oxford University Press.
Hinchliffe, G., and Jolly, A. (2011) 'Graduate identity and employability', *British Educational Research Journal*, 37, 563.

HM Government (2011) *Opening Doors, Breaking Down Barriers: A Strategy for Social Mobility*, London: Cabinet Office.

Holbrook, A., Krosnick, J., and Pfent, A. (2007) 'The Causes and Consequences of Response Rates in Surveys by the News Media and Government Contractor Survey Research Firms', in J. M. Lepkowski (ed), *Advances in Telephone Survey Methodology*, New York, NY: Wiley.

House of Commons' Education Committee (2012) *Education Committee – Second Report Appointment of Chair, Social Mobility and Child Poverty Commission*, London: House of Commons.

Hughes, D., and Gration, P. (2009) *Evidence and Impact: Careers and Guidance-related Interventions*, Berkshire: CfBT Education Trust.

Jencks, C., and Phillips, M. (1998) *The Black–White Test Score Gap*, Washington, DC: Brookings Institute.

Jepperson, R. L. (1991) 'Institutions, Institutional Effects and Institutionalism', in W. W. Powell and P. J. DiMaggio (eds), *The New Institutionalism in Organizational Analysis*, London: University of Chicago Press, pp. 143–163.

Jerrim, J., Vignoles, A., and Finnie, R. (2012) *University Access for Disadvantaged Children: A Comparison across English-speaking Countries*, Department of Quantitative Social Sciences Working Paper 12–11, University of London: Institute of Education.

Johnson, T. (1972) *Professions and Power*, London: Macmillan.

Jones, C., and Livne-Tarandach, R. (2008) 'Designing a Frame: Rhetorical Strategies of Architects', *Journal of Organizational Behavior*, 29, 1075–1099.

Kaufman, S. R. (2013) 'Fairness and the Tyranny of Potential in Kidney Transplantation', *Current Anthropology*, 54, Supplement 7 (Potentiality and Humanness: Revisiting the Anthropological Object in Contemporary Biomedicine), 56–66.

Kennedy, S. (2010) 'Key Issues for the New Parliament – Social Mobility: Missing an Opportunity?', *House of Commons Research Library*, London: House of Commons.

Kindon, S. (2003) 'Participatory Video in Geographic Research: A Feminist Practice of Looking?', *Area*, 35(2), 142–153.

Kirkpatrick, I., and Ackroyd, S. (2003) 'Archetype Theory and the Changing Professional Organization: A Critique and Alternative', *Organization Studies*, 10(4), 731–750.

Kotter, J. P. (1995) 'Leading Change: Why Transformation Efforts Fail', *Harvard Business Review*, 73(2), 59–67.

Kotter, J. P. (1999) *On What Leaders Really Do*, Cambridge, MA: Harvard Business School Press.

Kotter, J. P. (2008) *Force for Change: How Leadership Differs from Management*, New York, NY: Simon and Schuster.

Kotter, J. P. (2013) 'Management Is (Still) Not Leadership', *Harvard Business Review*, 9th January.

Krathwohl, D. R., Bloom, B. S., and Masia, B. B. (1964) *Taxonomy of Educational Objectives: The Classification of Educational Goals, Handbook II: The Affective Domain*, New York, NY: David McKay.

Kritzer, H. J. (1999) 'Legal Practice in a Post-professional World', *Law and Society Review*, 33, 713–762.

Kuhn, T. S. (1977) *The Essential Tension: Selected Studies in Scientific Tradition and Change*, Chicago, IL: University of Chicago Press.

Kuipers, B. S., Higgs, M., Kickert, W., Tummers, L., Grandia, J., and Van Der Voet, J. (2014) 'The Management of Change in Public Organizations: A Literature Review', *Public Administration*, 92(1), 1–20.

Kultgen, J. (1988) *Ethics and Professionalism*, Pennsylvania, PA: University of Pennsylvania Press.

Langlands, A. (2005) *The Gateways to the Professions Report*, London: Department for Education and Skills.

Larson, M. S. (1977) *The Rise of Professionalism: A Sociological Analysis*, Berkeley, CA: University of California Press.

Laurison, D., and Friedman, S., (2015) *Introducing the Class Ceiling: Social Mobility and Britain's Elite Occupations*, London: London School of Economics Sociology Department.

Lawrence, T. B., and Suddaby, R. (2006) 'Institutions and Institutional Work', in S. Clegg, C. Hardy, T. Lawrence, and W. Nord (eds), *The Sage Handbook of Organization Studies*, London: Sage, 215–53.

Layder, D. (1993) *New Strategies in Social Research: An Introduction and Guide*, Cambridge: Polity Press.

Lee, R. G. (2000) '"Up or Out" – Means or Ends? Staff Retention in Large Firms', in P. Thomas (ed), *Discriminating Lawyers*, London: Cavendish.

Legal Education and Training Review (2013) *Setting Standards: The Future of Legal Services Education and Training Regulation in England and Wales*, London: ILEX/BSB/SRA.

Legal Services Board (2011) *Increasing Diversity and Social Mobility in the Legal Workforce: Transparency and Evidence*, Consultation Paper, London: Legal Services Board.

Lemmings, D. (1990) *Gentlemen and Barristers: The Inns of Court and The English Bar, 1680–1730*, Oxford: Clarendon Press.

Leondari, A. (2007) 'Future Time Perspective, Possible Selves, and Academic Achievement', *New Directions for Adult and Continuing Education*, 114, 17–26.

Lewin, K. (1952) 'Field theory in social science', in D. Cartwright (ed), *Selected Theoretical Papers*, London: Tavistock Publications.

Lounsbury, M., and Crumley, E. (2007) 'New Practice Creation: An Institutional Perspective on Innovation', *Organization Studies*, 28(7), 993–1012.

MacDonald, K. (1995) *The Sociology of the Profession*, London: Sage.

Manderson, D., and Turner, S. (2006) 'Coffee House: *Habitus* and Performance Among Law Students', *Law & Social Inquiry*, 31(3), 649–676.

Mansbridge, J. (1990) *Beyond Self-Interest*, Chicago IL: University of Chicago Press.

Markus, H., and Nurius, P. (1986) 'Possible selves', *American Psychologist*, 41, 954–969.

Markus, H., and Ruvolo, A. (1989) 'Possible Selves: Personalized Representations of Goals', in L. A. Pervin (ed), *Goal Concepts in Personality and Social Psychology*, Hillsdale, NJ: Erlbaum, pp. 211–241.

Marshall, T. H. (1963) *Sociology at the Crossroads*, London: Heinemann.

Martens, L. (2012) 'The Politics and Practices of Looking: CCTV Video and Domestic Kitchen Practices', in S. Pink (ed), *Advances in Visual Methodology*, London: Sage.

Mauss, M. (1967) *The Gift: Forms and Functions of Exchange in Archaic Societies*, New York, NY: Norton.

Maute, J. L. (2011) 'Global Continental Shifts to New Governance Paradigm in Lawyer Regulation and Consumer Protection: Riding the Wave', in Francesca Bartlett, Reid Mortensen and Kieran Tranter (eds), *Alternative Perspectives on Lawyers and Legal Ethics: Reimagining the Profession*, London: Routledge.

McKinlay, J. B., and Arches, J. (1985) 'Towards the Proletarianization of Physicians', *International Journal of Health Services*, 15(2), 161–95.

McMorrow, J. A. (2016) 'UK Alternative Business Structures for Legal Practice: Emerging Models and Lessons for the U.S.', *Georgetown Journal of International Law*, 47, 665.

Melia, K. M. (1996) 'Rediscovering Glaser', *Qualitative Health Research*, 6(3), 368–373.

Merton, R. K., Fiske, M., and Kendall, P. L. (1956) *The Focused Interview*, New York, NY: Free Press.

Meyer, R. E., and Hammerschmid, G. (2006) 'Changing Institutional Logics and Executive Identities: A Managerial Challenge to Public Administration in Austria', *American Behavioural Scientist*, 49, 1000–1014.

Milburn, Rt. Hon. A. (2009) *Unleashing Aspirations: The Final Report of the Panel on Fair Access to the Professions*, London: Cabinet Office.

Milburn, Rt. Hon. A. (2012) *Fair Access to Professional Careers: A Progress Report by the Independent Reviewer on Social Mobility and Child Poverty*, London: Cabinet Office.

Milburn, Rt. Hon. A (2014) *Elitist Britain?* London: Social Mobility and Child Poverty Commission.

Milburn, Rt. Hon. A. (2015) 'Social Mobility Has Come to a Halt', *The Telegraph*, 25th May.

Morley, L. (2007) 'The X Factor: Employability, Elitism and Equity in Graduate Recruitment', *Twenty-First Century Society: Journal of the Academy of Social Sciences*, 2(2), 191–207.

Morse, J. M. (2003) 'Principles of Mixed Method and Multi-method Research Design', in C. Teddlie and A. Tashakkori (eds), *Handbook of Mixed Methods in Social and Behavioural Research*, London: Sage.

Mossman, M. J. (2006) 'The First Women Lawyers: Piecemeal Progress and Circumscribed Success', *Osgoode Hall Law Journal*, 45(2), 379.

Moyser, G. (1988) 'Non-standardized Interviewing in Elite Research', *Studies in Qualitative Methodology*, 1, 109–136.

Muzio, D., and Ackroyd, S. (2005) 'On the Consequences of Defensive Professionalism: Recent Changes in the Legal Labour Process', *Journal of Law and Society*, 32(4), 615–642.

Muzio, D., and Ackroyd, S. (2008) 'Change in the Legal Profession: Professional Agency and the Legal Labour Process' in D. Muzio, S. Ackroyd and J.-F. Chanlat (eds), *Redirections in the Study of Expert Labour: Established Professions and New Expert Occupations*, London: Palgrave Macmillan.

National Equality Panel (2010) *An Anatomy of Economic Inequality in the UK*, London: Government Equalities Office.

Nelson, R. L., and Trubek, D. M. (1992) 'Arenas of Professionalism', in R. L. Nelson, D. M. Trubek and R. L. Solomon (eds), *Lawyers Ideals/Lawyers' Practices: Transformations in the American Legal Profession*, Ithaca, NY: Cornell University Press.

Neuberger, Rt. Hon. Lord (2007) *Entry to the Bar Working Party: Final Report*, London: General Council of the Bar.

Noaks, L., and Wincup, E. (2004) *Criminological Research: Understanding Qualitative Methods*, London: Sage.

Nottingham Evening Post (2011) 'KCH Barristers Merges with Garden Square as Legal Services Act Lands', 10th May.

Nunn, A. (2011) *Draft Report on Fostering Social Mobility as a Contribution to Social Cohesion*, Strasbourg: Council of Europe.

Nunn, A., Johnson, S., Monro, S., Bickerstaffe, T., and Kelsey, S. (2007) 'Factors Influencing Social Mobility', *Research Report Number 450*, London: Department for Work and Pensions.

Ocasio, W. (1997) 'Towards an Attention-Based View of the Firm', *Strategic Management Journal*, 18(S1), 187–206.

Ogg, T., Zimdars, A., and Heath, A. (2009) 'Schooling Effects on Degree Performance: A Comparison of the Predictive Validity of Aptitude Testing and Secondary School Grades at Oxford University', *British Educational Research Journal*, 35(5), 781–807.

Papademetriou, D. G, Somerville, W., and Sumption, M. (2009) *Social Mobility and Education: Academic Papers Presented at a High-level Summit Sponsored by the Carnegie Corporation of New York and the Sutton Trust*, London: Sutton Trust.

Parsons, T. (1940) 'An Analytical Approach to the Theory of Social Stratification', *American Journal of Sociology*, 45(6), 841–862.

Paterson, A. A. (1996) 'Professionalism and the Legal Services Market', *International Journal of the Legal Profession*, 3(1–2), 137–168.

Pettigrew, A. (1990) 'Longitudinal Field Research on Change: Theory and Practice', *Organization Science*, 1(3), 267–293.

Pettigrew, A. M., Woodman, R., and Cameron, K.S. (2001) 'Studying Organizational Change and Development: Challenges for Future Research', *Academy of Management Journal*, 44(4), 697–713.

Pfeffer, J., and Salancik, G. R. (1978) *The External Control of Organizations: A Resource Dependence Perspective*, New York, NY: Harper and Row.

Pike, G., and Robinson, D. (2012) *Barristers' Working Lives: A Biennial Survey of the Bar 2011*, London: General Council of the Bar.

Pinnington, A., and Morris, T. (2003) 'Archetype Change in Professional Organizations: Survey Evidence from Large Law Firms', *British Journal of Management*, 14, 85–99.

Pirie, F., and Rogers, J. (2012) 'Pupillage: The Shaping of a Professional Elite', in J. Abbink and T. Salverda (eds), *The Anthropology of Elites*, Basingstoke: Palgrave Macmillan.

Polden, P. (2010) 'The Legal Professions', in W. Cornish, J. S. Anderson, R. Cocks, M. Lobban, P. Polden and S. Smith (eds), *The Oxford History of the Laws of England, Vol. XI: 1820–1914: The English Legal System*, Oxford: Oxford University Press.

Pollard, E., Tyers, C., Tuohy, S., and Cowling, M. (2007) *Assessing the Net Added Value of Adult Advice and Guidance, Research Report RR825A*, Nottingham: Department for Education and Skills.

Prest, W. (1986) *The Rise of the Barristers: A Social History of the English Bar 1590–1640*, Oxford: Clarendon.

Rajak, D. (2011) *In Good Company: An Anatomy of Corporate Social Responsibility*, Stanford, CA: Stanford University Press.

Rea, L., and Parker, R. (1997). *Designing and Conducting Survey Research*, 2nd ed, San Francisco, CA: Jossey-Bass.

Rogers, J. (2010) 'Shadowing the Bar: Studying an English Professional Elite', *Historical Reflections*, 36(3), 39–58.

Rogers, J. (2012) 'Representing the Bar: How the Barristers' Profession Sells Itself to Prospective Members', *Legal Studies*, 32(2), 202–225.

Rogers, J. (2014) 'Feeling Bad and Being Elite: A Comparative Analysis of the Anxieties and Uncertainties of Aspiring Barristers', *Comparative Sociology*, 13, 30–57.

Rolfe, H., and Anderson, T. (2003) *A Firm Decision: The Recruitment of Trainee Solicitors*, London: Law Society.

Sander, R. H. (2011) 'Class in American Legal Education', *Denver Law Review*, 88(4), 631–682.

Scheper-Hughes, N. (2007) 'The Tyranny of the Gift: Sacrificial Violence in Living Donor Transplants', *American Journal of Transplantation*, 7, 507–11.

Semple, N. (2015) *Legal Services Regulation at the Crossroads: Justitia's Legions*, Gloucester: Elgar.

Shah, S., Pascall, G., and Walker, R. (2006) *Future Selves: Career Choices of Young Disabled People*, University of Nottingham: School of Sociology and Social Policy website publication.

Shils, E. (1975) *Center and Periphery: Essays in Macrosociology*, Chicago, IL: University of Chicago Press.

Social Mobility Commission (2016) 'State of the Nation 2016: Social Mobility in Great Britain', London: Social Mobility Commission.

Sommerlad, H. (2007) 'Researching and Theorising the Processes of Professional Identity Formation', *Journal of Law and Society*, 34(2), 190–217.

Sommerlad, H. (2008) '"What are You Doing Here? You Should be Working in a Hair Salon or Something": Outsider Status and Professional Socialization in the Solicitors' Profession', *Web Journal of Current Legal Issues*, 2.

Spada (2012) *Social Mobility Toolkit for the Professions*, London: Spada.

Strauss, A., and Corbin, J. (1990) *Basics of Qualitative Research Grounded Theory Procedures and Techniques*, Newbury Park: Sage.

Strauss, A., and Corbin, J. (1998) *Basics of Qualitative Research Techniques and Procedures for Developing Grounded Theory*, 2nd ed, Thousand Oaks, CA: Sage.

Stringer, N. (2008) 'Aptitude Tests Versus School Exams as Selection Tools for Higher Education and the Case for Assessing Educational Achievement in Context', *Research Papers in Education*, 23, 1.

Suddaby, R. (2010) 'Challenges for Institutional Theory', *Journal of Management Inquiry*, 19(1), 14–20.

Sullivan, R. (2010) *Barriers to the Legal Profession*, London: Legal Services Board.

Thornton, M. (1996) *Dissonance and Distrust: Women in the Legal Profession*, Melbourne: Oxford University Press.

Thornton, P. H. (2004) *Markets from Culture: Institutional Logics and Organizational Decisions in Higher Education Publishing*, Stanford, CA: Stanford University Press.

de Tocqueville, A. (1899/1946) *Democracy in America*, translated by Henry Reeve, London: Oxford University Press.

de Tocqueville, A. (1980) *On Democracy, Revolution and Society*, selected writings edited by J. Stone and S. Mennell, Chicago, IL: University of Chicago Press.

Tolbert, P. S. (1988) 'Institutional Sources of Organisational Culture in Major Law Firms', in L. G. Zucker (ed), *Institutional Patterns and Organisations: Culture and Environment*, Cambridge, MA: Ballinger.

Waring, J. (2014) 'Restratification, Hybridity and Professional Elites: Questions of Power, Identity and Relational Contingency at the Points of 'Professional–Organisational Intersection', *Sociology Compass*, 8(5), 688–704.

Weber, M. (1947) *The Theory of Social and Economic Organisation*, New York, NY: Oxford University Press.

Wilkins, D. B. (1998) 'Fragmenting Professionalism: Racial Identity and the ideology of "Bleached Out" Lawyering', *International Journal of the Legal Profession*, 5, 141.

Wilkins, D. B. (1999) 'Partners Without Power? A Preliminary Look at Black Partners in Corporate Law Firms', *Journal of the Institute for the Study of Legal Ethics*, 2, 15.

Witz, A. (1992) *Professions and Patriarchy*, London: Routledge.

Wood, D. (2008) *Review of the Bar Vocational Course, Report of the Working Group*, London: Bar Standards Board.

Young Legal Aid Lawyers (2013) *Social Mobility and Diversity in the Legal Aid Sector: One Step Forwards, Two Steps Back*, London: YLAL.

Zimdars, A. (2010) 'The Profile of Pupil Barristers at the Bar of England and Wales – 2004–2008', *International Journal of the Legal Profession*, 17(2), 117–134.

Index

Abbott, A. 169
Abel, R.L. 154, 159
absolute social mobility 5
access: to information 182–92; mini-pupillages and 38–43; research 17–18
access programmes 3, 27, 182–208, 212; access to information 182–192; aims and objectives 193–196; changing the rules of the game 197–198; depiction of 92; ethics 205–207; experience of work experience through 137–139; extension of support 203–205; firm-level delivery 198–199; funding 133–134, 171, 196; general principles 182–198; incorporating into usual practice 202–207; mutual exposure and benefits 192–193; perception of 92–95; practical challenges 198–202; timing of 199–202; *see also* mini-pupillages, PASS, Pathways to Law
Access to the Bar awards 80, 82
Ackroyd, S. 78, 79–80
action approaches 48
adaptability 53–56
administration 171
advertising mini-pupillages 124, 149
aesthetics 39–43
affective domain 66, 72; loyalty 72, 85–89, 99, 210
agency: embedded *see* embedded agency; individual 27, 98, 103–105
aims of access programmes 193–196; PASS and meeting its aims 147–149
Alford, R.R. 57
altruism 60–61, 89, 91, 95–97
American Bar 63, 64
American Bar Association (ABA) 80, 146

applications for mini-pupillages 16–17, 124–133
approachability 92–93
approved regulators 11
aptitude tests 165–166
archetypes 51, 78–83
arenas 51, 114; altering the concept of professionalism within 111–114; transfer of values 114–118
Ashley, L. 13–14
Ashton, A.J. 34
aspirations, raising 140, 206–207, 214
attachment *see* loyalty
Auerbach, J.S. 64
average family income 9
axial coding 25

Bar, the 6–7, 26, 28–46; access programmes and perceptions of 208; Called to 32, 50, 151; caste-like appearance 35; central value system 67–72, 112, 113–114, 119, 143; challenges for the junior Bar 214–216; 'in crisis' 155; effects of post-professionalism on 177–180; evolution of the elite 209–210; historical perspective on social mobility 34–38; mini-pupillages and access 38–43; progress in social mobility 193–194; public perceptions of 15, 186–187; route to practise 32–34; as a social class 123–124; social norms 123–124, 135–137; structure of 28–32, 84, 116–118
Bar Council 30–31, 65, 72–73, 74, 117, 158; 'good practice' guide for mini-pupillages 127, 129–130; and legal aid cuts 75; and other sites of power 76–77, 81–82; statistics 12, 49; Working Lives Report 1, 170

Index

Bar Course Aptitude Test (BCAT) 165–166
Bar Placement Week 80, 82
Bar Professional Training Course (BPTC) 2, 30, 32, 33, 69, 154; cost 151, 152; professional education as cultural reproduction 161–165, 167–168; scholarships for 30, 173
Bar Standards Board (BSB) 12, 30, 31–32, 158, 159, 160; consultation on professional education 162–163; and other sites of power 76, 78
Bar Table veto 34, 35
Bar Vocational Course (BVC) 155, 156, 161
Barrow, J. 126
Battilana, J. 58, 104, 108
BCAT (Bar Course Aptitude Test) 165–166
Benchers 35, 68–69; embedded agency 103, 104–105; and post-professionalism 178–180
Boon, A. 159
Bourdieu, P. 6, 39–43, 104, 119, 142
BPTC see Bar Professional Training Course
Braithwaite, J.P. 58, 122
Bridge Group 8–9
British Dental Association 11
BSB see Bar Standards Board
Bucher, R. 51
Burns, A. 31
BVC (Bar Vocational Course) 155, 156, 161
BVC Review Group 165

Called to the Bar 32, 50, 151
capacity to effect change 56–59
careers advice 8–9, 183–185
central value system 52–53, 59; of the Bar 67–72, 112, 113–114, 119, 143; changes in 112, 113–114, 119, 143
chambers 28–29, 79, 108–109; financing mini-pupillages 134–135; firm-level access programmes 198–199; handling of applications for mini-pupillages 124–127, 129; mutual exposure and mutual benefit 192–193
chancery 189
change see organisational change
Charmaz, K. 24, 25
Chartered Insurance Institute 11
Chicago Bar Association 64

City Law School 167
Clegg, N. 7
clerkships, judicial 144–147
closure: and community 70–72; occupational 15, 38–39, 52–53; social see social closure
Cocks, R. 36, 37
coding 25
coercive power, lack of 80
cognitive standardisation 160–161
cohesiveness 115–118
COIC (Council of the Inns of Court) 162, 163
collective action 108–111
collective embedded agency 104
Commercial Bar Association (COMBAR) 16, 114, 135
committees 28–29, 74, 103–104, 173–175
community 70–72
conservatism 41
constraints 26, 27, 152–181; permeability of social fields 174–177; professional education 160–169; regulation 154–157, 158–160; structuring properties of the field 169–175
constructivist grounded theory 24
consultation 176–177
contacts within the profession 33
context 198–202
control over entry 154
Corbin, J. 24, 25
core category 25
Council of the Inns of Court (COIC) 162, 163
counter-associations 64–65
Cox, E. 37
Criminal Bar Association 75
Crooks, D.L. 24
cultural capital 39, 40–41
cultural reproduction 160–169

data collection 20–23
data interpretation 18
Davies, V. 31
dependency 96
deprofessionalisation 54, 177
DiMaggio, P.J. 68
diminished power of professional associations 44, 45–46, 153–160
direct applications for mini-pupillages 124–125, 128, 130, 132–133

direct work experience, privileging of 141–144, 211–212
diversity 12, 34–35, 68–69; as a competence 112–113; motivations for increasing 89–97
doxa 41–42

early intervention 5, 7–10, 150, 212; timing of access programmes 200–202
economic capital 39, 40
education: and applications for mini-pupillages 131–133; early intervention 7–10, 150, 212; permeability of social fields 174–177; professional education as cultural reproduction 160–169; stage of and timing of access programmes 199–202; state-school 170; support throughout 14
Education and Training Department 109
elite: evolution of 209–210; role in the central value system 68–69, 104, 209; *see also* Benchers
elite universities 13
embedded agency 55, 56, 99, 103–105, 119; paradox of 98, 103
embedded professional associations 56–59; field position of 83–89
employment 2; role in social mobility 9–10; second jobs 37–38, 215–216; self-employment 2, 29, 208
entry requirements 52; for the BPTC 164–165
Equality Act 2010 11
equality of opportunity 6
ethics: and access programmes 205–207; research 19–20
Evans, H. 215
evolution: of elite 209–210; of professionalism 44, 66–67, 158
expenses 134–135, 196
extension of support 203–205

family 174–177
Ferlie, E. 61
field positions 82, 104–105, 210; of embedded professional associations 83–89
financial problems, pupils' 155–156
financial support 37; *see also* funding
Finnie, R. 8, 200

firm-level access programmes 198–199
fit 25
fitting in 38–43
focus groups 22, 23
formal processes 101
Francis, A.M. 47, 55, 112, 114, 171
Freidson, E. 48
Friedland, R. 57
functionalism 48, 49
funding: access programmes 133–134, 171, 196; pupillages 155–156, 214; research 17–18
future selves 175

gate-keeping 43, 53, 122
GDL (Graduate Diploma in Law) 32, 52
Geddes, J. 100, 101
General Medical Council 11
geographical reach 203, 204–205
gifting 60, 96
Glaser, B.G. 23, 24, 25
Goldsmith, P. 155
Graduate Diploma in Law (GDL) 32, 52
Gration, P. 9
Gray's Inn 32, 156
Greening, J. 4
Greenwood, R. 57
grounded theory 23–26

habitus 41–42, 119; habituation to 160–169
Hale, Baroness 205–206, 214
Halliday, T.C. 63, 64
hard structuring properties 169, 170–175
Haug, M.R. 54
heterogeneity 72, 74–76
Hinings, C.R. 57
homogeneity 160–161
Hughes, D. 9

ICSL (Inns of Court School of Law) 161–162, 167, 168
identity: formation 38–43, 50, 121–122, 124–128, 191; multiple identities 191
ideology: ideological commitment to diversity 94; ideologies of the legal profession 49–51
inclusiveness 60; policy 174–175
incorporation of access programmes into usual practice 202–207

230 *Index*

individual agency 27, 98, 103–105
individual stories 44, 45, 98, 99, 119; importance of 100–103
individuals: challenging prevailing institutional logics 105–111; importance within professional associations 26–27, 98–120, 210, 213; power 103–105
informal mini-pupillages 125, 128–130
information: access schemes and provision of 182–192; medium of 188–192; quality and quantity 187–188; provision 14, 140, 205–207; sources 183–187
initiation of organisational change 72–83
Inner Temple 1, 26, 30, 32, 119, 156, 171–2, 213; altering institutional logics 106, 107, 115, 118; capitalising on barristers' loyalty 87–89; Education and Training Department 109; entrance exam 36–37; field position 83–85; loyalty to 77, 85, 86; Outreach Committee 103–104, 109, 172–173; PASS *see* PASS; relationships with other sites of power 76–77, 78, 80–82
Inns of Court 29, 30, 31–32, 46, 151, 212; barrister loyalty to 66, 72, 85–89, 99, 210; and chambers 29; collaboration between 75–76, 174; historical perspective on social mobility 34–38; initiating organisational change 73, 74, 75–76; lack of cohesiveness 115–117; as professional associations 62–65; scholarships for the BPTC 30, 173; *see also under individual Inns*
Inns of Court School of Law (ICSL) 161–162, 167, 168
institutional entrepreneurship 68, 108
institutional logics 55–56, 57–58, 105, 119; change in and changes in the central value system 113–114; challenging prevailing logics 105–111; individual and collective challenges to 108–111; institutionalisation of 194
institutional theory 55–56, 99–100
institutionalisation of change 195
inter-generational social mobility 5, 8
internal stratification 169

international comparisons 10; mini-pupillages and US judicial clerkships 144–147
interviews 22–23
intra-generational social mobility 5

James I 36
Jepperson, R.L. 195
Jerrim, J. 8, 200
judicial clerkships 144–147
junior Bar 214–216

Kennedy, S. 10
Kirkpatrick, I. 78, 79–80
Kotter, J.P. 62
Kritzer, H.J. 27, 43, 53, 54, 112, 177
Kuipers, B.S. 61–62

Langlands, A. 8, 9, 10
Larson, M.S. 39, 160, 161
Law Society 47, 55, 158
leadership 98–99, 210
Legal Aid Agency 214, 215
legal aid cuts 75, 135, 205, 214–215
Legal Education and Training Review (LETR) 12–13, 124, 149, 153, 159, 161
Legal Practice Course (LPC) 55, 167
Legal Services Act 2007 (LSA) 53, 154–155, 158, 159, 177
Legal Services Board (LSB) 11–12, 154, 159–160
Lewin, K. 194
Lincoln's Inn 32, 34, 35, 156
links between elite professions and young people 14
Lockhart, C. 101
London 133, 204
longitudinal extension of support 203–204
longstanding status quo 15
loyalty 66, 72, 85–89, 99, 210
LPC (Legal Practice Course) 55, 167
LSA (Legal Services Act 2007) 53, 154–155, 158, 159, 177
LSB (Legal Services Board) 11–12, 154, 159–160

maintaining the status quo 45, 143
Manderson, D. 136
margins, the 174
McGill University 'Coffee House' events 136
Melia, K.M. 25

mentoring 14, 203–204
merit and potential 4
meritocracy 15, 90, 101–102; as recruitment criterion 44, 45
methodology 3, 17–23; data collection 20–23; design 3, 18–19; ethics 19–20; funding and access 17–18; prior preliminary data collection 20
Middle Temple 30, 32, 35–36, 80, 82, 105, 156
Milburn, A. 7; Progress Report 13; Report 7, 9, 10, 13; Review 7, 8
minimum pupillage award 155–156, 214
minimum wage 155
mini-pupillages 27, 33–34, 121–151; and access 38–43; advertising 124, 149; applications for 16–17, 124–133; comparison with US judicial clerkships 144–147; experience of through an access programme 137–139; financial matters 133–135; identity formation 124–128; participating in 133–139; privileging of 141–144, 211–212; purpose of 139–141; securing 128–133; social norms at the Bar 135–137; *see also* PASS
mixed-methods research design 3, 18–19
modifiability 25
monopolistic theory 48, 52–53, 63, 95
motivations: for change 59–61; for increasing diversity 89–97; sources of motivation 92–97
multiple sites of power 76–83
mutuality 43, 192–193

National Association for Law Placement (NALP) 146, 147
National Equality Panel 9
Nelson, R.L. 50, 51
networking 185–186
Neuberger Report 156, 157, 176, 185
not fully legally qualified staff 53–54, 176–178
norms, social *see* social norms
North America 160; judicial clerkship in the USA 144–147
Nunn, A. 5, 6, 9–10

objectives of access programmes 193–196
occupational closure 15, 38–39, 52–53

Office for Legal Complaints 154
'One Bar, One Voice' event 215
ongoing support 203–204
open coding 25
organisational change 53–62; adaptability 53–56; capability to effect 56–59; initiating 72–83; motivations for 59–61; stages of 194; sustaining 61–62
outreach activity director (X) 107, 108, 110–111, 115, 117
Outreach Committee 103–104, 109, 172–173
'outsider' status 138

paradox of embedded agency 98, 103
parallel routes to mini-pupillage 130
Parsons, T. 6
participating in work experience 133–139
PASS (Pegasus Access and Support Scheme) 2, 3, 27, 45, 46, 121–151, 196–198, 211–212, 213; achievement of its aims 147–149; aims 193; applications for 16–17, 124–133; as case study 15–17; chambers and 28, 29, 73; coalitions and 77–78; comparison with judicial clerkships in the USA 144–147; data collection 19, 20, 22; experience of work experience through 137–139; firm-level delivery 198; identity formation 124–128; importance of Inns of Court 88; and participating in work experience 133–139; privileging of work experience 141–144; purpose of 139–141; securing work experience 128–133
Paterson, A.A. 114
Pathways to Law 3, 22, 70, 80, 107, 148; data collection 19, 20, 21
peer groups 175–177
Pegasus Access and Support Scheme *see* PASS
perception: of access programmes 92–95; access programmes and perceptions of the Bar 208; individual stories of access 102; public perception of the Bar 15, 186–187
performativity 108
Pettigrew, A.M. 61, 62
plausible story 25–26
playing the game 197–198

policy 4–15; early intervention 7–10; policy background 5–7
positional power 106
post-professionalism 27, 43, 53–54; effects on the Bar 177–180
potential 4
Potts, R. 98
power: approaches 48; diminished for professional associations 44, 45–46, 153–160; individual 103–105; multiple sites of 76–83; positional 106; relational 106
Prest, W. 34–35
privileging of mini-pupillages 141–144, 211–212
professional associations 26, 47–65, 210–211, 212–213; adaptability 53–56; and altering the concept of professionalism 111–114; capacity to effect change 56–59; constraints on interventions by *see* constraints; diminishing power of 44, 45–46, 153–160; field position of embedded professional associations 83–89; ideologies of the legal profession 49–51; importance of individuals 26–27, 98–120, 210, 213; initiation of organisational change 72–83; Inns of Court as 62–65; motivations for change 59–61; motivations for increasing diversity 89–97; multiple sites of power 76–83; occupational closure 15, 38–39, 52–53; size 72–73; sustaining change 61–62; values 26, 66–97; *see also under individual professional associations*
professional association-level access programmes 198
professional education 160–169
professional identity formation 38–43, 50, 121–122, 124–128, 191
professionalism 48; altering the concept of 111–114; differing forms within segments/arenas 114–115; evolution of 44, 66–67, 158; and social closure 69–72
professions: caste-like appearance 207; as occupations and social strata 38–39; role in social mobility 10–14; social mobility and in the 21st century 1–27
proletarianisation 54, 177
public perceptions of the Bar 15, 186–187

publicly funded work 170
pupillages 2; competition for 32–33; minimum pupillage award 155–156, 214; obtaining through informal routes 101; securing 164–165
purpose of mini-pupillages 139–141

Qualifying Sessions 30, 32, 50
questionnaires 20–22

Rajak, D. 96
regulation 154–157, 158–160; self-regulation 158–159
relational power 106
relative social mobility 5
relevance 25
re-professionalisation thesis 177
reputational gain 92–93, 94
research methodology *see* methodology
resilience 102
restratification 178–179
Rogers, J. 3, 60, 61, 157, 211, 213
rules of the game, changing 197–198

salaried staff 210; altering institutional logics 108–109; embedded agency 103
saturation of concepts 25
savings 37
school-based careers advice 183–184
second jobs 37–38, 215–216
securing a mini-pupillage 124–133
segments of a profession 114; altering the conception of professionalism within 111–114; transfer of values 114–118
selective coding 25
self-employment 2, 29, 208
self-interest 59, 60–61, 89, 95
self-regulation 158–159
Semple, N. 160
shorthand measures 83
sites of power: multiple 76–83; and the role of archetypes 78–83
size of professional associations 72–73
small-group work 187–188
snobbery 34
social capital 39–43, 123
social class, the Bar as a 123–124
social closure 38, 51, 67; tradition, professionalism and 69–72
social field positions *see* field positions
social fields: permeability of 174–177; structuring properties of 169–175

social mobility: absolute and relative 5; defining 5; inter-generational 5, 8; intra-generational 5; policy background 5–7; and the professions in the 21st century 1–27; role of the professions in 10–14; societal concern with 4–15
Social Mobility Commission 4, 38
Social Mobility Toolkit 11
social norms 38, 39–43, 121–122; the Bar as a series of 123–124, 135–137; participating in work experience 135–137
social strata 38–39
social stratification 6, 8; Bourdieu 39–43
societal concern with social mobility 4–15
soft structuring properties 169–170
Solicitors' Regulation Authority (SRA) 158, 159
specialists in education and access 177
Stanford Law School 145
state-school education 170
status quo: longstanding 15; maintaining 45, 143
Strauss, A. 23, 24, 25, 51
structuring properties of the field 169–175; hard 169, 170–175; soft 169–170
Suddaby, R. 57, 99–100
sustaining change 61–62
Sutton Trust 8
symbolism of access programmes 92–95

talent 13, 14, 90–91, 102, 161, 186; as recruitment criterion 44, 45
targeting of resources 8
television programmes 186
timing of access programmes 199–202
Tocqueville, A. de 39, 41, 75
Todd, M. 98, 103, 104
tradition 41; and social closure 69–72
transfer of innovation 99, 114–118
travel costs/expenses 133–134, 196
Trubek, D.M. 50, 51
Turner, S. 136

United States judicial clerkships 144–147
university careers advice 184–185
University of Wisconsin 145
usual practice, incorporation of access programmes into 202–207

values: central value system *see* central value system; challenges to transfer of 114–118; professional associations 26, 66–97
Vignoles, A. 8, 200

Weber, M. 38
work experience at the Bar *see* mini-pupillages
workability 25
Working Lives Report 1, 170
workshops on applications 202–203

Zimdars, A. 1

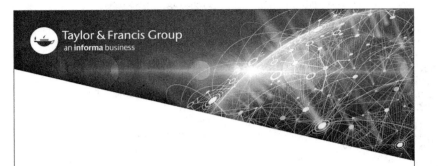